Instructor's Resource Manupany

Intercultural Communication in Contexts
Second Edition

by Judith N. Martin and Thomas K. Nakayama

Lisa Bradford
University of Wisconsin-Milwaukee

Mayfield Publishing Company
Mountain View, California
London • Toronto

International Standard Book Number: 0-7674-1235-4

Manufactured in the United States of America

10 9 8 7 6 5 4 3 2 1

Mayfield Publishing Company
1280 Villa Street
Mountain View, California 94041
(650) 960-3222

Printed on recycled paper.

CONTENTS

PREFACE

Teaching intercultural communication can be a challenging, sometimes frustrating, and incredibly exciting opportunity. This manual contains a combination of ideas and approaches for teaching intercultural communication using Judith N. Martin and Thomas K. Nakayama's *Intercultural Communication in Contexts*. I hope these ideas will be useful to you as you prepare for your teaching experience.

Martin and Nakayama go a step further than most of the available texts in presenting the study of intercultural communication from three diverse philosophical perspectives and then integrating these perspectives to inform students about important issues affecting the intercultural communication process. As such, the text represents a pluralistic approach to teaching intercultural communication. In a very real sense, its creation is a celebration of diversity in thinking about intercultural communication by the authors.

In an effort to present the study of intercultural communication from multiple perspectives, Martin and Nakayama invited me to compile ideas from my intercultural teaching experience and those of two other contributors, Jolanta A. Drzewiecka and Francisca Trujillo-Dalby, in this manual. To introduce you to the diversity of perspectives and experiences brought together in this manual, I would like to share a little background information about each of the contributors and myself.

Some materials in this manual were contributed by Jolanta A. Drzewiecka who co-edited the first version of this manual. She came from Poland as an international student; completed her doctorate at Arizona State University, with a strong emphasis in cultural studies; and is now at Washington State University. Several new activities in this manual were contributed by Francisca Trujillo-Dalby. She is a second-generation Latina, raised in California. She has a master's degree in communication from Portland State University and currently teaches there. During her summers she is a junior faculty member at the Summer Institute for Intercultural Communication.

I grew up in northern Utah and am European American. I have a doctorate in communication from Arizona State University, where I was trained in social science and interpretive approaches to studying intercultural communication. I have taught intercultural communication for the past 12 years in both culturally homogeneous and multicultural/multilingual classes. Presently, I teach and do research at the University of Wisconsin-Milwaukee, but I have previously taught communication courses at Brigham Young University, Brigham Young University-Hawaii, Arizona State University, and Arizona State University-West. In addition to meeting many international students and friends in the United States, I have many memorable intercultural experiences from the 17 months I lived in Honduras and from various trips to Mexico and Western and American Samoa.

As you can see from our diverse ethnic and national backgrounds and the diversity of our research and teaching perspectives and experiences, our contributions to this manual represent a variety of approaches and perspectives toward teaching intercultural communication. However, we are unified by our similar commitment to the goal of helping students understand the role of culture in our communication and the hope that you will enjoy teaching intercultural communication as much as we have.

I have divided this instructor's resource manual into four parts:

- Part I provides tips for organizing the course, including sample syllabi and general teaching tips for new course instructors.

- Part III consists of materials to assist instructors with lecture preparation: learning objectives, key words, extended chapter outlines, discussion questions, and classroom exercises and chapter assignments.

- Part IV provides test questions for each of the chapters, including multiple-choice, matching, true/false, and essay questions.

PART I
ORGANIZING THE COURSE

Here are some suggestions for organizing your course, including sample syllabi for both semester- and quarter-length courses. Your syllabus is a contract between you and your students, with obligations on each side. Include your expectations for student effort and behavior. Clearly explain grading and course content so that students will know what to expect and what they will learn. By thoroughly explaining course policies and procedures, you will reduce misunderstandings.

SAMPLE COURSE SYLLABUS
INTERCULTURAL COMMUNICATION SYLLABUS

Course Instructor:

Office & Phone:

E-mail Address:

Office Hours:

Course Place & Time:

Course Description

This course explores issues related to the intercultural communication process. We will consider the important role of context (social, cultural, and historical) in intercultural interactions. We will examine the complex relationship between culture and communication from three conceptual perspectives: the social psychological perspective, the interpretive perspective, and the critical perspective.

General Course Objectives

Traditionally, we have approached the study of intercultural communication primarily from a social psychological perspective. Although this perspective has yielded many important ideas about intercultural communication, other perspectives may also contribute to our understanding of intercultural communication, particularly in acknowledging the influence of context and power in our intercultural interactions. In this course, we apply three conceptual perspectives to the study of intercultural communication. Although these approaches are diverse, their contributions are integrated to provide a comprehensive picture of intercultural communication.

From applying these approaches to the study of intercultural communication, we will also come to appreciate the complexity and dialectical tensions involved in intercultural interactions. This learning process should enhance self-reflection, flexibility, and sensitivity in intercultural communication.

1

Required Course Materials

Martin, J. N., & Nakayama, T. K. (2000). *Intercultural communication in contexts*, (2nd ed.). Mountain View, CA: Mayfield.

Student Learning Objectives

During this course, students should:

1. Become familiar with the study of intercultural communication from the traditional social psychological perspective, the interpretive perspective, and the more recent critical perspective.

2. Discover the importance of the roles of context and power in studying intercultural communication.

3. Become more sensitive to the complexity of intercultural interactions.

4. Recognize the influence of their own cultural groups on intercultural communication interactions.

5. Become more willing, self-reflective, flexible, and open communicators in intercultural communication interactions.

Course Policies and Procedures

Attendance: Two **unexcused** absences are permitted during the semester. Three points will be subtracted from a student's course point total for each absence recorded beyond those permitted. The instructor may excuse certain absences such as those authorized by the administration for participation in athletics and personal **emergencies** (severe personal or family illnesses, personal or family tragedies, work-related emergencies). Proof for excused absences must be documented within two weeks of the absence and must clearly state that the emergency **required** that the student miss the course on the date and at the time of the absence.

Drop Policy: Students may drop the course with written approval of the course director through the date specified in the current schedule of classes. After this date, students with extreme emergencies may withdraw from the course by filing a written appeal and written permission from the instructor with their school/college advising office.

Incomplete: An incomplete will be awarded to students who have passing grades and who, in the last quarter of the course, become seriously ill or suffer tragedies that prevent them from otherwise completing the course. To receive an incomplete, the illness or tragedy must be documented in a written memo to the course director. The memo must clearly show that the emergency prevented the student from completing the remainder of the coursework.

Special-Student Resources: A variety of services are available to students who need special accommodations for success in this class. These students should contact the instructor during the first week of class.

Religious Observation and School Excused Activities: Students who miss class for these reasons are responsible for contacting the instructor to pick up returned assignments and to review class announcements. It is their responsibility to obtain class notes from other students. Students who miss exams or graded in-class activities as a result of their participation in a religious observation or school excused activity will be allowed to complete these activities or substitute activities on an alternative date. Contact the instructor at least two weeks prior to these absences to reschedule activities. Assignments should be submitted prior to the absence.

Grading: Grades will be determined by student performance in the following areas:

Exam 1	50 pts.
Exam 2	50 pts.
Final Exam	50 pts.
Term Project	75 pts.
Activity Reports	75 pts.
Class Activities	50 pts.
Total	350 pts.

Final grades will be based on the total number of points earned in the course. Letter grades will be assigned according to the following standard curve:

A	=	94%, 329–350	B–	=	80%, 280–293	D+	=	67%, 234–244
A–	=	90%, 315–328	C+	=	77%, 270–279	D	=	64%, 224–233
B+	=	87%, 304–314	C	=	74%, 259–269	D–	=	60%, 210–223
B	=	84%, 294–303	C–	=	70%, 245–258	F	=	59%, 209 and below

Grievances: Students with concerns or questions about assignment grading should address those grievances to the instructor in memo form within two weeks of receiving the grade. The graded assignment should accompany the memo. The instructor will consider the concern and respond or request a meeting with the student to discuss the matter. If a student feels that a correct response was marked incorrectly on a test, the student may submit a written case for his/her answer. This case should include evidence supporting the student's response from the text or lecture materials. Other concerns may be discussed with the instructor during regularly scheduled office hours or by appointment.

Course Standards: Students who enroll in this course are expected to demonstrate professionalism in the following areas:

1. *Course Assignments:* All class assignments submitted for grading should be neatly typed, double-spaced, on standard 8-1/2 × 11 paper. Students should attach the grade sheet to the front of the assignment.

2. *Course Communication:* Students are expected to show respect for instructors, teaching assistants, guests, and one another regardless of opinion, value, cultural, and other group differences. Students should give one another equal opportunity to express opinions, experiences, and ideas. All students should be supportive of a cooperative learning environment in the lecture hall. The instructor reserves the right to publicly address students whose behavior disrupts the learning environment and to arrange for disciplinary action according to policies set by the university.

3. *Course Facilities:* Students are responsible for keeping the room orderly and clean. No smoking is allowed in the lecture hall or building.

4. *Course Preparation:* Students are expected to read assigned material prior to class. They should be prepared to answer questions related to the material in the text and may be called on to do so. Students should also be prepared to ask questions about issues of interest or for clarification of concepts during class. No assignment will be accepted beyond two weeks past the due date without prior written consent from the instructor. No assignments will be accepted after the final exam.

Academic Misconduct: Students discovered cheating (turning in nonoriginal work, engaging in plagiarism, and so on) will lose points on the assignment/test in question. The instructor may also pursue disciplinary actions according to university policies and procedures.

Course Format

This course consists of lectures, class discussions, group activities, and special presentations. Students may be asked to write brief reaction papers, give group reports, or complete quiz questions that they will submit for class participation points. A total of 50 points for class activities is possible during the semester/quarter. Students who have excused absences for a class in which participation points were available are responsible for meeting with the instructor to find out how they can make up the points they missed. The lectures are designed to promote dialogue on issues addressed in text chapters and to provide additional information beyond what is included in the text.

Class discussions are designed to encourage students to express opinions, observations, share experiences, and ask questions. Students should use this time to clarify their understanding of concepts encountered in course materials. Personal issues such as test and assignment scores will not be addressed during this time. Students with these concerns should follow the guidelines presented in the syllabus for grievances.

Group activities will be arranged periodically to allow students to become acquainted with other class members and their ideas. They also provide opportunities for students to see the application of the principles introduced in course materials. The frequency and quality of the group activities largely depends on the cooperation of group members.

Special presentations may include guest lectures, media presentations, and so on. The instructor will schedule these according to available resources and time constraints.

Course Assignments

Term Project: [If you assign a term project, such as those listed in Part II of this manual, provide details here.]

Activity Reports: During the quarter/semester, students can earn up to 75 points from assignment options. These assignments are designed to motivate students to engage in and think about intercultural communication and the application of topics discussed in class. The instructor will provide a list of assignment options at the beginning of the course, along with suggested due dates. Students are encouraged to select those assignments that they think will be of most use to them personally. Grades on these assignments will be based on the depth of the observations, their thoroughness, and their overall quality (grammar, organization, style, and so on). **Note:** Students are responsible for the quality of learning experience they get from these assignments. Students who put little effort into them will get little out of them.

Examinations: There are two midterm examinations and one final examination. **The final will not be comprehensive.** Exams will consist of true/false, matching, multiple-choice, and some short-essay questions. Each exam will cover approximately one third of the material in the course. Students **must** take the exams when they are scheduled. Makeup exams are allowed in the case of excused absences and are arranged according to guidelines on attendance and religious observation.

SAMPLE SEMESTER COURSE SCHEDULE

Here is a sample course schedule for a 15-week, 45-hour semester.

Class Period	Topic	Weekly Reading
Week 1	Introduction to course Introduction activity Why study intercultural communication? Classroom exercise/video Development of the discipline	Chapter 1
Week 2	Theoretical approaches to intercultural communication Classroom exercise/video Applications of theoretical approaches	Chapter 2
Week 3	Dialectical approaches to understanding culture and communication Classroom exercise/video What is culture? What is communication? Classroom exercise/video	Chapter 3
Week 4	The relationship between communication and context The relationship between communication and power From history to histories History, power, and intercultural communication	Chapter 4
Week 5	Classroom exercise/video History and identity Intercultural communication and history Classroom exercise/video Catch up and review	
Week 6	**Exam 1** A dialectical approach to understanding identity Classroom exercise/video Social and cultural identities Identity, stereotypes, and prejudice	Chapter 5
Week 7	Identity development issues Identity and language Identity and communication Classroom exercise/video Thinking dialectically about language Cultural variations in language	Chapter 6

Class Period	Topic	Weekly Reading
Week 8	Discourse: Language and power Classroom exercise/video Moving between languages Language politics and policies	
Week 9	A dialectical approach to nonverbal communication The universality of nonverbal behavior Classroom exercise/video Defining cultural space Types of migrant groups	Chapter 7
Week 10	Classroom exercise/video Cultural shock Migrant host relationships Cultural adaptation	Chapter 8
Week 11	Identity and adaptation Catch up and review Classroom exercise/video **Exam 2**	
Week 12	Defining popular culture and folk culture Consuming and resisting popular culture Classroom exercise/video Representing cultural groups U.S. popular culture and power	Chapter 9
Week 13	Benefits and challenges of intercultural relationships Stages of relational development Classroom exercise/video Relationships across differences Context of intercultural relationships	Chapter 10
Week 14	Characteristics of intercultural conflict Interpersonal approach to conflict Classroom exercise Interpretive and critical approaches to conflict Managing intercultural conflict	Chapter 11
Week 15	Components of competence Classroom exercise Applying knowledge about intercultural communication What the future holds Catch up and review	Chapter 12
	Final Exam	

SAMPLE QUARTER COURSE SCHEDULE

Here is a sample course schedule for a 10-week, 40-hour quarter.

Class Period	Topic	Weekly Reading
Week 1	Introduction to course Introduction activity Why study intercultural communication? Classroom exercise/video Development of the discipline	Chapter 1 Chapter 2
Week 2	Theoretical approaches to intercultural communication Classroom exercise/video Applications of theoretical approaches What is culture? What is communication?	 Chapter 3
Week 3	Classroom exercise/video The relationship between communication and context The relationship between communication and power From history to histories History, power, and intercultural communication Classroom exercise History and identity Catch up and review	 Chapter 4
Week 4	**Exam 1** Social and cultural identities Identity, stereotypes, and prejudice Identity development issues Classroom exercise/video Identity and language Identity and communication	 Chapter 5
Week 5	Cultural variations in language Discourse: Language and power Moving between languages Language politics and policies A dialectical approach to nonverbal communication Classroom exercise/video The universality of nonverbal behavior	Chapter 6 Chapter 7
Week 6	Defining cultural space Classroom exercise/video Types of migrant groups Cultural shock Migrant host relationships Cultural adaptation Classroom exercise/video	 Chapter 8

Class Period	Topic	Weekly Reading
Week 7	Identity and adaptation	
	Catch up and review	
	Exam 2	
	Defining popular culture and folk culture	Chapter 9
	Consuming and resisting popular culture	
Week 8	Classroom exercise/video	
	Representing cultural groups	
	U.S. popular culture and power	
	Benefits and challenges of intercultural relationships	Chapter 10
	Classroom exercise/video	
	Stages of relational development	
Week 9	Relationships across differences	
	Context of intercultural relationships	
	Classroom exercise/video	
	Characteristics of intercultural conflict	Chapter 11
	Approaches to conflict	
	Managing intercultural conflict	
	Classroom exercise	
Week 10	Components of competence	Chapter 12
	Classroom exercise	
	Applying knowledge about intercultural communication	
	What the future holds	
	Catch up and review	
	Final Exam	

TEACHING TIPS

Intercultural communication may be considered an explosive "issues course" because discussions of cultural views and differences touch on our deeply held assumptions and evoke emotional responses. Students often come to class with strong opinions formulated by their cultural upbringing and especially influenced by home and mass media. They are rarely conscious of the racist implications of their views, and although they do admit that racism is a fact of life, they deny that they themselves are racist. Because the process of learning about cultural differences involves realizing that one person's view is one of many and certainly not universal, students respond with resistance and sometimes with anger. In this section, you will find suggestions for overcoming some of the challenges associated with teaching intercultural communication.

Intercultural Communication in Contexts uses a dialectical approach to connect traditional social science perspectives with interpretivist and critical perspectives. You and the students will be examining cultural experiences and rethinking deeply held assumptions. With the dialectical approach to intercultural communication, self-reflection becomes a crucial part of the pedagogical process.

Many thought-provoking issues are raised in the text to enhance students' sensitivity to issues affecting intercultural interaction. Because the dialectical approach is a more complex, yet powerful, approach for teaching intercultural communication, you may find that course preparation requires more effort on your part than traditional approaches. However, your efforts will improve the quality of the experience for you and your students.

Teaching from a dialectical perspective involves asking many questions. Instructors and students must question whose interests are being served by particular interpretations of social reality and intercultural interactions presented by the students or to the students in their environment (for example, from their parents or mass media). Teaching from this perspective requires raising questions of power and ideology, and it means that we must challenge those views of reality that students assume to be common sense, natural, normal, necessary, the only possibility, and/or universal (Ahlquist, 1992, Giroux, 1992). Prompt students to question the process by which we come to know about social reality, other cultures, and communication; that is, whose stories are being represented and whose stories are being excluded in this process and which views of social reality are encouraged by these selective inclusions and exclusions. As you teach from this perspective, try to make a connection between theory and lived experience; this might result in explosive discussions as theoretical issues touch on students' lives.

This dialectical perspective reflects a commitment to dialogue in research as well as in teaching. Although respect should be the basis of this dialogue, it should not preclude critiques that might lead to conflict. Managed conflict can deepen understanding of issues and encourage honest expressions and is a necessary stage in the pedagogical process (Giroux, 1992). From the dialectical perspective, no communication issue is ever resolved; a dialogue must continue.

Preparing to Teach the Class

Instructors are motivated to teach intercultural communication for a variety of reasons. Hence, they approach this opportunity from many different levels of experience and expertise. It is exciting to see an increase in instructors who have received training from excellent doctoral and master's programs in intercultural communication. At the same time, I can empathize with instructors assigned to teach intercultural communication by administrators who mistake travel and study abroad experience or membership in a particular racial/ethnic group as intercultural expertise. Although both intercultural experience and knowledge are critical components of preparation to teach intercultural communication, there are additional areas of preparation that you should consider. In addition to knowledge about cultural groups and a background in related research and theory, you should prepare yourself to teach a class in intercultural communication through a continuous self-reflection process that critically examines your cultural position and experiences. It is important to remember that this process is never finished and will be publicly conducted throughout the quarter or semester as students challenge your beliefs and assumptions. Take some time to question your own views about issues currently being discussed and attempt to identify your own resistance to viewing them from different social positions. It is helpful to think about your cultural upbringing and experiences and how they feed into your views of social reality and communication.

Ahlquist (1992) points out that it is often useful to use examples from your own experiences of discrimination and privilege to encourage students to rethink their own views. However, reveal your own experiences with caution. In some instances, students may mistakenly assume that personal experiences shared by instructors are accusations motivated by personal political agendas and a climate of defensiveness may emerge that inhibits the classroom dialogue. If you communicate feelings of genuine respect for students early in the quarter or semester, this is less likely to occur. Exercise caution when sharing personal intercultural experiences. Students should see your articulation of these experiences as an attempt to share cultural insights, not as a brag session. You can do this by posturing the experience as a personal discovery, supporting your experiences with those of others, and discussing both successes and failures throughout the course.

Because understanding intercultural communication is a process, I suggest that you increase your own understanding by searching out opportunities for intercultural experiences. You might try traveling or visiting other cultures, participating in international and other cultural group activities, and volunteering for community service projects that focus on cultural groups in your area. If these opportunities are not feasible, try to gain exposure to intercultural issues by reading about cultural groups and viewing videos on cultural themes. The important thing is to experience for yourself some of the ideas you will be discussing with your students and to think about cultural issues.

These experiences increase your credibility with students, enable you to illustrate class concepts with personal examples, and enhance your understanding of intercultural communication processes. Specifically, I suggest that new intercultural communication instructors work through some of the chapter assignments and term projects prior to assigning them to their students. This will provide you with some intercultural experiences, familiarize you with the assignments, and increase your sensitivity to student challenges and questions. You will also improve your ability to evaluate the quality of student effort on each assignment.

I suggest gaining a thorough knowledge of current events regarding cultural issues and policies because students frequently ask questions about political or cultural issues and events. You may be able to use these questions to introduce important ideas relevant to the course.

If you are uncomfortable teaching and contrasting the three perspectives Martin and Nakayama combine to form their dialectical perspective of intercultural communication, you could place less emphasis on the orientation to the perspectives found in Chapter 2, perhaps skipping the chapter altogether and instead explaining to students that the authors approach intercultural communication by combining different perspectives of intercultural communication. The combination of these approaches allows them to consider the role of history, power, and context in intercultural communication in ways other approaches sometimes fail to do.

Dealing With Difficult Topics

Prejudice

Students often approach the topic of prejudice with the idea that people either are or are not prejudiced and that they themselves are not. Your challenge is to show students that there are many different ways and levels in which people exhibit prejudice today. It is also helpful to explain to students that people are not necessarily racist because they are evil and have made conscious choices to be racist. Rather, people often perpetuate racism because of the positions they occupy within the cultural/social hierarchy, as those positions enable and encourage racist attitudes. In my experience, students appreciate this statement because it encourages them to examine the structures of society without guilt. If students understand that they are able to critically analyze social structures, they gain an awareness of their own involvement and the power to change those structures.

Another approach I have used to help students thoughtfully and openly discuss prejudice and related issues focuses on the relationship of cognitive information processing with labeling, stereotyping, prejudice, and discrimination. This begins with an exercise (see Chapter 5, Classroom Exercises and Chapter Assignments) in which a student is asked to categorize, name, and then describe the characteristics of category members. Then a discussion is conducted about the role of categorization in our information processing and its limitations. From the exercise, I can develop simple definitions of categorization, labeling, and stereotyping and suggest ways in which categorization often leads to negative stereotyping, prejudice, and discrimination. My goal is to help students recognize that stereotyping, prejudice, and discrimination often emerge without our awareness as we organize and interpret the information we receive.

Sexual Orientation

Discussions in the classroom about sexual orientation are often difficult because most students immediately want to define themselves as "not homosexual." Point out to students that this is what they are doing and ask them to explain. Try to use a strategy that does not put students on the spot. For example, you might say, "I noticed that several of you . . ." This might lead to a discussion of the term *homosexual* as a medical and cultural definition.

Difficult Discussion Topics

Many other difficult topics, such as xenophobia, affirmative action, and anti-Semitism, will emerge during class discussions. Attempt to create an atmosphere in which students feel they can express their opinions without fear of being punished. That does not mean that students should be able to express racist views without being asked to explain why they made those statements, the implications of their views, and how their opinions reflect on them and their participation in an intercultural communication class. However, students should be able to voice their opinions, rather than be silenced, because it allows them to examine and better understand their views as well as the reactions of others. When students do speak out, encourage them to critically evaluate what they have said rather than simply telling them they are wrong. You might ask students where they learned what they just said and what they think the implications are of their statements. Try to encourage an atmosphere of self-reflection and responsibility to others in the classroom for their contributions to the discussion (hooks, 1993).

Additionally, although you should encourage active participation in discussions, try to prevent some students from dominating the discussion, thereby prohibiting others from speaking. You might avoid eye contact with those who want to dominate and look directly at those who refrain from participation; another strategy is to state beforehand that you will ask those who do not participate for their opinions.

Houston (1992) suggests that many students do not speak out in the classroom because they fear sounding racist. One way to encourage student participation is to allow them to discuss issues hypothetically. Although this method is not as self-enlightening, it is still useful. For example, if the aim is to help students recognize how stereotypes influence intercultural communication, you might ask students to create a list of stereotypes they have heard about a particular cultural group and then have them suggest how these stereotypes might influence a person's communication with members of this group.

Teaching in Different Contexts

Students bring many different experiences to the classroom. Although some of these experiences are personal, some also represent the views of large numbers of people. For example, many European American students tend to have similar experiences or points of view. These students raise issues and require explanations that are somewhat different from students of color whose social positions lead to diverse experiences and opinions. Here I address some challenges you may face in different contexts.

Who Has Culture?

European American/White students often see themselves as universal human beings rather than as representatives of a specific culture. In their minds, it is other people who have culture, and "other" refers to racial or ethnic minorities. They do not see their whiteness as a racial category or their experiences as cultural experiences. This position leads them to regard themselves as the norm and to see others as deviating from that norm. Have students begin the process of learning intercultural communication by understanding that they do have culture and by specifying their position within the larger cultural framework. Students should be encouraged to understand that in order to communicate with others they first have to learn about themselves. Several chapters in the textbook provide theoretical perspectives that help students understand their location in cultural terms (for example, see Chapters 3, 4, and 5 on culture, history, and identity). I have included several classroom activities and assignments in this manual to facilitate this process.

In culturally diverse classes, there is sometimes a tendency to equate ethnic diversity with diversity of experiences. However, often the experiences of students are limited to their own group or the environment in which they grew up. Do not assume that students have had experiences outside their own group or that they will understand the perspective of others.

Lack of Historical Knowledge

Many European American students do not have adequate knowledge of the history of different racial and ethnic groups within the United States. The education of most students reflects a Eurocentric bias. Lack of knowledge about various cultural groups in the United States causes a variety of problems during classroom discussions, including limited or biased understanding of issues, and false cause–effect reasoning. Many students will insist that their education was objective and deny that it was structured by a racist societal ideology. When confronted with specific examples of events excluded from the general history they learned in school, many students react with anger and frustration directed at their schools. This often happens after students have watched a documentary. For example, when students learn the history of Japanese Americans in the United States during World War II and realize that many Japanese Americans were placed in internment camps with poor living conditions while sons and brothers fought with U.S. troops against the Japanese, they are shocked and angered. Help students by exploring why these events happened and why they have been excluded as general knowledge. Students should study how power in social and cultural contexts influenced these wartime events. It may be valuable to ask students to compare those conditions with present societal trends and to consider whether similar events could recur and, if so, how to avoid this.

Encourage students to see patterns in what has been excluded from their textbooks and the kinds of social, historical, and political realities these exclusions promote. Although there is not enough time in the term to present a history of all the different groups within the United States, you may find it helpful to present written or video material documenting critical moments in the history of different groups, such as the civil rights movement. You can also assign research projects that encourage students to investigate the histories of different groups within the United States or a family tree assignment, which raises students' interest in history and allows them to see the impact of history on their own families.

European American students may consider the study of history boring, may not see any connection to their lives, or may argue that it is time to forget past mistakes and move on to a better future. Here, you might provide examples of events that were repeated in history and ask why it would be useful to know the history before planning the future. You can make lectures on history more relevant to students by using discussions of the family tree assignment and video materials. These lectures should be designed to show the structural effects of history on individuals.

Attitudes toward history are different among students of color. History is often very important to them, and they understand the impact of history on the lives of individuals. However, some students may want to focus the discussion on their own groups whereas others may not want to deal with their own groups at all. Be aware of these feelings; encourage students to examine their experiences but do not expect them to speak for their groups. You should not select individual students to represent their groups in responding to questions; rather, ask for responses from all students.

Lack of Experiences and Contact With Different Cultural Groups

Surprisingly, some European American students claim that they have never had an opportunity to know on a personal level someone who is culturally/racially different from them. Here, you might encourage students to think abut the structure of society that allows them to interact only with people of their own group whereas others do not have this privilege. Additionally, you might question whether students who claim to have had no contact with culturally/racially different people really have never known a person who was different or have made choices not to interact when the opportunity was available. This could lead to an examination of what it means to have contact with someone or to say that one never had any contact with someone who is different.

Lack of Participation in Discussions

In every class there are students who do not participate in discussions. Some students do not talk because they are afraid to bring up a controversial issue, to disagree with other classmates, or to appear to be racist. This situation can be very difficult because certain students and their issues might be silenced by the majority. It is often helpful to assign journal writings in which students have a chance to discuss their views. This gives you an opportunity to respond to the student in writing or raise some issues in discussion (student anonymity should be maintained). It is important, however, that the students do not treat the journal writings as an easy way to earn points. There is also a danger that students will treat the journal writings as an opportunity to "spill their guts" rather than to critically reflect on their experiences and values in the context of theoretical issues discussed in class. It is helpful to provide students with strict guidelines for their journal writings (see the discussion on term projects in Part II).

Some students' lack of participation is determined by the norms of their cultures. Additionally, international students are often concerned about their language skills and using correct grammar, causing them to refrain from participating in discussions. Although there are strategies for making participation in discussions easier, sometimes it is best to allow international students to decide when and how they want to participate instead of putting them on the spot.

To encourage students to participate in discussions, it is helpful to ask them to bring to class written discussion questions based on their reading materials or the last lecture (it could be a way of earning class participation points). This encourages them to read and think about their reading assignments. Another strategy is to present discussion questions to students at the beginning of class and give them some time to think through their answers. Students are then more likely to volunteer their answers and may not be as anxious or embarrassed when you call on them.

Sometimes there will be only one or two students of color in class. It is *very* important that these students are not put in situations in which they are called on to speak for their groups. Although you might be careful not to do it, students may turn their heads and look at those whose race or ethnicity has been mentioned. This can be a good opportunity to raise the issue of representation and diversity of opinions within groups. You might ask students why they all looked at this person and why it is that we expect others to speak for the whole group but would feel uncomfortable doing it ourselves.

Prejudicial or Racist Comments

Prejudice and racism are very difficult topics to deal with. As mentioned previously, students often deny that they are prejudiced or racist and at the same time make racist comments. Students often do not realize they have made a racist remark or used sexist language, for instance, Oriental, Negro, stewardess, and so on. You might be surprised many times by students' lack of knowledge about appropriate and inappropriate terms. When students do make racist or prejudicial comments, ask them to repeat or explain their comments. Also, you can repeat their comments or questions using appropriate language and ask them whether this is what they meant.

Use of nonsexist and nonracist language should be the subject of ongoing discussion, as well as the topic of a separate class discussion. This may be especially important for diffusing potentially difficult situations in class, such as if you slip and say something that students challenge as inappropriate. Even experienced instructors with the best of intentions make mistakes. It is hard to erase culturally conditioned language patterns that have been perpetuated by family, social, political, and media influences. I have been in this situation before and was able to successfully deal with the consequences by immediately admitting the error, apologizing, and exploring with students the reasons it happened. Sexist language, in particular, seems to be a challenge for some instructors. Although it is important to be sensitive and careful, difficult issues should not be ignored in class discussions. Skipping over certain issues may communicate a lack of concern. You should do your best to prepare for subjects with which you are less comfortable, to monitor your use of language, and to learn strategies that will help you address potential mistakes.

Although blatantly racist comments are generally considered reprehensible, homophobic comments are not always negatively sanctioned by society. When such comments are made, you might ask students to think about the hierarchy of tolerances and why some comments are less acceptable than others even though they all express hostility toward people who are in some way different.

Students Reacting With Anger

Because deeply held beliefs and cultural assumptions are often challenged in the classroom, a few students may direct their anger or frustration at you. Some may accuse you of being wrong because your position is different from theirs. Students may express their feelings during class discussion or in their journal assignments. Although you may feel like responding emotionally, it is more productive to respond nondefensively and to ask students to explain their opinions and back them up. It is also helpful to redirect the discussion away from the issue of personality and toward theoretical and factual issues and to remind students that although they are entitled to their own opinions they should be prepared to back them up and to clarify them through critique and argumentation.

Tell students at the beginning of the course that discussions about deeply held cultural beliefs may result in hurt feelings; in such situations, they should ask themselves why they are reacting in this way and what it reveals about themselves. Questioning one's own reactions is part of understanding one's cultural identity.

Student Resistance

A class in intercultural communication will inevitably raise questions of racism and prejudice. Students can offer many examples of racist acts that they have witnessed, experienced themselves, or been exposed to through mass media. At the same time, however, they deny being racist themselves and attempt to explain racism as a fault of the past and older people ("old people are racist, young people are not"). Some will resist acknowledging racism in themselves, others will resist acknowledging racism altogether. It is helpful to bring in statistics and video materials dealing with issues of prejudice and discrimination. You might have the greatest impact, however, when you speak from your own experience. Presenting examples of prejudice in your own environment and being honest about your own participation in the racist ideology can be very powerful.

Discussing your personal experiences can be very risky if you are not ready to take an objective stance in critically evaluating your experience and, most important, in speaking to others about it. Although you will be vulnerable to student charges of racism, this strategy can be very useful as students can see that it is possible to speak of one's own experience without being defensive. You need to be careful not to turn the class into a confessional but to use personal experience to strengthen theoretical issues.

Often, students will be willing to discuss racism as it exists in other places, states, or countries, but they are unwilling to discuss racism in their own backyard. It is very useful for you to study the history of the region where your college or university is situated and use examples of ethnic and racial relations or cultural events in lectures, for example, the history of (de)segregation, enactment of laws, and so on. This strategy allows you to show the relevance of history to the present and to individual students by examining the residue of historical events.

It can also be helpful to bring in guest speakers to represent different positions or to provide current examples of how racism affects the communities in which the students live. For example, invite the fair housing council from the community in which the majority of students reside to describe instances of racism in the housing industry locally and nationally. The council will probably be eager to talk with students, and students will be surprised that racism is present to such an extent in their own community. This activity increases the relevance of the material discussed in class and its effect on individuals and the community.

Some students of color might also deny racist tendencies. Some will argue that one cannot be racist if one is not White. You might explain to the students that we all participate in racism that might be directed against our own group or against other racial, religious, cultural, or sexual orientation groups.

When the Instructor Is a Person of Color

Often when the instructor is a person of color, students project their own anxieties onto the instructor and think/say that the instructor has a personal agenda and/or "hates all White people." This is a very difficult situation, but it is something you should expect and be prepared for. How you deal with it depends on the context and your experience. It might be useful to be very explicit about your views and life experiences and about your goals as an instructor.

Respect Versus Guilt

When discussing sensitive issues, particularly those associated with prejudice and racism, it is important to use multiple teaching approaches for presenting information and ideas. It is a good idea to share different viewpoints from a variety of sources so that students do not feel that the instructor is "preaching" to them or is on a "soap box." Be sensitive in the way you present discussions of historical inequities. Sometimes certain students, particularly European American/White students, feel that they are being accused of responsibility for past and present actions of their cultural group. Although the discussion on history in Chapter 4 may help them to understand this better, frequently these students will respond by either feeling guilty or defensive. Although small doses of guilt may motivate some self-reflection, too much may have a negative impact on the learning process.

There are two very important reasons for being cautious about creating a learning context in which groups feel guilty about their cultural background. First, this outcome goes against the very objectives for teaching intercultural communication. The primary goal of teaching intercultural communication is to encourage people to learn respect for all people regardless of their differences. If one group is made to feel negatively about their own cultural group, regardless of where that group is positioned politically, they may begin to view their group negatively. Devaluing one's own group does not demonstrate a true value for diversity any more than devaluing another's group would.

Intercultural instructors need to be particularly sensitive to this. Unfortunately there have been some intercultural instructors who have become disillusioned with being from their own cultural group in the past as they have discovered more about their group's historical mistakes in intercultural and international relationships. As a result, they have consciously or unconsciously abandoned their cultural group by trying to adopt the identity of another group through dress, activities, and so on. In addition to personal issues about how this affects their own identities, of particular concern is what these behaviors and attitudes communicate to their students, especially those students who share the same cultural backgrounds.

Second, as corporate diversity trainers have already discovered, when one group feels guilty, diversity training may backfire or result in "backlash." For example, trainers have found that when White males experience feelings of guilt in diversity training programs, the training may contribute to, rather than resolve, tensions between different groups. This occurs because guilt is not a good motivator and in some cases may actually incite a degree of defensiveness that may turn into rebellion. These feelings may motivate an increase in negative feelings about and treatment of people from certain groups.

Instructors may be able to prevent these feelings by emphasizing respect and the positive contributions of many cultural groups. They may also help students deal more effectively with the implications of their groups' histories by allowing them opportunities in class discussions and assignments to explore these feelings in more detail. Familiarize students with the steps of majority and minority identity development found in Chapter 5 and spend time allowing them to explore the characteristics of a person in the final stage of these two models. Make it clear to them that persons who reach this final stage have arrived at a point where they can appreciate their own and other's diversity and cultural backgrounds.

FILM AND VIDEO DISTRIBUTORS

Here is a list of resource information on the distributors of the films and videos recommended in Part III: Chapter Materials.

Annenburg/CPB Project: (800) 532-7637; fax (802) 864-9846

Beacon Films: (800) 323-9084; fax (847) 328-6706

California Newsreel: (800) 621-6196; fax (415) 621-6522

Cambridge Documentary Films: (617) 484-3993; fax (617) 484-0754

CRM Films: (800) 421-0833, (619) 431-9800; fax (619) 931-5792

Encyclopaedia Britannica Educational Corporation: (800) 621-3900; fax (800) 480-0553

Facets Multimedia, Inc.: (800) 331-6197; fax (773) 929-5437

Fanlight Productions: (800) 937-4113; fax (617) 524-8838

Filmakers Library: (212) 808-4980; fax (212) 808-4983

Filmic Archives: (800) 366-1920; fax (203) 268-1796

Films for the Humanities and Sciences: (800) 257-5126; fax (609) 275-3767

Frameline: (415) 703-8650; fax (415) 861-1404

Goodmeasure, Inc.: (617) 621-3838

Griggs Productions: (800) 210-4200; fax (415) 668-6004

Indiana University: (800) 552-8620; fax (812) 855-8404

IRIS Films: (800) 343-5540; fax (510) 841-3336

Kit Parker Films: (800) 538-5838; fax (408) 393-0304

LCA (c/o New World Video): (310) 444-8100; fax (310) 444-8101

McGraw-Hill Publishing Company: (800) 338-3987

MPI Home Video: (800) 323-0442

MTI/Film and Video: See Phoenix Coronet

NAFSA Association of International Educators: (800) 836-4994; fax (412) 741-0609

New Day Films: (201) 652-6590; fax (201) 652-1973

PBS Video: (800) 344-3337; fax (703) 739-5269

Phoenix Coronet: (800) 221-1274; fax (314) 569-2834

Prentice-Hall Publishing Company: (800) 922-0579; fax (201) 767-2993

Pyramid Film & Video: (800) 421-2304; fax (310) 453-9083

Rosenstein Productions: P.O. Box 2483, Champaign, IL 61825-2483

Sai Communications: (800) 343-5540; fax (201) 652-1973

Society for Visual Education, Inc.: (800) 829-1900, (773) 775-9550; fax (800) 624-1678

SVE and Churchill Media: (800) 829-1900; fax (800) 624-1678

University of California Extension Media Center: (510) 642-0460; fax (510) 643-9271

Utah Valley State College, Behavioral Science Department: (801) 222-8083

Video Knowledge: (516) 367-4250; fax (576) 367-1006

West Glen Films: (800) 325-8677; fax (212) 944-9055

REFERENCES

Ahlquist, R. (1992). Manifestations of inequality: Overcoming resistance in a multicultural foundations course. In C. Grant (Ed.), *Research and multicultural education*. Washington, DC: Falmer.

Giroux, H. (1992). *Border crossings: Cultural workers and the politics of education*. New York: Routledge.

hooks, b. (1993). Transformative pedagogy and multiculturalism. In T. Perry & J. Fraser (Eds.), *Freedom's plow: Teaching in the multicultural classroom*. New York: Routledge.

Houston, M. (1992). The politics of difference; Race, class, and women's communication. In L. Rakow, (Ed.), *Women making meaning: New feminist directions in communication*. New York: Routledge.

PART II
COURSE ASSIGNMENTS AND EVALUATING STUDENT ACTIVITY PAPERS

PHILOSOPHY OF ASSIGNMENTS AND EVALUATION

The ideal assignment allows students to discover information that will be personally enlightening and salient. These assignments both support and extend course objectives. However, I recognize that the success of any assignment depends on the effort and enthusiasm the student contributes. For this reason, I make it very clear to students during the first class period that the value of the assignments is their responsibility. Those who put little effort into assignments will get little out of them. The number of assignments completed by students is not nearly as important as the quality of their learning experience, but requiring too little work will decrease students' opportunities to learn and may send a false message about your expectations regarding their scholarship. Expect students to work hard, but try not to overburden them with lots of projects. I base my approach to giving assignments on my perception of students' needs; I use assignments to create meaning for ambiguous concepts or add a sense of realism to abstract issues.

In this manual, you will find two types of sample assignments: term projects and chapter assignments. The term projects, described later in Part II, cover broad issues related to several chapters or ideas and require more student time, whereas the chapter assignments in Part III are shorter and focus on ideas specific to individual chapters. I also encourage you to look for ideas from other sources, including creating your own assignments. Because the needs of students differ by region, class composition, and other demographic factors, I have tried to avoid dictating the specific set of assignments that will be most beneficial to your particular classes. Rather, I have provided a variety of assignments and some suggestions for determining which assignments to choose. I would also encourage you to find ways to modify existing assignments so that they better respond to the needs of your students.

Analyze Your Audience

It is virtually impossible to determine individual student needs when you are organizing the course, but general ideas about the needs of the students taking your classes may be identified by researching the demographics of the college or university, the demographics of the communities from which the majority of your students come, and the reasons that outside departments suggest or require this course in intercultural communication. In addition, it may be useful to understand the current intercultural issues in the community.

Although assignment ideas are suggested for each chapter, I do not suggest requiring one assignment per chapter because that may overload students. The decision for the number of required assignments depends on the interest of your students and on your preferences. With too many assignments, students may become resentful, and with too few, students may not have the chance to learn concepts firsthand. New teachers should try out assignments to get a feel for the amount of time and effort they require. I typically have assigned one to two term projects and three smaller assignments (two to three pages in length) over the course of the semester. (This may be too much for a quarter-system course.) You could also give few, if any, term projects and increase the number of smaller assignments.

Talk With Colleagues

Speaking to colleagues in your department, particularly those with experience teaching intercultural communication, may be enlightening. These colleagues may give you valuable information about the student population and community that will help you make decisions. However, recognize that your experience in teaching the course and your relationship with your students will be unique.

Colleagues in your department and from other colleges and universities may also be willing to share ideas and assignments that they have used effectively. Many will be willing to share these ideas and are easily approached. The National Communication Association directory is a useful resource for finding out how to contact colleagues; regional and national conventions present opportunities to speak with many colleagues at once, and resources and chat rooms are emerging over the Internet.

Consider Your Own Expertise

Instructors bring different areas of expertise to the course. You should select assignments that you are comfortable helping students complete and grade. If you are a new instructor, you may want to complete the assignments you plan to use and discuss them with others who have experience teaching intercultural communication. When you are comfortable with and enthusiastic about the assignments, students get a better sense of the assignments' relevance and your willingness to help them.

Encourage Student Involvement

Although you cannot individualize course assignments for each class member, you can give students a choice. Providing assignment options to complete during the course and allowing students to choose from among the options is a useful strategy for getting students involved. Students will complain less about assignments, they will feel a greater sense of personal control and autonomy, and they will have more opportunity to explore intercultural issues of personal interest. Although grading various assignments initially may seem taxing, in the long run you will find it to be less tedious. Here are a few guidelines for those instructors who wish to use this approach:

1. Point values for all the options must be determined prior to the course so that students will know what combination of assignments they need to complete to receive the required number of assignment points.

2. Assignments with equivalent point values should require an equivalent amount of effort. If students find that one assignment is easier than another and both are worth the same number of points, they will typically choose the easier one.

3. Students will need clear written instructions for each assignment at the beginning of the course.

4. Due dates should be interspersed throughout the course. Students should submit one assignment at each due date instead of handing in a set at the end of the term. This breaks the grading into more manageable parts and prevents students from rushing to complete all the assignments at the end of the course.

Evaluation

A variety of techniques and philosophies can be applied to grading course assignments. I consider fairness and useful feedback to be two of the most important criteria in determining methods and approaches to grading. Fairness begins with the instructions given to students for completion of assignments. If you make the instructions for the assignments clear to students and they understand your expectations and requirements, they will be more inclined to feel that your evaluations of their work are fair. To be useful, feedback should indicate why students lost points. However, feedback may also perform other functions, such as challenging students to think in more depth about aspects of the assignment or their conclusions. Feedback can be used to provide encouragement and motivation to students who are extending themselves to really explore and understand issues in the course.

Consider a variety of evaluation approaches and choose one with which you are comfortable. English teachers have successfully used the grade sheet approach for student compositions, and I have modified it for class assignments in intercultural communication. This approach clarifies students' expectations of the assignment, provides an efficient way to give feedback, and increases grading consistency. The approach consists of creating a grade sheet for each assignment. The grade sheet lists the criteria the instructor will use in grading the assignment with a breakdown of the points. This grade sheet is given to students before they begin the assignment, and it can be a resource for completing the assignment. The grade sheet is submitted with the assignment, and the instructor uses the criteria on the grade sheet to evaluate the paper. Examples of two of these grade sheets follow.

Sample Assignment Evaluation Forms

Example 1—Ethnic Identity Chapter Assignment Grade Sheet

Content: The paper is a well-organized report of your observations about your ethnic background and how this background may or may not be an influence on your communication. At least four of the six thought questions are addressed in the report. ____ of 4 points

Depth of Observations: You have shown that you have thought carefully about the content questions by discussing the implications or applications of your observations to communication situations. ____ of 4 points

Quality: Ideas are expressed clearly with complete sentences, correct punctuation, and proper spelling. The paper is a minimum of 1-1/2 pages in length, double spaced in standard font size. ____ of 2 points

Total ____ of 10 points

Example 2—Term Project 1 Grade Sheet

Introduction: You have identified the culture you have chosen as the focus for your review, you have given a rationale for the importance of studying this culture, and you have provided a brief preview of the paper. ____ of 5 points

Content: The paper reports literature that is relevant in addressing at least four questions about the culture. It is clear from the discussion why the questions are important to understanding how to communicate completely in the culture. Sufficient literature is used to answer the questions thoroughly. The information comes from at least six sources, two of which are published research reports or ethnographies.   ____ of 15 points

Use of Sources: In the paper, proper citations (according to APA style) are given to support the conclusions you reach about aspects of the culture. There is no evidence of plagiarizing others' ideas or categories. Quotations are not "over used" and are punctuated according to style guidelines. At the end of the paper, you give a list of sources containing all of the references for the citations in the text of the paper.   ____ of 10 points

Organization: The literature is clearly organized in a logical framework. The answers to the questions are clear. You are careful not to go off on tangents, and you have clear transitions between ideas and paragraphs. Paragraphs are well organized and complete.   ____ of 10 points

Quality: Ideas are expressed in complete sentences, correct punctuation, and proper spelling. Format and length requirements are met.   ____ of 10 points

                                          Total   ____ of 50 points

SUGGESTIONS FOR TERM PROJECTS

Term Project 1—Research on a Specific Culture

Objective: To encourage the student to learn specific information about a culture of personal interest.

Description: The outcome of this research project is a literature review that summarizes the student's research on the culture he/she has chosen.

Part A: Instructions for Research Project

1.   Select a culture that you wish to research.

2.   Research this culture using research reports published in academic journals, published ethnographies, interviews, encyclopedias, and other published materials. A minimum of six sources should be used to document information in the literature review. Two of these sources should be research reports published in academic journals or published ethnographies. Students are encouraged to use members of the culture in their communities for at least two of the remaining four sources.

3.   The paper should have a cover page on the front that includes the title of the paper, the course number and title, and your student identification number. On the back of your paper, please print your name.

4. The literature review itself should be four to six pages, double spaced, and typed in a regular 10- or 12-point font. The literature review should begin with an introduction that identifies the culture you have chosen and why you think it is important to study. This introduction should be no more than 1-1/2 pages in length. The rest of the literature review should contain a logically organized and detailed report from the available literature that answers four to six of the questions listed in Part B.

5. The information included in the literature review should be cited using in-text citations (APA style).

6. At the end of the literature review, include a "works cited" or "reference" section that lists the full references for the citations used in the literature review. Include only those references that are actually cited.

7. Write the paper according to APA style guidelines. This especially applies to the use of in-text citations and the reference section. Note: This paper is a formal research paper and should be written in third person.

8. You are encouraged to meet with the instructor for help in completing this project. Please start your project immediately.

Part B: Suggested Term Project Questions

1. What are some of the value differences between this culture and your own?

2. What are the predominant religious beliefs espoused by members of this culture, and how do you think these beliefs influence their behaviors?

3. What are some nonverbal communication differences found in this culture?

4. What are some communication style differences found in this culture?

5. What are some language or dialectical differences found in this culture?

6. How are social roles/gender roles viewed in this culture?

7. Do the family structure and roles differ in this culture?

8. Are there differences in interpersonal/romantic relationships in this culture?

9. If you were a person traveling to do business in this culture, what information would you need?

10. For someone going to this culture for a study abroad or a brief work assignment, what information would aid his/her cultural adjustment?

11. How does this culture's history influence perception and communication between this culture and your own culture?

12. How does this culture's government influence perception and communication between this culture and your own culture?

13. What are some of the stereotypes people of your culture have about people in the culture you have chosen? Is there any truth to them?

14. Does the education system in this culture differ from the one in your own?

Note: this is not a comprehensive list. Many important questions could be investigated about the culture you have chosen. You may use other questions if they are approved by the instructor.

Term Project 2—Interaction Journal Entries

Focus: To provide an opportunity for the student to experience some of the elements of intercultural communication and to practice intercultural communication competence skills.

Objectives: These include, but are not limited to, (1) increasing the student's awareness of cultural variables that influence communicative interaction; (2) increasing the student's ability to explain cultural differences in communication; and (3) increasing the student's appreciation for the need to learn competence skills for intercultural communication.

Instructions: Each student will choose, either through the programs suggested by the instructor or through individual efforts, an individual or group from another culture to become acquainted with during the course. Each selection must be approved by the instructor. Choose someone who will meet with you at least ____ times (of a 1-hour minimum) during the course.

You should record your impressions and observations from these meetings in a journal. The instructor will ask for entries to be submitted periodically during the term (see the scheduled due dates on your syllabus). After you have completed the required interactions and journal entries, summarize your experience in a three-page double-spaced typewritten report. The report is worth up to 25 points. In this report you should address the following questions:

1. How did you feel when you first received this assignment? Have your feelings changed? If so, in what ways? If not, why?

2. Describe the interaction that was most enjoyable. What made it enjoyable?

3. What have you learned about intercultural communication competence from the experiences you have had with your partner? Be specific!

4. Evaluate the success of your experience. What was successful? What were some of the difficulties you faced? Did you overcome the difficulties? If so, how?

Guide for Journal Entries

Your journal entries are worth 10 points each and should be a minimum of 1-1/2 pages. The more thorough you are in writing the journal entries, the more helpful they will be when you write your final report. Your instructor will read these journal entries and will give you feedback occasionally with suggestions or questions for you to consider. Your instructor will maintain your confidentiality. Your grade will not be based on what you say or how you feel but on your thoroughness in recording your observations in the areas suggested and on evidence of a thoughtful evaluation of your experience.

Each entry should be dated. Briefly describe the setting and the purpose or activity that you chose for your interaction. In general, record any information or observations that you think will be useful in completing the final report. Specifically, you should provide information for these five areas:

1. During your interaction, what did you learn about your partner's or partners' culture(s)?

2. Did you notice any challenges in trying to communicate with your partner? For example, did any misunderstandings occur?

3. What did you enjoy most about this interaction? Be specific!

4. What did you learn about yourself as an intercultural communicator?

5. What did you learn from this experience that helped you understand what it takes to become a competent intercultural communicator?

Term Project 3—Class Journal Writing

Journals are a very helpful teaching tool; they allow you to monitor students' progress and address problems or uncertainties early on. Additionally, they give students an opportunity to voice their opinions on issues they feel uncomfortable discussing in class and encourage them to relate the theoretical material to their own lives. Many students have emotional reactions to discussions of intercultural issues, and journal writing helps them to critically evaluate their reactions and gives you a chance to respond to problems. However, you should ensure that students do not simply divulge personal stories without applying the theoretical material. To avoid this situation, it is helpful to provide students with specific guidelines regarding their journal assignments. I have found that it is very useful if the instructor treats student writing seriously and responds to their concerns or critiques in writing. This strategy makes students feel more responsible for what they are writing. I provide the following guidelines for students, which you can modify for your purposes:

1. You will be required to write journal entries and turn them in every week. The purpose of this assignment is

    a. to critically analyze your feelings and reactions to the theoretical material from class discussions or assigned readings.

    b. to apply concepts you have learned in class.

    c. to provide feedback for the instructor.

2. Do not just "emotionally dump." A discussion of feelings is helpful only when you can understand them using the theoretical material. Use the following guidelines in your writing:

    a. How did you feel during the discussion? Why did you feel this way?

    b. Is there something else you wanted to say in class? Are there questions you wanted to ask? Did any issue in class confuse or surprise you?

    c. Was something said that was important to you and your understanding of cultural dynamics?

    d. Do you agree or disagree with something that was said in class or the textbook? Why?

    e. Apply something you learned in class to an intercultural experience outside class. Did the concept/idea/theory help you better understand your experience? Describe how. If it did not, explain why not. How would you modify the concept or idea?

    f. Are there any ideas you wish we could explore further in a future class section?

In their first journal entry, students might discuss why they chose to take intercultural communication. Although some students might be enrolled simply because it fit their schedule or it was required, they should still think about what they would like to get out of the class. This assignment allows you to check students' expectations and to discuss them if they are not going to be met in this class.

You will need to determine the point value for each entry and how many entries will be submitted during the term. Toward the end of the semester or quarter, students may burn out a bit, so you may choose to limit entries to one per week or cut off this assignment a couple of weeks before the end of the course.

Term Project 4—Film Analysis

Students select and view a video/film that discusses some aspect of intercultural relations. Students can select a new film or an older one (for example, *Higher Learning, City of Joy, Philadelphia, Grand Canyon*). Next, students conduct a critical analysis of the film as a cultural context, focusing on several scenes that they think are most important to the plot. You can provide students with all or some of the following guidelines and directives, adding to and modifying them depending on the scale of the assignment and the number of points available.

1. Describe the context in which the action takes place. Which elements of the film give us information about the context? How does the context affect communication patterns between the main characters?

2. Describe different identities that emerge in the course of the film. How are these identities constructed (ascription, avowal, interpellation)? How can the communication perspective help us understand the identities of the main characters? How can we use the critical perspective to understand these identities? What is the relationship between identities and context? Identify different social and cultural identities. Does the identity of any of the main characters change in the course of the film? Do any of the characters undergo a process of identity development? What influenced this process?

3. How does history affect the standpoints of the main characters? What do we learn about history from the film? What is the relationship between history and identities of the main characters?

4. What can you say about communication styles and language use in the film? What did you learn about the characters from the way they use language? Identify social structures that affect how the language is used (discourse).

5. Analyze nonverbal codes and cultural space. How do the main characters use nonverbal communication? How are cultural spaces constructed in the film? Identify different elements that are used to construct these cultural spaces.

6. Identify cultural position(s) the film represents. How are the cultural positions represented in the film related to our present cultural and political contexts? To which cultural positions does the film appeal? Whose social interests (in terms of social positions) are represented in the film? Why are those and not other interests represented? How is power implicated in social positions that the film represents?

Students might write drafts of each section after discussions of appropriate chapters and then write the final analysis.

Term Project 5—Theoretical Approaches to Studying Intercultural Communication

Objective: To help increase students' understanding of the social science, interpretive, and critical perspectives to studying intercultural communication.

Instructions: Have students select a research topic in intercultural communication such as affirmative action, bilingual education, apartheid, or a conflict between cultural groups. After researching the topic, students should prepare a two- to four-page brief summarizing the history of the topic and current status. They should also submit a one-page description for each of the perspectives that includes a discussion about how the topic could be studied from that particular perspective and six to eight questions that might be answered from that perspective. Students may follow the Disneyland Paris example provided in Chapter 2 of the textbook.

PART III
CHAPTER MATERIALS

CHAPTER 1

WHY STUDY INTERCULTURAL COMMUNICATION?

LEARNING OBJECTIVES

After studying the material in this chapter, students should be able to:

Identify six imperatives motivating increased interest in intercultural communication.

Describe how advances in technology and increases in mobility have influenced intercultural communication.

List ways in which immigration patterns affect relationships between nations and cultures.

Explain how the history of immigration influences cultural relations within the United States.

Describe how the study of intercultural communication is important to the economy of the United States.

Identify ways in which studying intercultural communication may contribute to promoting world peace.

Explain how understanding other cultures improves our awareness of our own cultures.

Describe some of the ethical issues that arise in the study of intercultural communication.

Explain what it means to be an ethical intercultural communicator.

KEY WORDS

Anglocentrism	global village	mobility
colonialism	heterogeneity	multinational corporations
demographics	immigrants	multiphrenia
diversity	intercultural communication	nativistic
enclaves	*maquiladoras*	self-reflexivity
ethics	melting pot	
ethnocentrism	microwave relationships	

EXTENDED CHAPTER OUTLINE

Intercultural communication is a rapidly growing area of study. You will be exposed to a variety of approaches used to study intercultural communication. The authors attempt to link intercultural communication theories and practices to increase your understanding of the theories. The authors will share personal intercultural experiences to increase your understanding of their perspectives. Do not be overwhelmed by the complexity of intercultural communication, but accept this as a part of the intercultural communication process.

I. The Technological Imperative: The term **global village** coined in the 1960s by Marshall McLuhan suggests that technological advances in electronic media have made it possible for us to communicate and form complex relationships with people throughout the world whom we have not met face to face.
    A. Technology and Human Communication
        1. Advances in electronic media have influenced how we think about ourselves and how we form intercultural relationships.
            a. Kenneth Gergen suggests that our social relationships have multiplied exponentially. We can be involved in multiple relationships simultaneously without making face-to-face contact.
            b. Family interactions have become **microwave relationships**. The family is frequently seen as a pit stop between technological devices.
            c. Gergen suggests that lack of time and space barriers to communication have lead to **multiphrenia**, or the splitting of the individual into multiple selves.
            d. This ability to communicate through many channels without being physically present may contribute to increasing notions about what one ought to do, self-doubts, and irrationalities as a result of our ability.
        2. How do these advances influence intercultural communication? We increasingly come into contact with people different from us in ways that we often do not understand. Sometimes these contacts end in hostility.
    B. Mobility and Its Effect on Communication
        Mobility in our society places us in physical contact with more people.
        1. Our society is increasingly more mobile; U.S. families move an average of five times during the lifetime of the family.
        2. Mobility changes our society and the individuals involved.
        3. Divorces contribute to mobility; only 50% of American adolescents live with both birth parents. The rest have other arrangements, and many are shuttled between parents across various geographical regions.
        4. Families also relocate for economic reasons.
II. The Demographic Imperative: There are two sources for recent and future changes in the U.S. population:
    A. Changing U.S. **Demographics**
        According to the Workforce 2000 study, the U.S. workforce population will change by the 21st century. The mean age of workers will increase to 36, women will comprise 48% of the workforce, and they will be more ethnically and racially diverse.

B. Changing Immigration Patterns
  1. Influence of Immigration
      a. The United States is often described as a nation of **immigrants**, however, it is important to understand that it is also a nation that subjugated its original inhabitants and permitted slavery.
      b. Immigration patterns have shifted since the 1960s when most U.S. immigrants came from European countries. Today, 90% of the one million immigrants to the United States are from Latin America and Asia.
      c. The Census Bureau predicts that by 2030 nearly half of the population will be African American, Asian, Hispanic, and Native American.
      d. Increased **heterogeneity** presents opportunities and challenges for intercultural communication students including:
          i. Acknowledgment of minority group fears, tensions, and treatment by politically dominant groups.
          ii. **Diversity** in society provides opportunities to expand our horizons linguistically, politically, and socially as we are exposed to different lifestyles and ways of thinking.
  2. Intercultural relations in the United States today can be understood by reviewing our immigration history.
      a. The United States has always been a nation of immigrants, but this overlooks the presence of the 8–10 million Native Americans who were already here.
      b. As the number of colonizing Europeans increased, the Native Americans decreased.
  3. African American Immigrants
      a. African Americans represent a special type of immigrant because they did not voluntarily choose to come to the United States and most were subjugated to slavery.
      b. Slave trade lasted 350 years and was outlawed in Europe much earlier than in the United States.
      c. An estimated 10 million Africans were brought to the United States, many additional Africans died on the slave boats in route.
      d. The history of African slavery has profound and unique effects on contemporary interracial relations in the United States.
      e. Slavery was a moral dilemma for many Whites and continues to be. As a result, many Whites prefer to ignore this part of history, but West (1993) suggests it is important to both acknowledge this historical mistake and recognize its historical consequences.
  4. Relationships with New Immigrants
      a. Relationships among the residents and immigrants have always been filled with tension and conflict.
      b. In the 19th century Native Americans were often caught in the middle of European rivalries.
      c. Later, **Anglocentrism** characterized history as tensions arose between new and more established European immigrants (mainly British) who wanted to protect their norms, language, and culture.

      d.   The **melting pot** metaphor emerged as way of describing established immigrants' feelings that all immigrants should work to assimilate into the mainstream culture.

      e.   Late in the 19th and early in the 20th centuries, the **nativistic** movement emerged. This anti-immigrant movement advocated violence against newer immigrants and received government support in the form of anti-immigrant acts that prevented groups, particularly Asians, from entering the United States.

      f.   By 1930, it unified European immigrant groups and focused racial hostilities on non-White immigrant groups (for example, Asians, Native Americans, and so on). This was devastating because of the economic split that resulted between White and non-White citizens.

      g.   Throughout the world, economic conditions have influenced attitudes toward immigration. When economic conditions are bad, attitudes toward immigrants become more negative.

      h.   Tensions between cultures exist today as exemplified by the conflicts that have occurred in Los Angeles and across Southern California.

      i.   These conflicts may become exacerbated when cultural groups in an area settle in **enclaves**.

5.   Immigration and Economic Classes

      a.   Some group tensions may result from economic disparities between different immigrant groups.

      b.   Most Americans do not like to acknowledge the existence of class structures and how tough it is to move up in this structure.

      c.   Failure to acknowledge the rigidness of the class structure not only reinforces the beliefs of upper-class members in their own abilities but promotes among lower classes the false hope that they can get ahead.

      d.   Cases of successful upward mobility are rare, and the reality is that the income gap between rich and poor in the United States is greater than in most industrialized countries.

      e.   Particularly since the mid-1970s, the rich have fared much better than the middle class or the poor, partly due to the loss of stable industrial jobs as companies have moved to cheaper overseas labor markets.

6.   Demographic Diversity

      a.   Immigration also contributes to religious diversity.

      b.   This diversity adds to the challenge of intercultural communication.

      c.   The challenge is to look beyond stereotypes and biases, to recognize diversity, and then apply intercultural communication skills.

      d.   It is important to recognize the inadequacy of the melting pot metaphor—people cannot be expected to assimilate in the same way.

      e.   Today a better metaphor may be a "salad" or a "tapestry," which recognizes that each group will retain its own characteristics and yet contribute to the whole.

      f.   The United States is not a model of diversity, nor is it the most ethnically diverse country.

      g.   Diversity can be a positive force providing linguistic richness, culinary variety, new resources to meet social challenges, as well as domestic and international business opportunities.

III. The Economic Imperative:
   A. The U.S. economy depends on global markets. In 1986, Japan surpassed the United States as an international creditor. The next year their per capita income exceeded that of the United States. Within two more years Japan had the 11 largest banks in the world.
   B. This motivated U.S. experts to study Japanese business practices. They found that Japanese have a greater belief in effort for its own sake. Evidence of this value difference is found in both the workforce and the education system. Japanese employees are motivated to work longer and have more persistence. Japanese students out perform American students on standardized exams.
   C. Japan differs in many ways from the United States, although neither good nor bad, these ways have been right for Japan.
   D. U.S. Americans have traits for success as well, but to compete effectively with other nations, we need to think in more sophisticated ways about the relationship between cultural patterns and economic success.
   E. Unfortunately, in contrast to companies in other countries, many American companies spend little time learning how to do business in other countries.
   F. Trends toward globalization present new issues in the form of **multinational corporations**. Many U.S. companies have established manufacturing plants along the U.S.–Mexican border, known as *maquiladoras*, which present intercultural challenges between Mexicans and U.S. Americans.
   G. Domestic diversity also motivates businesses to be attentive to cultural differences. Positive outcomes can emerge from positive responses to diversity.
IV. The Peace Imperative:
   A. Can diverse groups of people live together and get along?
      1. Historically the answer is not optimistic. Contact among different groups has often led to disharmony.
      2. There are many examples today of cultural conflicts.
      3. Some conflicts are tied to the history of **colonialism**. Colonialism occurred when groups with diverse languages, cultures, religions, and identities were united by European powers to form one state.
      4. Other conflicts are tied to economic disparities coupled with the influence of U.S. technology and media.
      5. Simply understanding intercultural communication may not end conflicts between cultural groups, but the existence of conflict underscores the importance of the need to learn more about other groups because ultimately people, not countries, negotiate peace.
      6. Interpersonal communication is important, but remember that individuals are influenced by conflicts in the societies they are born into as well.
V. The Self-Awareness Imperative: A less obvious reason to study intercultural communication is that it helps us understand our own cultural identity.
VI. The Ethical Imperative:
   A. Studying intercultural communication helps us address the ethical issues of living in an intercultural world.
      1. **Ethics** are principles of conduct that help govern behaviors of individuals and groups that often arise from a community's perspective of what is good and bad behavior.

2. Ethics focus more on degrees of rightness and wrongness in human behavior than do values.
3. Cultures may hold different notions of ethical behavior, and conflicts arise when the ethical systems of two cultures collide.
4. In this text the authors stress the relativity of cultural behavior—no cultural pattern is inherently right or wrong.
5. The decision about whether there is any universality in ethics depends on an individual's own perspective.
   a. An extreme universalist would insist that fundamental notions of right and wrong are universal and that cultural differences are superficial.
   b. An extreme relativist position holds that any cultural behavior can only be judged within the cultural context in which it occurs.
6. Some scholars have tried to develop universal ethical guidelines. Hatch (1983), for example, assumes that people can evaluate culture without succumbing to **ethnocentrism**, that all individuals and cultures share a fundamental humanistic belief, and that people should respect each others' well-being.
7. Studying intercultural communication should help us address ethical issues in intercultural interaction.

B. How to Be an Ethical Student of Culture
1. **Self-Reflexivity**
   a. Understanding oneself and one's position in society are vital to studying intercultural communication.
   b. The process of learning about other cultures will often teach us about ourselves.
   c. Sometimes this can be confusing because intercultural experiences change who we are and who we think we are.
   d. By understanding which social categories we belong to and their implications, we should better understand how to communicate.
2. Learning About Others
   a. The study of cultures is the study of other people.
   b. It is important not to forget that when we study cultures we are studying real people with real lives and that our conclusions about them may have real consequences for them and us.
   c. Students of cultures should speak "with" and "to" others instead of "for" and "about" others.
   d. In other words, it is important to listen and to engage others in dialogues about their cultural realities.

C. Changing Through Intercultural Contact
1. Sometimes communities lose their uniqueness because of intercultural contact.
2. Some cultures resist the influence of contact whereas others do not.
3. All education may be transformative, but intercultural communication may be more so because it deals with such fundamental aspects of human behavior.
4. Learning about intercultural communication may cause us to question the very core values and frameworks of our thinking.

5. There are unethical applications for intercultural information.
   a. Pursuit of intercultural information with the end to proselytize others without their consent.
   b. Trainers who misrepresent or exaggerate their abilities to change prejudices or racism in brief one-shot training sessions.

DISCUSSION QUESTIONS

Questions from the Text

1. How do electronic means of communication (E-mail, the Internet, fax, and so on) differ from face-to-face interactions?

2. How does increased mobility of our society affect us as individuals? How does it affect the way we form relationships?

3. What are some of the challenges that organizations may face as they become more diverse?

4. How might organizations benefit from increased diversity in the workplace? How might individuals benefit?

5. How do economic situations affect intergroup relations?

Additional Questions

1 Which cultural groups do we have the most information about? Why?

2. How do economic situations affect intergroup relations?

3. What roles do ethics play in intercultural communication?

Specific Questions About Each Imperative
(as suggested by Martin and Nakayama)

The Technological Imperative

1. How can we maintain good relationships in a multiphrenic age?

2. How can we rise to the challenges of high-tech communication?

3. Who can have access to these communication media and who cannot?

4. How do these technological developments reinforce power and privilege?

5. Whose language dominates?

6. How does physical mobility influence communication?

7. What are the implications when some groups move voluntarily and others are forced to move?

The Demographic Imperative

1. Why are some immigrant groups subject to prejudice whereas others are not?

2. How can a culturally diverse society maintain cordial relations among groups?

3. How are intercultural relations influenced when some groups have power and others do not?

The Economic Imperative

1. How does communication in business vary across cultures?

2. What can we learn about communication in cross-cultural (multinational) companies?

3. Why are some cultural groups successful at cross-cultural business and others are not?

4. How can diverse groups of people work together successfully in business?

5. Why are scholars focused primarily on understanding cross-cultural communication of more powerful nations?

The Peace Imperative

1. When does intercultural communication result in harmonious relationships among groups?

2. What kind of communication is most likely to promote resolution of conflict?

3. How can we understand how larger social forces are affecting us in our intercultural interactions?

4. How are these forces affecting others with whom we communicate?

5. How can understanding the dialectic between interpersonal and societal levels inform intercultural practices?

The Self-Awareness Imperative

1. How can we understand another's cultural position and space?

2. How can we understand the variety of cultural styles that come along with our cultural identities?

3. How do these communication styles vary?

The Ethical Imperative

1. How can we understand our own cultural background and others in an ethical stance?

2. Are there any ethical guidelines that transcend particular cultural contexts?

3. What are guidelines that transcend particular cultural contexts?

4. What are guidelines for ethical behavior in intercultural interaction?

5. How can we apply what we learn about intercultural communication in an ethical way?

CLASSROOM EXERCISES AND CHAPTER ASSIGNMENTS

1. Introduction Exercise: At the beginning of the course, it is useful to provide opportunities for the students to become familiar with each other so that they will feel more comfortable contributing to class discussions. This may be facilitated by dividing students into pairs. Each student is given 5 minutes to play the role of the interviewer and 5 minutes to be interviewed. At the end of 10 minutes, the student pairs take turns introducing each other to class members. The following questions are useful in becoming acquainted with students and the repertoire of cultural experiences they bring to the class:

a. Where did you grow up?

b. What other languages besides English do you speak?

c. What areas outside the United States have you visited?

d. Have you lived outside of the United States? Where?

e. Describe one intercultural experience you have had.

f. Describe one ritual your family practiced as you were growing up.

g. Why are you taking this class?

h. Would you like to live in another country? Why?

The length of time needed for this exercise depends on class size and the number of questions the instructor suggests to the students. Typically, 10 to 15 minutes are provided for the interviewing with the instructor alerting students when it is time to switch from being the interviewer to the interviewee. The oral introductions average about 2–3 minutes per pair. If you need to cut down the time allotted for the oral introductions, limit the students to telling four or five things they learned about their partners.

2. Intercultural Issues Exercise: Use this activity to increase student awareness of the impact and prevalence of the imperatives (for example, technological, demographic) described in this chapter. You need an edition (if the class size is large, multiple editions may be used) of a fairly large local newspaper. Divide the class into groups of two to four individuals and give each group a section of the paper with news articles of some type (for example, local, state, national, international, sports, business). Then assign the groups of students to skim through their sections of the paper for articles that report on issues related to the imperatives, with one member of the group keeping track on a piece of paper of the number of articles found for each imperative and writing a brief description of the subject of each article. (You may want to show them one or two examples from another paper/edition.) Students will need 10–20 minutes to work as groups, unless their assigned sections are small. When they have finished, record on the board the number of articles found by each group for each imperative. After tallying the total in each column, ask students to discuss why there were more articles concerning some initiatives than others (were there any precipitating events that generated more articles?) and to share examples of some of the articles.

3. Local Immigration Assignment: The focus of this assignment is to familiarize students with the way immigration patterns may have affected their own communities. Assign students to research the community in which they grew up or currently live to discover some of the motives for immigrants to move to the community. This assignment may be given as an individual project or to groups. Suggested information sources could be state or local histories, reference librarians at local libraries, tourist information, the chamber of commerce, local historians, or longtime residents of the community. Students compile the information in a written or oral presentation form. Some questions to guide their research include:

a. What ethnic backgrounds/countries are represented in your community?

b. From what ethnic backgrounds/countries are the majority of the people in your community?

c. What were some of the reasons people from different ethnic backgrounds/countries came to your community?

d. How did the people from these different ethnic backgrounds/cultures influence the community?

e. Are there any visible evidences of the cultures these people came from in the community today (celebrations, traditions, architecture, and so forth)?

f. Were there large groups of people from other ethnic backgrounds/countries who came to the community and have since left? Why did they come and go?

4. Video Assignment: Students may select a video to watch that depicts the experience of immigration to the United States for a particular ethnic group or individual (for example, *Far and Away*). After they have watched the video, students should describe the immigration experience using these questions as a guide:

a. What factors influenced the group/individual to move to the United States?

b. What were the primary challenges this group/individual faced in trying to get along in the United States?

c. How did the group/individual react to these challenges?

d. Were there any people or events that aided the group/individual?

5. Assessing Cultural Behavior—Ethics Exercise: This activity is designed to help students begin to explore their personal ethics and the challenges created by viewing intercultural communication in a relativistic rather than in a universalistic manner. Instructors should be prepared to discuss difficult issues that may arise during this activity and help students view ethics within a more complex framework by applying the guidelines in this chapter. For this exercise, ask students to find an ethical issue that they feel strongly about from a news broadcast, newspaper article, or the Internet. Instruct them to come prepared to describe the issue and the ethical challenge or dilemma it poses. Challenge students to describe the position a relativist and then a universalist would take on this issue. After all the students have presented their issues (in a large class they could do this in dyads or small groups), ask students to describe ways in which ethical intercultural communicators would handle these dilemmas using the guidelines in this chapter. Reinforce to students that many ethical issues are difficult and that the guidelines for ethical communication are challenging to use so it is important to listen patiently to each other and then help each other sort out the issues by asking questions like the ones suggested in the following hypothetical example. Suppose a student chose the debate over teaching Ebonics vs. standard English in California schools. The ethical issues raised in this debate may include whether Ebonics is a "real" language, whether students of Ebonics will be disadvantaged by not learning standard English, and what message is being communicated to African Americans and speakers of other languages in the United States. The instructor might then encourage students to apply the ethical guidelines in their thinking by asking questions such as:

a. How can teaching both Ebonics and standard English help us to respect others?

b. Can we practice empathy by striving to "see" the value of Ebonics (or standard English) from another point of view?

c. How might teaching Ebonics in the public schools eliminate oppression?

d. What are possible ways to share responsibility with others when dealing with this issue?

6. Early Experiences With Cultural Differences: This introductory activity is useful for helping students explore their initial experiences with diversity. Ask students to write a one-page essay about their recollection of the first time they were aware of meeting someone who was different from themselves. The difference could have been based on culture, ethnicity, physical disability, religion, or economic class. Students should describe in their essay:

a. The circumstances of the meeting.

b. What made them aware that this person was different?

c. How they reacted?

d. Whether they felt the interaction was positive, negative, or neutral?

e. Whether they told anyone about the interaction and how that person reacted?

f. How this first interaction has affected future interactions with persons from the same group?

7. Cultural Artifacts Exercise: To encourage students to become more aware of their own cultural backgrounds and to emphasize the "hidden" nature of culture, ask students to bring to class an article or object from home that they believe exemplifies their cultural background and its values. During class, the students (if a large class, have them do this in small groups) "show and tell" their object and explain how the article is representative of their culture's values and beliefs.

8. Cultural Bingo Warm-Up: This is a fun and active way for students to meet and to begin to develop relationships with each other. Each student is provided with a list or a grid with boxes next to 10–15 statements (the number will depend on how many students are participating and the amount of time you want to use). You may want to choose questions that will help identify some of the diversity existing among the students. For example, find someone who:

Speaks a language other than English.

Is in love.

Wants to be a rock star.

Was born in a county other than the United States.

Has parents who speak more than one language.

Saw a movie last week.

Has a pet.

Students move around the room asking each other these questions until they find someone who can answer one of them affirmatively. That person signs his or her initials in the box or next to the question. The "game" continues until a student gets all the boxes or questions answered or until the instructor determines the game is over. The student who gets the most questions initialed "wins." This activity can be debriefed with questions such as:

a. How did the winner (or others) get so many questions answered?

b. What assumptions did you make about the others so as not to waste time asking questions a person could not answer "yes" to?

c. Did you learn anything surprising while doing this activity?

d. What types of diversity exist among the members of this class?

Note: If time is limited or it is not feasible for students to move around the room, this exercise could be used with the entire class at the same time. Statements could be read by the instructor, and students could be instructed to raise their hand if the question described them. This approach would still give students an opportunity to learn about each other.

SUGGESTED VIDEOS

1. Video: *The Amish: Not to Be Modern.* Produced by V. Larimore & M. Taylor. New York, NY: Filmakers Library; NY: dist. Modern Educational Video Network, 1992. This video shows aspects of the Amish community and examines how their religious beliefs provide the background for their lifestyle choices. (57 minutes)

2. Video: *The Asianization of America.* Produced by WNET/Thirteen. Princeton, NJ: Films for the Humanities, 1993. This video depicts the role of Asians in American business and society. (26 minutes)

3. Video: *Becoming American.* WNET/Thirteen. Produced by Iris Film and Video; producers, K. Levine & I. W. Levine. Franklin Lakes, NJ: New Day Films, 1983. The video relates the immigration experience of a Hmong refugee family to the United States and shows some of the obstacles they encountered. (30 minutes)

CHAPTER 2

THE HISTORY OF THE STUDY OF
INTERCULTURAL COMMUNICATION

LEARNING OBJECTIVES

After studying the material in this chapter students should be able to:

Describe the purpose of the Foreign Service Institute and how it initiated the study of intercultural communication.

Explain Edward T. Hall's contribution to the study of intercultural communication.

Describe how the initial emphasis on practical issues influences the study of intercultural communication today.

Identify the contributions of other disciplines to our understanding of intercultural communication.

Describe the three approaches to studying intercultural communication.

Explain the strengths and weaknesses of these approaches.

Describe the dialectical approach to studying intercultural communication.

Define culture, communication, context, and power.

KEY WORDS

Afrocentricity	etic	proxemics
collectivist	field studies	qualitative methods
communication	functionalist approach	quantitative methods
accommodation theory	individualist	rhetorical approach
conceptual equivalence	intercultural	Sapir-Whorf
critical approach	competence	hypothesis
cross-cultural training	interdisciplinary	social reproduction
dialectic	interpretive approach	social science approach
dialectical approach	macrocontexts	textual analyses
distance zones	metaphor	translation equivalence
diversity training	paradigm	variable
emic	perception	worldview
ethnography	processual	

EXTENDED CHAPTER OUTLINE

I. The Early Development of the Discipline: The study of intercultural communication is influenced by its origins in the United States and by the research philosophies of those who pursue its study. Interest in intercultural communication began post-World War II when business and government employees were having difficulties dealing with people in the cultures they were assigned to live and work in across the globe. In response, the U.S. government passed the Foreign Service Act in 1946 and began the Foreign Service Institute (FSI). Prominent scholars (Edward T. Hall, Ray Birdwhistell, and George Trager) were hired to develop training and materials to help overseas workers.

A. Nonverbal Communication
   1. At the institute nonverbal communication was emphasized as studies recognized that nonverbal communication varied by culture.
   2. E. T. Hall pioneered these systematic studies of culture and communication with publication of two books that greatly influenced the beginnings of this field.
      a. *The Silent Language* introduced **proxemics** or the study of how people use personal space to communicate.
      b. *The Hidden Dimension* continued by introducing four personal **distance zones** that influence communication and vary by culture.

B. Application of Theory
   1. There was little initial effort to construct theories because overseas workers were more interested in practical guidelines for helping them get along in the countries they worked in.
   2. This emphasis also contributed to the formation of a parallel "discipline," **cross-cultural training,** which expanded in the 1960s to include training for students and business personnel.
   3. Recently, **diversity training** has been included to help improve communication among various gender, ethnic, and racial groups who work together.

C. Emphasis on International Settings
   1. Initially intercultural scholars and trainers defined culture narrowly, primarily focusing on comparisons between nations to help middle-class professionals become successful overseas.
   2. Although the United States was in the middle of the civil rights movement, little attention centered on domestic contexts.
      a. This may have been due to the emphasis the FSI placed on helping overseas personnel.
      b. Perhaps it was because most of the researchers were from the middle class and their intercultural experience was gained abroad.

D. Interdisciplinary Focus
   1. Scholars in the FSI came from a variety of disciplines, bringing the theories from these disciplines into their study of communication. This **interdisciplinary** focus continues today.
   2. Contributions from several of these fields continue to form the integrated approach used today.

3. Linguists contributed
   a. an understanding of the importance of language.
   b. information about the relationship between language and reality such as that given by the **Sapir-Whorf hypothesis,** which suggests that our language affects our perceptions.
   c. information about how learning languages can contribute to **intercultural competence**.
4. Anthropologists contributed
   a. an understanding of the role of culture in our lives.
   b. an understanding of the importance of nonverbal communication.
   c. an awareness of the role of the researcher's cultural bias in cultural studies, underscoring the need for an interdisciplinary focus.
5. Psychologists contributed
   a. an understanding of the role of stereotyping and prejudice in intercultural communication.
   b. information about how variables such as nationality, ethnicity, personality, and gender influence intercultural communication.
6. Today intercultural communication has become increasingly centered in the communication discipline, with continued contributions from other disciplines.

II. Perception and Worldview of the Researcher: A second influence on the current study of intercultural communication is the **worldview** or research **paradigm** of those who study it.
   A. People select, evaluate, and organize information from the external environment through **perception**.
   B. These perceptions determine how they interpret the new information they obtain through their research and how they are influenced by their cultural groups (for example, ethnic, age, gender).
   C. Group-related perceptions are called *worldviews*, or value orientations, and are so fundamental that they are rarely questioned.
   D. Academic research is a cultural behavior, and research traditions have been influenced by worldviews about the nature of reality and how research should be conducted.
   E. Research worldviews are often held as strongly as cultural or spiritual beliefs, and there have been serious worldview conflicts among scholars.
   F. One recent example of such conflicts between scholars can be found in the social sciences where some scholars feel that reality is external and can be measured and studied, whereas others believe that reality is internal and can only be understood by living and experiencing it.
   G. These different perceptions of reality and how to study it have influenced research in intercultural communication.
   H. Presently, three worldviews characterize the study of culture and communication, and they reflect a blend of disciplines.

III. Three Approaches to Studying Culture and Communication: The three approaches include the social science approach, the interpretive approach, and the critical approach. Each approach is based on different assumptions, has different limitations, and makes unique contributions to our understanding of the relationship between communication and culture. These approaches differ in assumptions about human behavior, research goals, conceptualization of culture and communication, and preferred research methodologies. The text examines them using the problems of Euro Disney to illustrate how each approach can contribute toward understanding a communication dilemma.

A. The **Social Science Approach**: This approach, also known as the **functionalist approach**, was most popular in the 1980s and is based on research in psychology and sociology.
   1. Assumptions:
      a. The existence of a describable external reality.
      b. Human behavior is predictable.
   2. Goals: Describe and predict behavior.
   3. Procedures:
      a. **Quantitative methods**
      b. Data is usually gathered by questionnaires and sometimes by observing subjects firsthand.
   4. Culture is assumed to be a **variable** that can be measured, and the research goal is to predict specifically how culture influences communication.
   5. Methods:
      a. From the Euro Disney example researchers using this approach would want to identify cultural differences between French and American communication and then predict the park's success or failure based on these differences.
      b. Several contemporary research programs take a social science approach.
         i. Gudykunst's uncertainty reduction studies have found that people in **individualist** or **collectivist** cultures vary in their strategies for reducing uncertainty during initial encounters.
         ii. **Communication accommodation theory** originated from studies focused on identifying when and how people change their communication patterns to accommodate others during an interaction.
         iii. Some social science studies explain how communication styles vary from culture to culture.
         iv. Other studies have investigated how travelers adapted overseas.
   6. Strengths and Limitations: Many of these studies have made useful contributions; however, this approach has limitations.
      a. Many scholars now realize that human communication is often more creative than predictable.
      b. Reality is not just external but may be constructed by human beings.
      c. We cannot identify all of the variables that affect our communication.
      d. We cannot predict exactly why one intercultural interaction seems successful and others do not.
      e. Some of the methods used have not been culturally sensitive, and researchers have sometimes been too distant from their subjects.

7. To overcome some of the methodological problems, social scientists have developed strategies to achieve better equivalency in their measures.
   a. Brislin (1993) suggests that researchers need to establish at least two types of equivalency:
      i. **Translation equivalence** requires that research materials go through multiple steps of translation using different translators until versions are obtained in both languages that give the research concepts equivalent meanings.
      ii. **Conceptual equivalence** is obtained by making sure that the notions being investigated have similar meanings at various levels.

B. The **Interpretive Approach**: This perspective became prominent in the late 1980s, and one approach, the **ethnography** of communication, was founded in sociolinguistics. Ethnographers of communication perform descriptive studies of communication patterns within specific groups.
   1. Assumptions:
      a. Reality is constructed by humans.
      b. Human experience, including communication, is subjective.
      c. Human behavior is creative, not determined, and not easily predicted.
   2. Goals: Understand and describe human behavior (not predict).
   3. Procedures:
      a. **Qualitative methods** derived from anthropology and linguistics.
      b. Data is gathered using **field studies**, observations, and participant observations.
      c. Researchers are expected to be intimately involved in the research, often becoming good friends with members of the communities they study.
      d. The **rhetorical approach** is another example of interpretive research. In this approach researchers examine and analyze texts or public speeches and try to interpret the meanings they had in the contexts in which they occurred.
   4. Interpretivists see culture as created and maintained through communication.
   5. Two terms often used to distinguish the social science and interpretive approaches are **etic** and **emic**.
      a. Social science research usually seeks universal generalizations or etics.
      b. Interpretive research usually focuses on understanding communication patterns within specific cultures or behaviors that are emic to specific cultural communities.
   6. Methods:
      a. Jarvis and his research team did an interpretive study of Euro Disney.
         i. They obtained permission to live at the park for a month, went through new employee training, and conducted dozens of interviews.
         ii. Their goal was to understand as clearly as possible the meanings the Euro Disney employees made of their experience from their own perspectives.
         iii. They discovered serious conflicts between U.S. and non-U.S. employees, particularly with regard to the meanings for management and workers.

      b.   Other examples are studies that have investigated the language patterns of many different cultural groups.

          i.   Smith and Eisenberg investigated **metaphors** used by employees and management of Disneyland U.S.A. and found that over the years the metaphor had changed from drama to family, particularly among employees, and this change affected the way they interpreted common events.

         ii.   Philipsen (1990) did an interpretive study of communication patterns of men and women in a working-class neighborhood of Chicago ("Speaking Like a Man in Teamsterville").

        iii.   Carbaugh (1990) analyzed the communication rules on *Donahue*, a U.S. talk show.

      c.   Asante's (1987) notion of **Afrocentricity** is another interpretive approach. This approach emphasizes that understanding and describing communicative rules must be grounded in the beliefs and values of the people in the culture, suggesting that European research perspectives are not applicable to African American communication. Asante's framework of shared African assumptions has been used to understand contemporary African American communication.

   7.   Strengths and Limitations:

      a.   One strength is that the approach provides a more in-depth understanding of communication patterns in communities because of the emphasis on investigating communication in context.

      b.   One limitation is that there are few interpretivist studies of intercultural communication; for example, scholars have typically not been concerned with what happens when two groups come into contact with each other, although there are some comparative cultural studies.

      c.   The research is primarily conducted by outsiders to the research communities.

C.   The **Critical Approach:**

   1.   Assumptions:

      a.   Critical researchers share many of the interpretivists assumptions—they believe in subjective reality.

      b   They emphasize the importance of studying the context in which communication occurs but usually focus on **macrocontexts**, for example, political and social structures.

      c.   Unlike social science and interpretive researchers, they are interested in the historical context of communication.

      d.   They are interested in understanding power relations in communication, and identifying cultural differences is important only in relation to power differentials.

   2.   Goals: Understand and change the lives of everyday communicators. Researchers assume that by examining and writing about how power functions in cultural situations people can learn to resist forces of power and oppression.

   3.   Procedures:

      a.   **Textual analyses.**

      b.   They analyze cultural "products" such as TV, movies, and essays.

4. Culture is seen as a site of struggle where multiple interpretations come together under a dominant force.
5. Methods:
   a. A critical scholar might study Euro Disney as a site of cultural struggle. The U.S. Disney managers may see the exportation of Disney icons as benign international trade, whereas the French may see it as an example of cultural imperialism. They may feel that Disney icons are being imposed on them to replace French cultural values (love of literature, French style of savoir faire, savoir vivre).
   b. Another critical analysis could be made on Euro Disney public relations. Some French journalists believe that Disney's approach has been heavy handed because Disney people controlled access to information and rarely returned phone calls. They also strictly regulated interviews.
   c. A critical analysis could also study the aspects of U.S. culture and history that are being exported from Euro Disney and how these represent the American experience and whose view is being represented.
   d. A recent example of a critical analysis is Peck's (1993/94) study of Oprah Winfrey segments on racism, which identified three discourses about racism: liberal, therapeutic, and religious.
   e. Nakayama (1994) used the critical approach to analyze the movie *Showdown in Little Tokyo,* which depicts two Los Angeles police officers (one blond European American and one European Asian American) investigating a murder. He found that the European American character is favored over the Asian American character.
   f. Moon (1997) did a critical analysis of gender and social class communication by analyzing interviews with White women from working-class backgrounds. Among other findings, the study identifies strategies used by women to resist **social reproduction**.
6. Strengths and Limitations:
   a. One strength of this approach is its emphasis on power relations in intercultural interactions and the importance of social and historical contexts.
   b. One limitation is that it does not focus on face-to-face intercultural interaction but rather tends to focus on popular media forms of communication.
   c. Further, it does not allow for much empirical data.
   d. Another limitation is that this approach is rarely used to study international contexts. Most studies emphasize culture and communication in domestic settings.

IV. A Dialectical Approach to Understanding Culture and Communication
   A. What Is the Dialectical Approach?
   The authors see the three perspectives operating in interconnected and sometimes seemingly contradictory ways. Hence, they take a **dialectical approach** to understanding intercultural communication research and practice. The advantage of a dialectical approach is that it encompasses many different kinds of intercultural knowledge.

1. It emphasizes the **processual** aspect of intercultural communication, assuming that cultures change and so do individuals.
2. It emphasizes the relational aspect of intercultural communication, highlighting relationships among various aspects of intercultural communication and the importance of viewing these holistically rather than in isolation.
3. It permits holding contradictory ideas simultaneously. This type of thinking is difficult because it goes against the dichotomous thinking formal education in the United States emphasizes.
4. An understanding of intercultural communication can be enriched by combining the three research perspectives. As the Euro Disney example shows, each perspective provides an understanding of the problems and challenges that would be missed if only one perspective was used.
   a. The social science perspective helped researchers identify how specific cultural differences might predict communication conflicts.
   b. The interpretive perspective enabled researchers to confirm social science findings.
   c. The critical approach raised questions about the exportation of popular culture and the neutrality of our assumptions about intercultural experiences.
5. The knowledge gained by any of the three approaches is enhanced by the knowledge provided by the others.
6. Taking the dialectical approach requires that we not only recognize the contributions of each perspective but that we accept simultaneously the assumptions of all three perspectives.

B. Six Dialectics of Intercultural Communication: A list is provided of six **dialectics** of intercultural communication, others may be identified as one gains a greater understanding of intercultural communication.
   1. Cultural–Individual Dialectic: Intercultural communication is both cultural and individual.
      a. Communication is *cultural*, suggesting that we share some communication patterns with members of the groups we belong to.
      b. Other communication patterns are idiosyncratic or unique to the individual.
   2. Personal–Contextual Dialectic: Although individuals communicate on a personal level, the context of the communication is also important. In different contexts individuals take on different social roles.
   3. Differences–Similarities Dialectic: Human beings are simultaneously both different from and similar to each other.
      a. Overemphasizing differences can lead to prejudice and stereotyping.
      b. Overemphasizing similarities may prevent us from noticing the important cultural variations that exist.
   4. Static–Dynamic Dialectic: Intercultural communication is both static and dynamic because some cultural patterns remain relatively constant over time while others shift.
   5. History/Past–Present/Future Dialectic: To better understand intercultural communication, it is important to think not only about the present but also about how history affects our present interactions.

6. Privilege–Disadvantage Dialectic: Cultural members may be simultaneously privileged and disadvantaged, or they may be privileged in some contexts and disadvantaged in others.
    C. Keeping a Dialectical Perspective: The authors advise readers to keep the dialectical perspective in mind as they read the text because the dialectics introduced relate in a variety of ways to the topics discussed. The dialectical approach is not a theory but a lens from which to view the complexities of intercultural communication.

DISCUSSION QUESTIONS

Questions from the Text

1. How have the origins of the study of intercultural communication in the United States affected its present focus?

2. How did business and political interests influence what early intercultural communication researchers studied and learned?

3. How have the worldviews of researchers influenced how they studied intercultural communication?

4. How have other fields contributed to the study of intercultural communication?

5. What are the advantages of a dialectical approach to intercultural communication?

Additional Questions

1. How did Edward T. Hall's work contribute to the origins of the field of intercultural communication?

2. What are the strengths and limitations of using *only* the social science approach to studying intercultural communication?

3. What are the strengths and limitations of using *only* the interpretive approach to studying intercultural communication?

4. What are the strengths and limitations of using *only* the critical approach to studying intercultural communication?

5. Why do critical scholars see culture as a site of struggle?

6. What are some dialectics found in examining the process of intercultural communication?

CLASSROOM EXERCISES AND CHAPTER ASSIGNMENTS

1. Dialectical Approach Assignment: In this assignment students assume the position of researcher and analyze their culture using the three different approaches described in the chapter: social science, interpretivist, and critical. The students should describe what each approach would allow them to see and understand about their culture and what it would hide from them. The goal of this exercise is to help the students understand the strengths and limitations of each approach, understand the value of the dialectical approach, and become more conscious of their cultural position. This exercise could be used as a follow-up or a part of the "Becoming Culturally Conscious" assignment in the text.

2. Dialectical Approach Exercise: This variation of the "Dialectical Approach" assignment presented here could be used as in-class preparation for writing the paper. Students pretend that they are researchers interested in culture and assume the perspectives described in the chapter. Working alone, they prepare research questions that are appropriate for these perspectives. Next, they should pick partners and interview each other about their cultural backgrounds using the questions they have prepared. Three or four of the student pairs could be given a few minutes to present the information they discovered to the class. Debrief the exercise by leading a discussion about the advantages and disadvantages of each approach, stressing that a combination of the approaches gives a fuller picture of each person's position.

3. Mini Ethnography Exercise: Explain that one of the methods used by anthropologists to learn about cultural variations in nonverbal communication is observation and recording of behaviors. Students are then assigned to go in pairs to a public place on campus for 20–30 minutes where they can unobtrusively observe a specific nonverbal behavior (for example, how far apart people sit at the bus stop, what types/colors of clothing people wear to school). They should take notes on their observations, recording different behaviors and the frequency of their occurrence. When they return to class, they should look over their notes for recurring behaviors and see if they can identify the conditions under which these occurred. Are there any ways to classify the behaviors they observed into categories? Explain that ethnographers go through a similar process after their observations to identify patterns in the groups they have observed. Debrief the exercise by having students share ideas about what was challenging in trying to do the exercise and some limitations in their observations that might limit the generalizability of their conclusions to other groups.

4. Ethnography of Communication Assignment: Students are required to read Donal Carbaugh's *Donahue* study (referenced in the text, Chapter 1) and complete a mini duplication of his study by using his communication rules to analyze four segments of another talk show. Students should write a report that outlines their findings and discusses whether their findings support or contradict Carbaugh's. If they discover that Carbaugh's rules do not fit the show they have observed, they should identify other rules and provide a rationale for their conclusions.

5. Fieldwork Assignment: Students go to a setting they are not very familiar with (for example, a bar for someone who does not go to bars, bus stops for people who rarely take the bus) and observe for an hour on two different occasions. They should record observations of what they see and experience during these two hours. After finishing their observations, they should read over their notes to identify any behavioral patterns that may suggest what rules and norms exist in this setting for people's behavior. Students should hand in their field notes along with a discussion of their conclusions and rationale for them. They should also attempt to draw conclusions about what it would be like to communicate in this setting without a knowledge of the rules and norms.

6. Dialectical Approaches in Research Assignment: This assignment will help students become familiar with how researchers use each of the three approaches (social science approach, interpretive approach, and the critical approach) to study intercultural communication. Students are asked to locate one research article or book chapter that is based on one of the three theoretical approaches. Depending on the abilities of the students, instructors may have to provide them with lists of journals and books and/or refer them to the bibliography at the end of the chapter for ideas. Students should then write a one-page review of the article, or if the class is small, they could give a brief report on the article in class. The review/report should include:

a. The complete title, author, year, publication information.

b. The theoretical approach used by the researchers.

c. A summary of the article or book chapter.

d. A description of how the research was conducted.

e. The research findings.

If the assignment is presented in the form of class reports, debrief the activity by encouraging the students to contrast and compare the approaches used in the different articles. Invite students to discuss what might have happened if a researcher had chosen to use a different approach in a study. For instance, if the researcher had used a critical approach rather than a social science approach, what different information might the researcher have discovered or what different methods might the researcher have used?

7. Perception Exercise: This exercise is designed to demonstrate how differing perceptions can affect communication. Students write (or tell) a partner about a situation they were involved in with one other person where miscommunication occurred because their perceptions of the interaction were different from each other's. Instruct students to begin by briefly describing the "facts" of the situation, and then to briefly describe their own perspective of the situation. Then ask students to try to switch perspectives and attempt to describe the situation from the perspective of the other person involved, even if they disagree with that person's perspective. Partners will read (or listen) to each other's presentation. The readers (or listeners) will provide feedback to their partners about whether they have presented the other's perspective as completely and nonjudgmentally as possible. Debrief this activity by leading students in a class discussion about the difficulties involved in trying to see events from others' perspectives, particularly when one is emotionally committed to one perspective. Encourage them to identify reasons it might be important to consider others' perspectives in intercultural interactions.

8. Dialectics and Current Events Activity: This exercise is designed to give students the opportunity to practice using a dialectical approach for examining intercultural events. Prior to class, find newspaper articles describing current intercultural situations such as a political conflict, a business concern, an effort between two cultural groups to reach some shared goal, and so forth. Bring these articles to class and share one with the class for a class discussion or distribute one each to groups of three to five students. Instruct students to discuss how each of the three (social science, interpretive, and critical) approaches could be used to obtain an understanding of these situations.

9. Perception Process Activity: This activity is designed to help students review the steps of the perception process. Prior to class, choose three sheets of colored paper. Each piece should be a different color. On one of the pieces write a brief message in large ink that fills the page (Examples: "Today we will have a treat in class." or "Today we will learn about dialectics of intercultural communication."). Stack the pieces of paper together and cut them into medium-sized puzzle pieces (about 8). Then drop them in a container and mix up the pieces. During class, select a volunteer to come up to the front. Tell the class that you are going to give the volunteer a message and you want them to watch how he/she perceives it. Dump the message onto a table in front of the volunteer and ask him/her to make sense of it. Generally the volunteer will immediately begin to select out the pieces with words on them.

Stop the volunteer and ask the class what the volunteer is doing with the pieces of paper. Prod them until they suggest that the volunteer is sorting out or selecting the pieces with writing. Remind them that this is the first step of the perception process—sensory selection. Let the volunteer continue until you see him/her trying to put the pieces with words on them together. At this point, stop the exercise and ask the students what the volunteer is doing. They will generally note that he/she is now putting the pieces together, at which point you will ask if they could also say that he/she is organizing the puzzle pieces. Remind them that the second perception step is organization. Let the volunteer finish putting the puzzle together and ask him/her to interpret the message for the class. Remind the class that the third step in the perception process is interpretation. Then lead a discussion that reviews the steps and how our cultural backgrounds influence them. The following questions may help:

a. What determines which information we select from our environment to pay attention to?

b. How does our past experience influence how we organize the information we select?

c. How does our past experience influence how we interpret the information we select?

d. How might our cultural backgrounds influence the steps in the perception process?

CHAPTER 3

CULTURE, COMMUNICATION, CONTEXT, AND POWER

LEARNING OBJECTIVES

After studying the material in this chapter students should be able to:

Understand several dimensions to thinking about culture and how they inform our approaches to intercultural communication.

Understand the role of "low culture" (pop culture) in studying about cultures.

Identify characteristics important to defining communication.

Explain the relationship between communication and culture.

Describe the relationship between communication and context.

Discuss the role of power in communication interactions.

KEY WORDS

communication	high culture	norms
communication ritual	long-term versus	performative
cultural studies	short-term orientation	popular culture
cultural values	low culture	power distance
culture	masculinity/femininity	symbolic significance
ethnography of	value	uncertainty avoidance
communication		

EXTENDED CHAPTER OUTLINE

I. What Is Culture? **Culture** is considered the core concept in intercultural communication.
  A. Culture functions largely at a subconscious level, making it difficult for us to recognize our own cultural **norms** and assumptions until we encounter some that are different.
  B. Culture has been given a variety of different definitions and is complex, so it is important to reflect on the centrality of culture in our own interactions.
    1. Williams (1983) described culture as "one of the two or three most complicated words in the English language."
    2. Culture is more than just a part of the practice of intercultural communication. Even how we think about culture frames our ideas and perceptions.

3. One definition of culture is too restrictive, and the dialectical approach advocates looking at culture with multiple definitions and perspectives.
   a. Social science researchers do not focus on culture per se but rather on how culture influences communication.
   b. Interpretive researchers focus on cultural patterns within specific contexts.
   c. Critical researchers often view communication—and the power to communicate—as instrumental in resisting power and oppression.
4. It is also important to investigate culture as practitioners.
C. High Culture and Low Culture
   1. Arnold's definition of culture "the best that has been thought in the world" carried an emphasis on quality.
   2. Many Western societies make a distinction between high and low culture.
      a. **High culture** includes the cultural activities of the European elites: ballet, symphony, opera, great literature, and fine art.
         i. These are also sometimes referred to as international because they are supposedly appreciated by audiences in many cultures and time periods.
         ii. Universities devote courses and departments to study aspects of high culture.
      b. **Low culture** refers to cultural activities of the nonelite: graffiti, music videos, advertisements, game shows, wrestling, stock car racing, toys, talk shows.
         i. They were considered unworthy of serious study.
         ii. They were of little interest to museums or universities.
   3. The eliticism reflected in these distinctions was indicative of greater tensions in Western social systems.
   4. In the 20th century, particularly in the 1960s, social changes spawned an interest in ethnic studies, women's studies, and gay and lesbian studies in universities.
   5. These area studies did not rely on distinctions between high and low culture and contributed to a new framework that legitimized cultural forms traditionally categorized as low culture (now **popular culture**).
   6. Although the distinction between high and low cultures has been minimized, it has not disappeared and continues to reinforce a predominantly European-elite view of the world.
D. Shared and Learned Patterns of Beliefs and Perception
   1. Anthropological Definitions of Culture: Intercultural communication has been most influenced by definitions of culture from anthropologists and psychologists. Anthropologists have been more concerned about definitions of culture.
      a. Anthropologists Kroeber and Kluckhohn (1952) categorized and integrated 150 definitions for culture from various disciplines.
         i. Some definitions emphasized culture as a set of patterns of thought and beliefs.
         ii. Others emphasized culture as a set of behaviors.
         iii. Some focused on nonmaterial or material manifestations of culture.

      b. Geertz's (1973) definition of culture was probably the most widely accepted by early anthropologists and in communication studies.

      c. The traditional concept of culture continues to be the learned, shared patterns of belief.

  2. Psychological Definitions of Culture

      a. Psychologist Hofstede (1984) defined culture similarly, as the "programming of the mind" and the "interactive aggregate of common characteristics that influence a human group's response to its environment" (p. 21).

      b. The social psychological definition of culture is centered in the mind of the individual.

      c. Hofstede notes that these patterns are developed through interactions with various groups in our social environment. Thus, culture becomes a collective experience because it is shared with the people who live and experience the same social environments.

      d. Both the approaches from anthropology and psychology have been influential in the social science perspective of intercultural communication.

E. Definitions Borrowed from Ethnography: **Ethnography of communication** is a specialized area of study within the field of communication.

  1. Ethnographers of communication look for symbolic meanings of verbal and nonverbal activities to understand patterns and rules of communication within groups.

  2. These researchers define culture broadly (for example, talk show participants, and Vietnam War veterans)

  3. Carbaugh suggests that the concept of culture should be reserved for patterns of symbolic action and meaning that are deeply felt, commonly intelligible, and widely accessible.

  4. Cultural patterns only exist if the activity holds **symbolic significance** or evokes feelings that extend beyond itself.

  5. These patterns must also endure over time and are passed from person to person.

  6. Hymes' eight-part framework is a tool for studying naturally occurring speech in depth and context.

      a. Scene: the setting of the communication event

      b. Participants: the people who perform or enact the event

      c. Ends: the goal of the participants

      d. Act Sequences: the order of the phases of the event

      e. Key: the tone of the conversation

      f. Instrumentalities: the communication channel

      g. Norms: the rules people follow

      h. Genre: type or category of talk

F. Culture as a Contested Zone: In the 1960s the arrival of British cultural studies, which held the critical perspective, changed our thinking about culture and how we study communication.

  1. **Cultural studies** began with the establishment of the Centre for Contemporary Cultural Studies at the University of Birmingham and was fiercely multidisciplinary and committed to social change.

2. Stuart Hall envisioned that the group would utilize intellectual resources to understand everyday life and its antihumanness.
3. This approach motivated other fields to focus on applying academic work to everyday life.
4. Due to differing cultural and political situations, the format of cultural studies differs from place to place.
5. In the United States cultural studies is primarily located in communication departments.
6. The influence of cultural studies in communication has been profound, surpassing the influence of ethnic studies.
   a. It challenged the distinction between high and low culture.
   b. It argued that low culture was significant because it captured the contemporary and dynamic everyday representations of cultural struggles.
   c. As a result, overlooked cultural phenomena (for example, soap operas, music videos) gained importance in research.
   d. The conceptualization of "culture" from this approach, viewing culture as a contested site or zone, is very different from previous perspectives and addresses criticisms of earlier anthropological research.
   e. Seeing culture from this perspective increases our appreciation for the struggles of various groups who attempt to negotiate their relationships and well-being in the United States.
   f. It opens new thinking about intercultural communication.
7. The dialectical approach enables us to see culture as both shared and learned patterns of beliefs and perceptions that are mutually intelligible and widely accessible and as a site of struggle for contested meanings.

II. What Is Communication? **Communication** is as complex as culture, but its defining characteristic is meaning. It could be said that communication occurs whenever someone attributes meaning to another's words or actions. It is a "symbolic process whereby reality is produced, maintained, repaired and transformed" (Carey, 1989, p. 23).
A. Communication is symbolic: the words and gestures we use have no inherent meaning but that which is agreed upon by the communicators.
   1. The symbols are verbal and nonverbal, including some powerful social symbols.
   2. Each message can have multiple layers of meaning.
   3. Communicators assume that their listeners take the meaning they intend, but this assumption may be wrong, particularly when listeners have different cultural backgrounds and experiences.
B. The communication process is dynamic.
   1. Communication is ongoing and relies on other communication events to make sense.
   2. It occurs simultaneously, and boundaries where it begins and ends are blurry.
   3. When meaning is negotiated, we are creating, maintaining, and transforming reality.
   4. A person cannot communicate alone.

III. The Relationship Between Culture and Communication: There is a complex relationship between communication and culture. The two concepts are both interrelated and reciprocal.

A. How Culture Influences Communication

    1. Intercultural scholars have used broad anthropological frameworks to identify cultural differences in communication.

    2. Kluckhohn and Strodtbeck (1961) extended Geertz's earlier work in their study of contemporary Navajo, descendants of Spanish colonists, and Anglo Americans in the Southwest to better understand their **cultural values**.

        a. Values are the most deeply felt, zero-order beliefs shared by a cultural group and reflect what ought to be, not what is.

        b. They suggested that values stem from five questions all cultural groups must answer.

            i. What is human nature?

            ii. What is the relationship between humans and nature?

            iii. What is the relationship between humans?

            iv. What is the preferred personality?

            v. What is the orientation toward time?

        c. They concluded that there are three possible responses to each question and that every culture has one or possibly two preferred responses to each question.

        d. The preferred responses indicate predominant cultural values.

        e. This framework can be extended to cultural groups based on gender, class, nationality, and so on.

    3. The Nature of Human Nature

        a. Fundamental Goodness: This value is manifest in societies that emphasize rehabilitating lawbreakers. Religions such as Buddhism and Confucianism also espouse this orientation.

        b. Combination of Good and Evil: Many groups in the United States hold this perspective, though it has been shifting and now there is less talk about rehabilitation and reform and more about punishment. The United States currently has a higher percentage of citizens in prison than any industrialized country.

        c. Essentially Evil: Societies with this value are not interested in rehabilitation but rather punishment. This orientation may be related to the Christian view that humans are essentially evil and born with sin.

    4. Relationship Between Humans and Nature

        a. Humans Dominate Over Nature: Evidence of this is found in the United States where scientists attempt to modify or control nature to better accommodate human needs or desires.

        b. Nature Dominates Over Humans: In cultures with this perspective, people are more willing to accept what nature brings.

        c. Harmony Between Humans and Nature: In cultures (for example, Japan and Native Americans) with this perspective, people believe in respecting nature and believe that nature plays a vital role in the spiritual and religious life of the community.

5. Relationships Between Humans
   a. Individual (Individualism): Importance is placed on the individual rather than on the family, work teams, or other groups. Some claim this is the most important European American cultural value.
   b. Group-Oriented (Collectivism): More emphasis is placed on the family, work teams, or other groups.
   c. Note: These values may be related to economic class or rural/urban distinctions.
   d. They also may have strong influences on patterns of communication.
   e. Some people have the challenge of belonging to cultural groups with contradictory values.
6. Preferred Form of Activity
   a. Doing: This orientation emphasizes productivity and is the most common perspective in the United States. Higher status is accorded to those who do rather than to those who think.
   b. Growing: Importance is placed on the spiritual aspects of life, and few cultures practice this value, perhaps only Zen Buddhists. Some cultures, like Japan, may practice a combination of the doing and growing orientations.
   c. Being: Emphasis is placed on a kind of self-actualization in which the person is fused with the experience. Found in some Central and South American societies, Greece, and Spain.
7. Orientation to Time
   a. Future: Typical of most U.S. cultural communities. Examples of this orientation are savings accounts for the future or keeping appointment books of future appointments.
   b. Present: Typical in Spain and Greece, the emphasis is placed on the importance of the present and the value of living and realizing the potential of the present moment.
   c. Past: European and Asian societies typically emphasize the past, believing that history has something to contribute to understanding the present.
8. Not everyone in a society will hold the dominant value, but most cultural members will hold approximations of the dominant value.
9. Intercultural conflicts are often the result of conflicting value orientations, and these conflicts may be further complicated by power differentials.
10. Hofstede proposed a similar value framework based on his cross-cultural study of IBM subsidiaries in 53 countries.
    a. Hofstede identified five areas of common cultural problems, the answers to which form dimensions of cultural values.
       i. **Power distance:** acceptance of social inequality and relationship with authority. In low power distance cultures (for example, Denmark, Israel, New Zealand), people believe that less hierarchy is better and power should only be used for legitimate reasons. High power distance societies (for example, Mexico, Philippines, India) value social hierarchies, and decision making and relationships between people with different statuses are more formalized.

    ii. Individualism versus collectivism: emphasis on the individual or the group.

    iii. **Masculinity/femininity value**: the social implications of having been born male or female. This is a two-dimensional value referring both to how gender-specific roles are valued and what emphasis is placed on so-called masculine and feminine values. People in Japan, Austria, and Mexico tended to score high on masculinity, and people in northern Europe tended more toward femininity.

    iv. **Uncertainty avoidance**: addresses the degree of threat people feel about ambiguous situations and how they choose to deal with them. Cultures (for example, Great Britain, Sweden, Ireland, Hong Kong, United States) with low uncertainty avoidance have fewer rules, accept dissent, and are comfortable with risk taking. Cultures (for example, Greece, Portugal, and Japan) with high uncertainty avoidance prefer more rigid rules and seek consensus about goals.

    v. **Long-term versus short-term orientation** to life: This dimension was added to Hofstede's original four by Chinese researchers who did a similar study as a result of criticisms over the western European bias of Hofstede's framework. It reflects a society's search for virtue or truth. Cultures with a short-term orientation are concerned with possessing truth and may emphasize quick results in endeavors and social pressure to conform. Cultures with a long-term orientation will respect the demands of virtue and focus more on thrift, perseverance, and tenacity in one's activities and value a willingness to subordinate oneself for a purpose.

11.   The limitation of these frameworks is that people tend to assume a particular group characteristic will be manifested by all cultural members at all times and in all contexts.

12.   The dialectical approach reminds us that people from other cultures may both have differences and share similarities in their value systems and that the context may determine which value a person manifests at a given time.

B. How Communication Influences Culture: Culture is enacted through communication and so is influenced by communication. This can be understood by examining works of cultural communication scholars.

  1. They describe how aspects of culture are enacted in speech communities *in situ*, or in contexts. They seek to understand communication patterns situated socially and give voice to cultural identity.

  2. Specifically, they examine how cultural forms (terms, ritual, myth, and social drama) are enacted through structuring norms of conversation and interaction.

  3. These patterns are not viewed as being connected in a deterministic way to any cultural group.

  4. In one study, Katriel (1990) used Hymes' SPEAKING framework to describe the middle class Israeli **communication ritual** of "griping."

  5. A related approach from cultural communication studies sees culture as **performative**.

  a. This metaphor assumes that instead of studying an external (cultural) reality culture is observed in the way people enact and represent their worldviews.

  b. Phillipsen's (1992) Teamsterville study represents this approach.

 6. These interpretive studies frequently use cultural values as a way to explain cultural patterns.

 7. An example is Fitch's (1994) study comparing how people in Bogatá, Columbia and Boulder, Colorado persuaded others to do what they wanted, a form of sociolinguistics known as *directive*.

C. Communication as Resistance to Dominant Society: Resistance is the metaphor used in cultural studies to conceptualize the relationship between culture and communication.

 1. Based on this metaphor, researchers try to discover how individuals use their own space to resist dominant society.

 2. For example, they may study floating bars (illegal temporary warehouses distributing alcohol with no liquor license and no tax payments) in New York as a context in which people circumvent the system to discover how they can interpret their behavior as resistance to the dominant cultural system.

IV. The Relationship Between Communication and Context: Traditionally, context has been viewed as the physical and/or social aspects of a communication situation.

A. People communicate differently depending on the context.

B. Context is not static or objective, and it can be multilayered.

C. Context may consist of the social, political, and historical structures in which communication occurs.

 1. The social context is determined on the societal level, by the majority of citizens for that particular time period.

 2. The political context consists of those forces that attempt to change or retain existing social structures and relations.

 3. The historical context consists of reputations built in the past.

V. Communication and Power: Power is always a part of communication interactions, though its influence may not be evident or obvious.

A. Individuals rarely have equal power in communication interactions.

B. People in power consciously or unconsciously create and maintain power systems that support their own ways of thinking and communicating.

C. There are two levels of group-related power:

 1. Primary dimensions, which are more permanent in nature (for example, age, ethnicity, gender, physical abilities, race, and sexual orientation).

 2. Secondary dimensions, which are more changeable (for example, educational background, geographic location, marital status, and socioeconomic status).

D. Dominant communication systems ultimately impede those who do not share them.

E. Power also stems from social institutions and the roles we occupy in them.

F. Power is dynamic; power may be asserted and negotiated.

G. Dominant cultural groups perpetuate positions of privilege in many ways.

H. Disempowered people may find creative ways to negotiate power.

I. Power is complex; some inequities are more rigid, and multiple roles may influence its negotiation.

J. Intercultural communication cannot be understood without considering the power dynamics in interactions.

K. A dialectical perspective looks at the dynamic and interrelated relationships between culture, communication, context, and power.

DISCUSSION QUESTIONS

Questions from the Text

1. How have the notions of high and low culture influenced people's perspectives of culture?

2. How do the values of a cultural group influence communication with members of other cultural groups?

3. What techniques do people use to assert power in communication interactions?

4. How is culture a contested site?

Additional Questions

1. How does power influence intercultural communication interactions?

2. What is the difference between the traditional way of looking at context and communication and the new way? How does context affect communication?

3. What does it mean to think of culture as a contested site?

4. What are the implications of defining communication as a process?

5. What are some contributions that cultural studies have made to understanding intercultural communication?

6. What can intercultural researchers gain from studying low culture?

CLASSROOM EXERCISES AND CHAPTER ASSIGNMENTS

1. Defining Culture Exercise: This is a class discussion exercise designed to help students understand the difficulties in conceptualizing culture. Ask students how they would define culture, and based on their ideas, play the "devil's advocate" by suggesting different individuals/cultural groups that may challenge the definition. You may also use the following questions to stimulate thinking about how culture is defined:

    a. Does each country represent a separate culture?

    b. Is it possible for a country to have more than one culture?

    c. Is each culture composed of a single race of people?

    d. Is it possible to distinguish people from different cultures based on physical characteristics?

    e. What culture is a person from who was born in one culture and raised in another (for example, a baby born in Romania and raised in the United States)?

    f. What culture is a person from whose parents are originally from one culture but who was born and raised in another (for example, Japanese Americans, Latino Americans, and so forth)?

2. Defining Communication Exercise: Divide your students into groups of four to six individuals and assign the students to come up with the best definition that they can for communication. Suggest that as part of this discussion a list be created of the different characteristics of communication. After 10 minutes have passed, ask the students to share their lists and the definition of communication they have come up with. This could be followed by a discussion of the characteristics of communication and discussion about why there are so many different definitions for communication. At the conclusion of the discussion, you might want to propose the question "How would you define intercultural communication?" and lead the students in a discussion about how the definition may be modified to define intercultural communication. You may also want to discuss how the characteristics of communication they have listed would influence the process of intercultural communication.

3. Building Communication Models Exercise: At the beginning of this exercise, explain to the students that sometimes when we talk about processes we use models to illustrate the process. Show students a communication model (for example, Berlo's Sender/Receiver Model). Basic communication course, public speaking, or interpersonal communication textbooks are all good sources for finding an example model. Discuss the model with the students. Identify the characteristics of communication shown in the model, and have them suggest aspects of communication they feel are missing from the model. Then divide the students into small groups and challenge them to create an original model that they feel adequately illustrates the communication process. Tell them they have about 15 minutes to complete their models. One or two students from each group should be designated by the group members to draw the model on the board and explain the rationale behind its design. This exercise with the discussions could take close to one hour.

4. Ethnicity and Communication Assignment: This assignment is designed to motivate students to think about their own ethnic backgrounds and the extent to which their ethnicity influences their communication. Instruct students to research their own family background or that of the family in which they were raised to gain a sense of their own ethnic identity. They should talk with parents and other family members to find out where each generation of their ancestors was raised. Then they should find out what stereotypes and labels are found for these groups in the United States. With this information they should address the following questions:

   a. What is your ethnic background?

   b. To what extent do you feel your ethnic background influences who you are?

   c. If you think your ethnic background has little influence on you today, what other variables do you feel have a significant influence on your behavior?

   d. In what way, if any, does your ethnic background influence who you are comfortable communicating with (for example, What groups would you not feel comfortable communicating with? What groups might feel uncomfortable communicating with you?).

   e. To what extent do you think people are aware of your ethnic background? Do you think this influences the way they communicate with you?

5. Values Exercise: The goal of this emotionally powerful exercise is to allow students to experience firsthand the depth of meaning that values hold for us. Be aware that this may be upsetting for some students, particularly immigrants who may have lost something they value. Allow students to opt out of the process at any time if they find

the exercise too upsetting. The exercise will probably work better with a class that is willing to be self-reflective. First, give students 5 to 10 pieces of paper (determine the number by class size and time restraints). Then follow these steps:

a. Ask the students to write one of their values on each piece of paper.

b. Instruct them to organize the pieces of paper according to how important each value is to them, with the most important value at the top and the least important on the bottom.

c. Then invite students to throw away (literally into the middle of the room) the value they think is the least important one to them.

d. Ask them how it felt to throw away that value, even considering it was their least important one.

e. Instruct them to throw away their most important value.

f. Discuss how it feels to even figuratively throw away their most significant value.

g. (Optional) Ask each person to take one of the values from the person on their left and throw it away.

h. Ask how this feels.

After the exercise use the following questions to debrief the exercise.

a. How do you feel about the values you have in front of you?

b. How did it feel to lose values? To keep values?

c. What does this say about the power and the meaning our values have for us?

d. Did you feel differently when another person threw away one of your values than when you did?

e. Can you think of a situation where people have lost values?

f. Are there examples of situations in which people have taken other people's values away from them?

g. How did they react? How might you react in a similar situation?

h. What impact has this had on these people?

Invite students to retrieve "tossed" values at the conclusion of this exercise.

6. Power and Privilege Exercise—"Stand Up": This exercise allows students to identify themselves as belonging to a particular group or groups by standing up when a particular statement pertains to them. It is designed to bring into awareness the types of privilege we all have depending on the context. The instructor reads each statement and allows time for students to "stand up" in response to the statement. Students are encouraged to stand up only if they are comfortable doing so, and the exercise is done silently and without comment by others. The statements can be chosen to fit a particular topic or context, and the list that follows merely contains suggestions. The instructor may want to begin with statements that are not very personal and move to those that require more intimate self-disclosure. This list of questions is designed to highlight class issues. Stand up if:

You were born in the United States.

You were an only child.

You moved more than two times while growing up.

You were raised in the country (rural setting).

You grew up in an apartment.

Your family had few resources (students determine what "few" means).

Your family had more than enough resources.

You parents are divorced.

You have more resources than your parents have.

You are working to pay your way through school.

After the exercise examine each of the statements with the class and ask them how being a part of the group identified in the statement would affect their ability to communicate with people from other groups. Which groups would be most comfortable communicating with them? Which groups would be least comfortable communicating with them?

7. Self-Analysis Assignment: The goal of this assignment is to motivate students to think critically about their social responsibility with regard to patterns of dominance. Assign students to write an essay discussing ways that they can avoid enacting patterns of dominance in their personal, student, and professional lives.

SUGGESTED VIDEOS

1. Video: *True Colors.* Produced by North Brook, IL: MTI/Film & Video, 1991. This video questions our accomplishments in the fight for equality since the 1960s by testing various levels of prejudice. (19 minutes)

2. Video: *Still Killing Us Softly: Advertising's Image of Women.* Produced by Jean Kilbourne and Cambridge, MA: Cambridge Documentary Films, 1987. The producer and director, Margaret Lazarus, describes the portrayal of women in advertising and how this portrayal influences women, men, and children. It also suggests ways that advertising's portrayal of women affects the images men and women form of themselves. (32 minutes)

3. Video: *Black Views of Discrimination.* Distributed by Filmic Archives. Produced by the Educational Film Center for NYT Educational Media. New York, NY: New York Times Company, 1995. This video has four modules that deal with Black Americans' views of racial discrimination. (17 minutes)

4. Video: *Ain't Scared of Your Jails.* Produced by Blackside, Inc. Alexandra, VA: PBS Video, 1986. This video shows some of the different tactics used by college students involved in the civil rights movement. The video shows four related situations: the lunch counter sit-ins, the beginning of the Student Nonviolent Coordinating Committee (SNCC), the influence of the movement on the presidential campaign in 1960. and the 1961 freedom rides. (60 minutes)

CHAPTER 4

HISTORY

LEARNING OBJECTIVES

After studying the material in this chapter, students should be able to:

Understand the role of history in intercultural communication interactions.

Describe some of the histories that influence our communication.

Describe how power has influenced the recording and acknowledgment of history.

Explain why it is necessary to recover "hidden" histories.

Discuss how the resulting power from our histories influences intercultural communication.

Understand the importance of narratives in developing our identities.

Explain how diasporic histories influence intercultural interactions.

Identify the antecedents of our intercultural contacts.

Describe the contact hypothesis.

List the conditions under which contact may facilitate positive attitude change toward another culture.

Explain how we can negotiate histories in interactions.

KEY WORDS

absent history	ethnic histories	national history
colonial histories	family histories	political histories
contact hypothesis	gender histories	postcolonialism
cultural-group histories	grand narrative	racial histories
	hidden histories	sexual orientation history
diaspora	intellectual histories	social histories
diasporic histories	modernist identity	

EXTENDED CHAPTER OUTLINE

I. Introduction: Our knowledge of history and how we feel about it are influenced by our cultural background.
    A. In intercultural encounters, differences may become hidden barriers to communication.
    B. The influence of history on our interactions is frequently overlooked, but many intercultural interactions involve a dialectical interplay between past and present.

C. Although European American students often want to de-emphasize history, many current situations cannot be understood without knowing their historical background.

D. Further, how we think about the past influences how we think about ourselves and others.

E. A dialectical perspective enables us to understand how history positions people in the different cultural places from which they communicate with and interpret others' messages.

F. This chapter will focus on the history/past–present/future dialectic.

II. From History to Histories: To understand the dialectics in everyday interaction, we need to think about the histories that are part of our various identities.

A. Political, Intellectual, and Social Histories
   1. Some people restrict their notion of history to documented events.
   2. **Political histories** are written histories that focus on political events.
   3. **Intellectual histories** are written histories that focus on the development of ideas.
   4. **Social histories** are accounts of the everyday life experiences of various groups in the past.
   5. **Absent history** is a historical event that was never recorded.
   6. An absent history is not an insignificant history, but acknowledging absent histories requires more complex thinking about the past and the ways it influences the future.

B. **Family Histories**
   1. These occur at the same time as other histories, but on a more personal level.
   2. Often they are not written down, but passed along orally from one generation to the next.
   3. Families vary in their knowledge of and feelings of importance for their family histories.
   4. Many family histories are deeply intertwined with ethnic-group histories.

C. **National History**
   1. The history of any nation is important to its people.
   2. This history is taught formally in school, and we are expected to recognize certain historical events and people.
   3. National histories give people a sense of who they are and solidifies their sense of nationhood.
   4. Even if people do not fit into their national narratives, they are expected to know them in order to understand references used in communication.
   5. We rarely receive much information about the histories of other nations unless we study other languages.
   6. Historical contexts shape language.

D. **Cultural-Group Histories**
   1. Cultural groups in each nation have their own histories.
   2. These may be hidden, but they are related to the national history.
   3. They are not always part of the national history, but they are important in the development of group identity, family histories, and the contemporary lives of these co-cultures.

4. The authors feel that history should be viewed as many stories about the past rather than as one story on a singular time continuum.
5. Ignorance of others' histories may lead to potential misunderstandings.

III. History, Power, and Intercultural Communication

Power is a central dynamic in the writing of history. A culture's power structure influences what information is transmitted as history and how it is transmitted.

A. The Power of Texts
1. History is vital for understanding identity, but it is only accessible to us in a textual, narrative form.
2. Not everyone has an equal chance to write and produce historical texts.
3. Sometimes lack of access to political participation and forbidden languages have made it impossible to write histories.
4. The availability of political documents and how they reflect powerful inequities influences what can be written as history.
5. The seeming unity of the past, the linear nature of history, is merely a reflection of **modernist identity**, grounded in Western tradition.

B. The Power of Other Histories
1. In this period of rapid change, the "**grand narrative**" of the past has lost credibility, and we are rethinking cultural struggles and cultural identities.
2. Histories that have been suppressed, hidden, or erased are being rewritten as cultures that were dominated in the past are being empowered.
3. This restoration of history enables us to examine what cultural identities mean and to rethink the dominant cultural identity.

C. Power in Intercultural Interactions
1. Power is the legacy of past history and leaves cultural groups in particular positions.
2. We are never "equal" in intercultural encounters because history has left us in unbalanced positions, and though we may chose to ignore it, this imbalance will still influence our interactions and identities.

IV. History and Identity

A. Histories as Stories
1. Although people are tempted to ignore all the levels of history that affect them, this only masks their influence.
2. Telling stories is a fundamental part of the human experience.
3. Histories are stories we use to help us make sense of ourselves and others.
4. A strong element in our U.S. cultural attitudes encourages us to forget history.
5. The desire to forget history tells us significant information about how our culture negotiates its relationship to the past and about how we view the relationships of other cultures with their pasts.
6. Ignoring history can sometimes lead to wrong conclusions about others that reinforce stereotypes.
7. It is a paradox that even if we ignore history we cannot escape it.

B. Ethnic and Racial Histories
1. Minority groups have had to struggle to retain their histories.
   a. They have not learned them in school, but the histories are vital to their understanding of who they are.

     b.   Mainstream U.S. history has neither the time nor space to include all **ethnic histories** and **racial histories**.

     c.   Some people feel these histories question or undermine the celebratory nature of a national history.

     d.   However, these histories act as markers in the maintenance of cultural identity for many groups of people (for example, Japanese, Jewish).

     e.   Histories are never isolated but are interwoven and place cultural groups in differential power positions are: sometimes the victim, sometimes the victimizer, and sometimes both.

     f.   Blanchot (1986) suggests that we have responsibilities for histories that happened even before we were born.

     g.   Displacement of populations is part of the history of every migrating or colonizing people.

     h.   All our lives are entangled in the web of history from which there is no escape, only denial and silence.

C.   Hidden Histories: Revealing histories hidden from the mainstream can help those cultural members with the construction of their personal and cultural identities and offer them an opportunity to reconcile the events of history. Awareness of **hidden histories** helps others understand how groups have negotiated cultural attitudes in the past that are relevant today.

   1.   Gender Histories

     a.   Feminist scholars have insisted that much of the history of women has been lost.

     b.   Although there is interest in women's history today, **gender histories** are difficult to document because of restrictions against women's access to public records.

   2.   Sexual Orientation Histories

     a.   Much of the **sexual orientation history** of homosexuals has been suppressed.

     b.   This happens when people try to construct a specific understanding of the past and may prevent us from acknowledging significant historical lessons.

     c.   Relationships with the past are tied to issues of power.

     d.   People have even tried to reconfigure Nazi history, with homosexuals as the perpetrators rather than the victims, to motivate negative attitudes toward gay identity.

   3.   Racial and Ethnic Histories

     a.   Injustices by one culture to another are also frequently suppressed (for example, Japanese internment).

     b.   Simply acknowledging lost history does not remove the effects of that history.

     c.   Some histories cannot be suppressed because of their marks on our identity (for example, being French but looking Chinese).

     d.   One intercultural communication problem is that our desire to view the world in discrete units motivates us to overlook the displacement and migration of other people.

4. Diasporic Histories
   a. Also overlooked in intercultural communication are the international relationships many racial and ethnic groups have with people who share their racial and ethnic heritage and history.
   b. These relationships resulted from migrations, slavery, transnational capitalism, religious crusades, and so forth.
   c. It is important to recognize transnational cultural groups—diaspora.
   d. A **diaspora** is a massive migration caused by war, famine, or persecution that disperses a unified group.
   e. **Diasporic histories** chronicle these migrations.
   f. Sometimes these migrations cause people to cling more tightly to their group's identity, though with time people tend to acculturate to their new home countries.
   g. History helps identify the connections among people who have been affected by diasporas and other transnational migrations.
5. Colonial Histories
   a. A better understanding of the dynamics of intercultural communication today comes from understanding **colonial histories**.
   b. Colonialism has been significant in determining what languages are spoken in various countries today.
   c. Many nations have attempted to resist the influences of colonialism by reclaiming their native languages.
   d. The languages we speak are determined by the histories of the societies we are born into.
   e. Colonial history is filled with incidents of oppression and brutality.
   f. As a result, many advocate a position of **postcolonialism,** which is an intellectual, political, and cultural movement beyond colonialism that calls not only for independence of colonialized states but of colonialist ways of thinking.
6. Socioeconomic Class Histories
   a. Though frequently forgotten, class issues and economics motivated many people to emigrate to the United States.
   b. People who are socioeconomically privileged also emigrate.
   c. These histories are helpful in understanding interactions and politics between different groups.
V. Intercultural Communication and History: A number of perspectives are important for understanding relationships between communication and history.
   A. Antecedents of Contact: It is important to recognize that we bring elements of our personal histories into each intercultural interaction including:
      1. Childhood experiences concerning other cultures.
      2. Historical myths about other cultures.
      3. The language we speak.
      4. The tendency to be affected by recent, vivid events.
   B. Contact Hypothesis
      1. The **contact hypothesis** is the notion that better communication between groups of people will occur if they are simply put together in the same place and allowed to interact.

2. Though this notion has no historical support, many public policies and programs in the United States and abroad are based on this hypothesis.
3. Allport (1979) and Amir (1969) have tried to identify conditions under which the contact hypothesis holds true. Their studies and subsequent ones show that the histories of the groups heavily influence the outcomes of contact and that eight conditions must be more or less met for contact to facilitate positive attitude change and intergroup communication.
   a. Members of both groups should be of equal status both within and outside of the contact situation.
   b. Strong normative and institutional support for contact should be provided.
   c. Contact should be voluntary.
   d. Contact should not be superficial but have the potential to extend beyond the immediate situation and to occur in a variety of contexts with a variety of individuals from both groups.
   e. Cooperation within groups should be maximized, and competition between groups should be minimized.
   f. An equal number of members from each group should meet.
   g. Group members should have similar beliefs and values.
   h. Individuation of group members should be promoted.
4. This list helps us understand how domestic and international contexts vary, and it is easy to see how the history within a nation-state may lead to conditions and attitudes that are more difficult to facilitate.
5. This list is incomplete, and meeting each condition does not always guarantee positive outcomes when diverse groups of people interact.
6. It simply represents a starting place.
C. Negotiating Histories Dialectically in Interaction
   1. To negotiate histories in our interactions, we need first to recognize that we have them (both known and hidden) and to understand the role they play for those with whom we interact.
   2. We need to understand the role histories play in the identities we bring into the interaction.
   3. Sometimes the past–present dialectic operates along with the disadvantage-privilege dialectic, and we need to think dialectically about history and class.
   4. Both dialectics affect our view of the past, present, and future.
   5. Who we are today is greatly influenced by how we understand the past, as well as by the ways we live and the culture we believe to be our own.

DISCUSSION QUESTIONS

Questions from the Text

1. What are some examples of "hidden" histories, and why are they hidden?

2. How do the histories of the United States influence our communication with people from other countries?

3. What kinds of histories are likely to influence your interactions with an international student of the same gender and age?

4. What factors in your experience have led to the development of positive feelings about your own cultural heritage and background? What factors have led to negative feelings, if any?

5. When can contact between members of two cultures improve their attitudes toward each other and facilitate communication between them?

6. How do histories influence the process of identity formation?

7. What is the significance of the shift from history to histories? How does this shift help us understand intercultural communication?

8. Why do some people in the United States prefer not to talk about history? What views of social reality and intercultural communication does this attitude encourage?

Additional Questions

1. How does a dialectical perspective help us to understand the role of history in communication interactions between people of different cultures?

2. How do national histories influence citizens' identities?

3. How does power influence the writing of history?

4. Why do the authors argue that we are never "equal" in intercultural encounters?

5. What dangers are there in ignoring history?

6. Why does Blanchot (1986) suggest that we have responsibilities for histories that happened even before we were born.

7. What makes diasporic histories unique from other types of histories?

8. What does the contact hypothesis tell us?

CLASSROOM EXERCISES AND CHAPTER ASSIGNMENTS

1. Defining History Exercise: Ask students what the term history means to them. Ask them to explain their answers (in a heterogeneous class, students will probably give a variety of different answers, in a monocultural class, answers might be more unified, suggesting that history is not very important). This exercise should be conducted before most students have a chance to read the chapter as an introduction. The instructor should list all the types of responses on the board and ask the students to think about them as they read the chapter, respond in a journal entry, or use them to start a lecture and a discussion about the relationship between different histories and social positions.

2. Interview Assignment: Assign students to work with four to six other students to interview two individuals who vary in gender, age, ethnicity, and race about their attitudes toward history. Interviews should be completed for an assigned class period. On that day, an hour of class time is given to the groups to meet and compile the information. Have them attempt to specify how social positions influence individuals' attitudes toward history and what factors influence whether an individual sees history as an important element of his or her identity. Their conclusions could be shared in class, or they could each write a brief report and turn it in with summaries of their interviews.

3. Family/Local History Assignment: The focus of this assignment is to help students become more familiar with their own personal family history or the history of their community. Students are assigned to interview an elderly (at least 70 years old) family member or member of their community (preferably someone who has spent the majority of his or her life in the community). Students should prepare questions for the interview that invite the interviewees to talk about what they remember about growing up; changes that they have seen occur (social, technological, economical, and so on) and how they feel these have affected the family/community; information about the origin of the family/community in the United States; how they think growing up today is different from when they grew up; whether they feel that values in society have changed and what effect this change has had on life today. Students should take notes or ask permission to record the interview. After completing the interview, students should write a paper that addresses questions such as:

   a. How do you think growing up in your family/community is different today than it was for your interviewee?

   b. What are some of the changes that have occurred in the United States during the lifetime of your interviewee, and how do you think those changes have affected your family/community?

   c. Have there been any shifts in values that have affected your family/community?

   d. What new information did you learn about your family/community?

   e. What did you learn about the origins of your family/community in the United States?

   f. Of the information you gained, what information was the most interesting/meaningful to you?

   g. How do you think the history of your family/community has influenced your life experience and how you think about yourself?

4. History of Groups in Conflict Assignment: Students are to select two cultural, national, or religious groups presently involved in conflicts (for example, Serbs and Albanians, Palestinians and Israelis, and so forth). Assign them to work in teams with one partner researching the history of each group. Their goal is to determine what events, people, and/or beliefs in the histories of these two groups have perpetuated the present conflict and how these have been interpreted by the members of each group. Students should try to identify what the conflict is about and how the groups' perceptions of their experiences and positions differ. After gathering this information, students could be assigned to present it in oral or written form as either a dialogue between members of the cultural groups they researched or from the perspective of peacekeepers assigned to help negotiate the resolution of the conflict.

   Note: With minor expansions to the requirements, this assignment could easily be made into a term project.

5. Negotiating History Exercise: This exercise is designed to encourage students to investigate an event in United States history from different cultural perspectives. Have students research videos, magazine articles, and so on that reported events surrounding the 500th Anniversary of Christopher Columbus "discovering" America from a pre-assigned cultural viewpoint such as Native American, European American, African American, Asian, Latino, European, or Spanish. It is likely that students will need to dig deeply and look in a variety of nonacademic resources for this assignment. In addition, students may want to interview cultural informants, asking for their opinions of this event. During class, students will present this event

from their assigned perspective. Encourage students to defend/support (using their research findings) why the group they represent perceived the situation from their particular view. This assignment could also be researched and presented in teams of three or four students.

6. History Assignment: This assignment is designed to encourage students to learn about someone whose culture is different from theirs by reading about a particular person's life. Students read an autobiography or essay of a person whose culture, religion, sexual orientation, or social class status is different from their own. The person may be famous, but this is not necessary for meeting the goals of this assignment. The students can either make a verbal presentation to the class or be asked to write a two- to four-page report about the person's life. Ask students to point out how events in the person's cultural, gender, socioeconomic, or other histories influenced that person's life.

7. Dialectic Approach to Current Issues: Select a current issue in the United States about which there is conflict between two groups (for example, women in the military, teaching Ebonics, or bilingual education). Randomly divide the students in the class into two groups and assign each group to represent one side in this conflict. Random assignment will prevent people who might be members of the groups in the conflict from choosing the side they favor or forcing members of groups associated with the conflict to defend their positions against members on the other side of the conflict. Then split each student group into two subgroups. Assign the members of one subgroup to research issues in the history of the group they represent that provide a context for the position of their assigned group. Instruct members of the second subgroup to research the present conflict from the position of their assigned group to gather details about how the conflict is being negotiated. Have them work together to prepare an oral report that will explain the current position and conflict from the position of each group and that explains events in the past that helped inform and motivate their group's position. After each group has presented its report, debrief the activity by asking students:

   a. Were there any historical events shared by the two groups? How did the outcomes of these events affect the current issue?

   b. How does the history of each group affect their current position?

   c. How does understanding the history of each group aid us in understanding the current issue?

   d. What might people miss toward understanding this issue if they are ignorant of the history of one group? Both groups?

SUGGESTED VIDEOS

1. Video: *Black Athena.* Distributed by San Francisco, CA: California Newsreel, 1991. This video depicts the debate based on Martin Bernal's book about the African origins of Greek culture. In his book, Bernal argues that 19th-century scholars intentionally covered up the relationships between the Greek culture and non-European cultures. (52 minutes)

2. Video: *Awakenings.* Distributed by Alexandria, VA: PBS Video, 1986. This video is the first episode of the *Eye on the Prize* series. It reviews the history of the segregation of Blacks in the south. (60 minutes)

3. Video: *Black History: Lost, Stolen, or Strayed.* CBS News production released by West Glen Films, 1968. In this video Bill Cosby describes how the history of White and Black relations have affected African Americans. He gives examples of achievements made by African Americans that have been omitted from history texts and shows the changing of the Hollywood stereotype for African Americans.

4. Video Series: *Eyes on the Prize II.* Distributed by Alexandria, VA: PBS Video, 1986. This is a series of videos on the history of American civil rights from 1965 to 1985. There are eight episodes in this series beginning with *Ain't Gonna Shuffle No More.*

5. Video: *Minorities: From Africa, Asia and the Americas.* Distributed by Phoenix/Coronet, 1972. This video reviews the history of America's non-White minorities and how they have all contributed to U.S. society. (16 minutes)

6. Video: *Before Stonewall: The Making of Gay and Lesbian Community.* Distributed by MPI Home Video. This video relives the emotionally charged start of today's gay rights movement, focusing on events that led to the 1969 riots at a New York City gay bar (Stonewall Inn) and many other milestones in the gay movement for acceptance.

CHAPTER 5

IDENTITY

LEARNING OBJECTIVES

After studying the material in this chapter, students should be able to:

Describe from a social psychological perspective how identity is formed.

Explain how identities are developed through our communicative interaction with others.

Identify some of the ways in which people communicate their identity.

Explain how the context of the larger society contributes to the formation of identity.

Discuss responses to the social and political ascriptions of identity.

Identify some of the major social and cultural identities that are manifest in our communication.

Distinguish between racial and ethnic identity.

Explain differences in how identities are developed for minority versus majority group members in the United States

Describe the relationship between identity and language.

Discuss the ways in which one's own identity and perception of other's identities influence our communication.

KEY WORDS

age identity	ethnic identity	minority identity
ascription	gender identity	national identity
avowal	global nomads	prejudice
class identity	hyphenated Americans	racial identity
core symbols	identity	regional identity
cultural brokers	interpellation	religious identity
discrimination	majority identity	stereotypes

EXTENDED CHAPTER OUTLINE

Identity is a bridge between culture and communication. We communicate our identity to others and form our identity through communication with others. Sometimes identity conflicts occur in our interactions. This chapter explores relationships between communication and identity and the role of identity in intercultural communication.

I. A Dialectical Approach to Understanding Identity: In this chapter, the static–dynamic and personal–contextual dialectics will be used to explore the characteristics of **identity** as well as three main contemporary perspectives (social psychological, communication, and critical).

    A. Social Psychological Perspectives

        1. Identity is created partly by self and partly through group membership.

        2. The self is composed of multiple identities and is culture bound.

        3. Identities are self-created, formed from a series of identity conflicts, diffusion, confusion, and crises.

        4. Identity formation occurs in spurts, some negative, with periods when we don't think much about ourselves and our identities.

        5. Identity development involves an exploration of one's abilities, interests, options, and values, often in relation to group membership.

        6. Many groups (gender, race, ethnicity, class, sexual orientation, religion, nationality) affect us while we are growing up as we compare ourselves and others to them.

        7. Gender identification (1–3 years of age) occurs earlier than racial/ethnic (7–9 years of age) identification, and minority group members seem to develop a sense of their identity before majority group members.

        8. Due to different group memberships, we have multiple identities that come into play at different times, given the context.

        9. Emphasis for developing identities varies across cultures.

    B. A Communication Perspective

        1. Identities are not created by self alone but are co-created through communication with others.

            a. Identities emerge during the communication process.

            b. They are negotiated, co-created, reinforced, and challenged through communication.

            c. Presenting our identities is complex and sometimes the received image conflicts with the presented image.

        2. Avowal and Ascription Processes

            a. **Avowal** is the process by which an individual portrays him- or herself.

            b. **Ascription** is the process others use to attribute identities to individuals.

            c. Sometimes what is avowed is the same as what is ascribed; sometimes these conflict.

        3. Different identities are emphasized depending on the person we are communicating with and the conversation topic.

        4. Intercultural communication competence is communication that affirms the most salient identity in the conversation.

        5. The central idea in this perspective is that identities are expressed communicatively.

a. Identities are expressed in core symbols, labels, and norms.

b. **Core symbols** tell us about the fundamental beliefs/central concepts that define a particular identity.

c. They are expressed through communication and created and shaped through communication.

d. Labels are a category of core symbols and are the terms used to refer to aspects of our own and others' identities.

e. Certain norms of behavior are associated with particular identities.

C. Critical Perspective

1. Contextual Identity Formation: This approach is motivated by the attempt to understand identity formation within the contexts of history, economics, politics, and discourse.

a. Due to the ethnic, socioeconomic, or racial positions of our parents, identities are ascribed to us even before we are born.

b. Identities that others ascribe to us are socially and politically determined.

2. Resisting Ascribed Identities

a. Although we may resist them, we begin with the identities ascribed to us.

b. This is the process of **interpellation,** which establishes the foundation from which interaction occurs.

3. The Dynamic Nature of Identities: Because social forces are always changing, our identities are dynamic.

II. Social and Cultural Identities

A. Gender Identity

1. The formation of **gender identity** begins in infancy.

2. Gender is not the same as biological sex.

3. Cultural notions influence what it means to be male or female, and some activities are considered more masculine or more feminine.

4. Media has a role in how people socialize with others, contributing to gendered contexts.

5. Cultural shifts modify the notion of what is masculine or feminine so these notions are constantly changing, driven by commercial interests, advertising, and other cultural forces.

6. We situate ourselves in relation to these changing notions and act out aspects of gendered identity to communicate our masculinity or femininity.

B. Age Identity

1. **Age identity** is influenced by cultural notions of how people our age should act and look.

2. Notions of age and youth are based on cultural conventions.

3. These notions of age may change as we grow older.

4. Social constructions are the other part of the identity process.

a. Different generations have different philosophies, values, and ways of speaking.

b. Slang creates ingroups within generations.

C. Racial and Ethnic Identity
   1. Racial Identity
      a. **Racial identity** is largely a modern phenomenon, and in the United States today it is both a sensitive and a pervasive issue, although many people feel uncomfortable about discussing it.
      b. Initially (15th to 16th century) the debates on race centered on religious questions concerning whether there was "one family of man" and what rights those who were different should have.
      c. Debates about which groups were "human" or "animal" were popular and provided a rationale for slavery.
      d. In the 18th and 19th centuries scientists tried unsuccessfully to classify races according to gene pools and/or cranial capacity.
      e. Scientists now approach race from a social and historical context instead of biologically because they recognize that racial categories are constructed in social and historical contexts.
      f. There are several reasons against the physiological basis for race:
         i. Racial categories vary widely throughout the world.
         ii. A variety of definitions are used in U.S. law to determine racial categories.
         iii. Racial categories are fluid and have shifted over time in the United States.
      g. Racial categories are based to some extent on physical characteristics, but they are also constructed in fluid social contexts so it makes more sense to talk about *racial formation* than racial categories.
      h. How people construct the complex social meanings associated with race influences their communication with others.
   2. Ethnic Identity
      a. **Ethnic identity** is a set of ideas about one's own ethnic group.
      b. Dimensions of ethnic identity include: self-identification, knowledge about ethnic culture, and feelings about belonging to a particular ethnic group.
      c. Some U.S. residents see themselves has having a very specific ethnic identity because they feel connected to an origin outside the United States.
      d. For others ethnicity is a vague concept, and they see themselves as "American" instead of **hyphenated Americans.**
      e. What does "American" mean, how is this identity formed, and how does it influence communication with hyphenated Americans?
   3. Racial Versus Ethnic Identity
      Scholars have differing views on whether racial and ethnic identity are the same or different and which should be emphasized. If we never talk about race, but only ethnicity, can we consider the effects and influences of racism?
   4. Bounded Versus Dominant/Normative Identities
      a. One way to distinguish race and ethnicity for White people is to differentiate between bounded and dominant/normative identities.
      b. Bounded cultures are groups that we belong to that are specific (for example, Irish, Amish, German, Japanese) but not dominant.

    c. Membership in the dominant/normative White culture is difficult to define, though real.

    d. Our sense of racial and ethnic identity develops over time, in stages, as a result of communication with others.

    e. The stages of development depend on the type of group to which people belong and are affected by oppression.

    f. The strong identities of some groups may have ensured the survival of their cultural groups.

D. Religious Identity

1. **Religious identity** can be an important dimension in people's identities as well as a source of intercultural conflict.

2. It often gets conflated with racial or ethnic identity, suggesting that it is problematic to try to distinguish between various identities (racial, ethnic, class, national, regional).

3. Religious differences are often at the root of intercultural conflicts.

4. For some, religion is taken very seriously, and people are willing to fight or give their lives for their beliefs.

5. Conflicts arise when the religious beliefs of some individuals are imposed on others who do not share them.

6. Some people communicate their religious beliefs overtly by their clothing.

7. Because religious identities are less salient, everyday interactions may not invoke religious identity.

E. Class Identity

1. We typically do not consider socioeconomic class as an important part of our identities, but class often shapes our reactions to and interpretations of culture.

2. **Class identity** is reflected in the kinds of magazines we read, the foods we eat, and the words we use.

3. Because we feel it is impolite to ask about others' class backgrounds, we use communication strategies to place others in a class hierarchy.

4. These strategies are not always accurate.

5. Most people in the United States can recognize class associations but deny that the society has class divisions.

6. This increases the complexities of class issues because it indicates that we frequently do not know the criteria for class.

7. Further, people in the majority/normative class (the middle class) tend not to think about class, whereas the working class are often reminded that their styles of communication and lifestyles are different from the norm.

8. People assume that with enough work and persistence they can move up in class standing, but overwhelming evidence proves otherwise.

9. The poor are generally blamed because poverty persists—a classic case of blaming the victim.

10. Although class identity is not as clearly identifiable as other kinds of identity, it influences our perceptions and communication with others just as much as they do.

11. Race, class, and sometimes gender identity are interrelated, but race and class are not synonymous.

F. National Identity
    1. **National identity** refers to one's legal status in relation to a nation.
    2. Although nationality may seem clear-cut, this is not true when a nation's status is unclear.
    3. In many instances people have identified themselves with a nation that may or may not have emerged (for example, Confederate States of America).
    4. Sometimes nations have disappeared permanently or temporarily, but in all instances, citizens have various ways of thinking about nationality.
    5. Some people feel more strongly about their national identity than their ethnicity and vice versa, which is indicative of the complex and dynamic relationship between ethnicity and nationality.
G. Regional Identity
    1. Many regions of the world have separate cultural identities or **regional identities**.
    2. In the United States, regional identities are important but decreasingly so as the nation moves toward homogeneity.
    3. Regional identities can lead to national independence movements; they are often affirmed by distinct cuisines, dress, manners, and languages.
    4. Understanding regional identities may be important in intercultural communication, particularly if different regions speak different dialects.
H. Personal Identity
    1. Identity issues are closely tied to one's notion of self.
    2. Each person has a personal identity, but it may not be unified or coherent.
    3. We are who we think we are at the same time that outside influences constrain and influence our self-perception.
    4. We have many identities and sometimes they conflict.
    5. A dialectical perspective sees contradictions between identities as real and present challenges for communication and everyday living.
    6. Personal identities are important to us, and we try to communicate them to others.
    7. The success of our ability to communicate our personal identity depends on how others respond to us, and we use various ways to construct identity and portray ourselves as we want others to see us.
III. Identity, Stereotypes, and Prejudice: Identity group characteristics sometimes form the basis for stereotypes, prejudice, and racism. Their origin lies in both individual and contextual elements.
    A. To make sense of the immense amount of information we receive, we categorize and generalize the information, sometimes relying on stereotypes.
    B. **Stereotypes** are widely held beliefs about a specific group of people.
        1. They are positive or negative and help us know what to expect from people.
        2. They are detrimental when they are negative and when they are held rigidly.
        3. People tend to remember information supporting a stereotype better than contradicting information.
        4. Stereotypes come from many sources including the media and bad experiences.
        5. Because stereotypes operate at an unconscious level and are persistent, people have to work consciously to reject them.

          a.   Recognition of the stereotype is the first step.

          b.   The second step is finding information to counteract it.

C. **Prejudice** is a negative attitude toward a cultural group, based on little or no experience.

    1.   Prejudice may arise from the need to see our own groups as more positive than others or from perceived threats.

    2.   Tensions between groups, negative past contacts, status differences, and perceived threats can lead to prejudice.

D. **Discrimination** consists of overt actions to exclude, avoid, or distance as a result of stereotyping or prejudice.

    1.   It may be based on race, gender, or other group differences.

    2.   It can range from very subtle nonverbal behavior to verbal insults, job discrimination, physical violence, and systemic exclusion.

    3.   Discrimination can be interpersonal, collective, or institutional.

    4.   Recently, interpersonal racism has become subtle and indirect, but persistent.

    5.   Institutionalized or collective discrimination is also a problem.

IV. Identity Development Issues

    A. **Minority Identity** Development

       U.S. minority group members tend to develop a sense of racial and ethnic identity earlier than majority group members because Whites tend to take their culture for granted. They may develop strong ethnic identities, but lack awareness of their racial identity. The stages of minority development may apply to other minority identities (for example, class, gender, sexual orientation).

       1.   Stage 1: Unexamined Identity

          a.   Characterized by a lack of ethnicity exploration.

          b.   Minority members may accept the values and attitudes of the majority, including negative views of their own group.

          c.   They may have the desire to assimilate into the dominant culture and may express positive attitudes toward it.

          d.   Ideas about identity may come from parents or friends or the person may simply be disinterested in ethnicity.

       2.   Stage 2: Conformity

          a.   Characterized by an internalization of the values and norms of the dominant group and a strong desire to assimilate into the dominant culture.

          b.   Minority members may have negative attitudes toward themselves and their group.

          c.   They may be labeled negatively by members of their own group.

          d.   This stage may continue until people encounter situations that cause them to question their pro dominant culture attitudes.

       3.   Stage 3: Resistance and Separatism

          a.   Triggered by events, including negative ones that contribute to a period of dissonance or awareness that not all dominant group values are beneficial.

          b.   This may motivate the need to clarify the personal implications of heritage.

      c. It may be characterized by a blanket endorsement of one's group and accompanying values and attitudes and subsequent rejection of the values and norms of the dominant group.

    4. Stage 4: Integration
      a. Ideal outcome of the identity process.
      b. It is characterized by a strong sense of one's own ethnicity and an appreciation of other cultural groups.
      c. There is an awareness of the reality of racism and other forms of oppression, but any anger is redirected toward positive ends.
      d. The result is a confident and secure identity and the desire to eliminate all oppression, not just that aimed at one's group.

B. **Majority Identity** Development

Hardiman's (1994) model of dominant group identity development:

    1. Stage 1: Unexamined Identity
      a. Same as for minority individuals.
      b. People may have an awareness of differences, but they do not fear other groups or feel superior to them.

    2. Stage 2: Acceptance
      a. Characterized by the internalization (conscious/unconscious) of a racist ideology.
      b. This may be accepted passively or actively, but people are unaware that they have been programmed to accept this worldview.
      c. In the passive acceptance stage, individuals have no conscious identification with being White.
        i. Their assumptions, based on acceptance of society inequities, are subtly racist.
        ii. In this stage, majority members either avoid contact with minority members or patronize them.
      d. In the active acceptance stage, individuals are conscious of being White and may express feelings of superiority collectively.

    3. Stage 3: Resistance
      a. Characterized by a major paradigm shift.
      b. Individuals move from blaming minority individuals for their conditions to blaming their own groups for racial problems.
      c. May take the form of passive or active resistance.
      d. Passive resistance: Little behavioral change in individuals.
      e. Active resistance: Ownership of racism—individuals may feel embarrassed and try to distance themselves from other Whites.

    4. Stage 4: Redefinition
      a. Whites begin to refocus their energy on redefining whiteness in nonracist terms.
      b. They move beyond society's definition to seeing positive aspects of being European American and become comfortable with being White.

    5. Stage 5: Integration
      a. Whites integrate their whiteness into all other facets of identity.
      b. They also appreciate other groups.
      c. This integration affects all other aspects of personal and social identity.

C. Characteristics of Whiteness
   What does it mean to be White in the United States? What are the characteristics of a White identity? Frankenburg suggests that whiteness can be defined as the following set of related dimensions:
   1. A Location of Structural Advantage
      a. Privilege and White are not synonymous because not all whites have equal access to power.
      b. Boundaries between Americanness and whiteness are more fluid for White ethnic groups than for people of color.
      c. Some Whites today perceive themselves as being in the minority.
      d. Some feel that being White is a liability because they are prejudged as racists, blamed for social conditions they did not cause, and miss opportunities open to minorities.
      e. The accuracy of their perceptions is not as significant as the way they are negotiated through communication because people act on perceptions, not on reality.
      f. White people may have stronger White identities in states where there are a higher percentage of non-Whites.
   2. A Standpoint From Which to View Society
      a. Something about being White versus Black influences how we view the world and ultimately how we communicate with others.
      b. For example, a majority of Whites believe that Blacks have achieved equality with Whites on issues that motivated the civil rights movement in the 1960s, but Blacks believe racism and discrimination are on the rise.
      c. White women have divergent views about whether being White is a positive or negative trait.
   3. A Set of Cultural Practices
      a. Some views and cultural practices may be held primarily by Whites.
      b. They are most visible to non-Whites who are excluded.
D. Multiracial and Multicultural People
   1. There are approximately 2 million multiracial (ancestry of two or more races) people in the United States.
   2. The development of their racial identity is a fluid process of complex transition between the child and the social environment.
   3. **Global nomads** are children who grew up in many different cultural contexts because their parents moved around a lot (for example, children of missionaries, military, or international business employees).
   4. People with long-term romantic interethnic or interracial relationships also tend to develop multicultural identities.
   5. These individuals may develop identities following the stages described earlier but may gain a less clear sense of their cultural identity—they may feel marginalized, struggling with two sets of cultural realities.
   6. They may receive criticism from both cultures.
   7. A multicultural person is one who comes to grips with a multiplicity of realities, defined by a new psychocultural style of self-consciousness.

8. Milton Bennett's (1993) stages for the development of an ethnorelative perspective:
   a. Denial or ignorance of difference.
   b. Recognition of difference and negative feelings about it.
   c. Minimization of the effect of difference.
   d. Acceptance of cultural differences.
   e. Adaptation—changing behavior to adapt to others.
   f. Integration—becoming a multicultural person or culture broker.
9. Majority and minority individuals may experience Bennett's stages differently.
10. **Cultural brokers** are people who can facilitate cross-cultural interaction and conflict.
11. Multicultural people experience stresses and tensions.
   a. They may have difficulty deciding what is important.
   b. They may feel multiphrenic or fragmented.
   c. They may suffer a loss of their own authenticity.
12. Janet Bennett (1993) suggests there are two types of marginal individuals:
   a. Encapsulated marginals become trapped by their marginality.
      i. They feel disintegrated in shifting cultures.
      ii. They have trouble making decisions.
      iii. They have difficulty with ambiguity and feel pressure from both groups.
      iv. They try to assimilate, but never feel comfortable.
   b. Constructive marginals thrive in their marginality.
      i. They see themselves as choice makers.
      ii. They are able to make commitments within the relativistic framework.
13. Multicultural identities are constantly being negotiated and explored, and it is never easy with society's preference for easy categories.

V. Identity and Language
   A. Labels referring to particular identities are significant in intercultural communication because of their relational meanings.
   B. These labels construct relational meanings in communication situations for the interactants.

VI. Identity and Communication
   A. Identity has a profound influence on intercultural communication.
   B. The individual–cultural dynamic helps us to understand the issues that arise when we encounter people whose identities we do not know.
   C. Sometimes we assume knowledge about others' identities based on their memberships in particular cultural groups, causing us to overlook their individual characteristics.
   D. The dialectical perspective helps us recognize the importance of balancing both the individual and cultural aspects of others' identities.
   E. The information overload and the number of identities that we negotiate daily lead to problematic communication and tension.
   F. Dimensions of our identities are personal and remain fairly consistent, but we cannot overlook the contextual constraints on our identity.

DISCUSSION QUESTIONS

Questions from the Text

1. How do our perceptions of our own cultural identity influence our communication with others?

2. What are some of the ways in which we express our identities?

3. How does being White affect one's experience in the United States?

4. What is the role of avowal and ascription in the process of identity formation?

5. What are some of the ways members of minority cultures and members of majority cultures develop their cultural identities?

Additional Questions

1. Why is it important to use a dialectical perspective to understand the formation of our identities?

2. How does the communication perspective explain the formation of identities?

3. How does the critical perspective explain the formation of identities?

4. What are some of the historical perspectives about racial differences?

5. How is the process of identity formation different for hyphenated Americans versus other Americans?

6. Why are many people reluctant to discuss class hierarchy in the United States?

7. What can people do to overcome the tendency to use stereotypes?

8. How do Milton Bennett's stages for the development of an ethnorelative perspective help us understand the development of our identities?

CLASSROOM EXERCISES AND CHAPTER ACTIVITIES

1. Multiple Identities Exercise: Have students list labels they would use to identify who they are to others. Ask several students to read the lists they made, and ask all of the students what they notice about those lists. Explain to students that these labels represent multiple identities they have. In which contexts are some identities more important to students than others? (You might ask them what happens to their identities when they go back home to visit their parents.) Can students characterize the identities they have listed in terms of the typology presented by the authors of the textbook?

2. Race and Ethnicity Exercise: Ask the students to write down a definition of race, and then ask them to read their definitions. As they read them, write each different definition on the board and explain that "race" does not have a fixed meaning but is a socially constructed term. Although we often assume that it has a commonsense meaning, people use it to mean a variety of different things such as phenotypical variations (skin color), cultural characteristics, nationality, ethnicity, region of origin, biological differences, environmental influences, and so on. If the students' definitions are limited, prepare examples of these different meanings. *Racist Culture* by David Goldberg provides a complete list of examples of these different social constructions of race. (Goldberg, D. [1993]. *Racist culture: Philosophy and the politics of meaning*. Cambridge, MA: Blackwell.)

3. Definition Exercise: Frequently when people talk about labels, stereotyping, prejudice, and discrimination, they use these terms interchangeably. This exercise is designed to provide students with simple general definitions for these terms and to help them see how closely these processes are related to the cognitive processes we use to interpret the information we receive through our senses. The instructions are written for an instructor who is working with one volunteer in front of the class but could be modified to include the participation of every class member. For this exercise you will need a set of 12 to 15 pens and pencils of assorted sizes and colors (include at least two red ones). Some of these can be similar or identical. You also need one pen and pencil set in which the pen and pencil look very much alike. Prior to class put all of the pens and pencils, except the pencil from the pen and pencil set, which you will keep in your pocket, together in an envelope or box. When you are ready to begin the exercise with your students, ask for one volunteer. Invite the volunteer to the front of the room and have him/her sit in a desk or at a table. Suggest that the other students watch as he or she does the exercise. After the volunteer is seated, proceed with the following steps:

   a. Hand your volunteer the envelope with the pens and pencils. Ask him or her to organize them into groups for you.

   b. Once they are organized, ask the volunteer to explain why he or she chose to put them in those groups.

   c. Explain to the students that the process the volunteer just completed was categorization. Have the students suggest ideas for defining categorization. Suggest that the categorization process is the way we organize all of the information that we get from our senses into groups. People, ideas, objects, and impressions are all categorized so that we have an organized way for recording them in our minds. Typically, people organize according to the most obvious (generally physical) attributes of people and objects.

   d. Now ask the volunteer to give each group a name. Explain that we give our groups/categories names so that we can refer to them easily. For example, if we want to talk about methods of transportation, we do not have to describe a vehicle in detail to give someone a general idea of what kind of car it is. We just say it is a convertible, station wagon, sports car, and so forth. This process is called labeling. Discuss the nature of the label with the students. Does it refer to physical characteristics, functions, or other characteristics? How many characteristics of the group does the label identify?

   e. Ask your student volunteer to describe the characteristics of the pens/pencils in each of the categories she or he has created. Then give the student the pencil that you had in your pocket. Ask her or him to categorize it. The student volunteer will generally choose to place it in the category with the pen that it matches. If this happens, point out that although the pencil looks like the pen it really has some differences and ask your volunteer why he or she put it there. Sometimes the student will place it with all of the other pencils. Ask the volunteer why he chose to put it in that group even though it looks just like an object categorized in another group. On occasion the student will create another category with just the pencil. After asking the student to explain his or her decision, explain that this is not the common approach we take to dealing with new information. Generally, we try to push new information into existing categories so that we can maintain a small number of categories. Discuss with students the pros and cons of these tendencies when we are categorizing people. Thank your volunteer and invite her or him to sit with the class, but leave the categories as they are.

f. Suggest that when we decide that an object belongs in a group we also have a tendency to assume that it will have the same characteristics as the other group members. This is stereotyping, or the projection of traits and characteristics on people or objects because of their assumed group membership. Discuss with the students the pros and cons of stereotyping. Consider with the students whether it is possible to both negatively and positively stereotype people. Ask them when stereotypes become a problem.

g. Now pick up one of the red pens (other colors may be substituted) and suggest to the students that after all of the school you have been to and all of the graded papers professors have returned to you with red correction marks you have come to have a negative feeling about red pens. Suggest that feeling is a prejudice. Prejudice is a feeling or attitude about a group. Ask the students whether it is possible to have positive prejudices as well as negative prejudices. Discuss conditions under which prejudices become damaging to our communication with others.

h. Pick up the red pen and tell the students that sometimes when you see red pens you just want to hurt them. Drop the red pen on the floor and step on it or slam it down on the table as you say this. Suggest to the students that what you have just done represents discrimination. Explain that discrimination occurs when a person acts out the prejudice he or she feels. Ask students whether it is possible to positively discriminate. Discuss some different types of discrimination that people use to communicate negative feelings about other groups.

(Note: Many of the definitions in the exercise are based on discussions of these concepts in Gordon Allport's [1979], *The Nature of Prejudice*, New York, NY: Addison-Wesley Publishing Company, Inc. You may want to use this source for additional discussion ideas.)

4. Exploring Stereotypes Assignment: The purpose of this assignment is to encourage students to recognize the stereotypes they have been exposed to for other cultural groups and how these stereotypes may influence communication between members of different cultural groups. Instruct the students to choose one cultural group represented in the United States and write a report that addresses the following issues:

a. Identify and describe the culture, using the stereotypes you can remember. Write honestly as your identification and description of the stereotypes is not an indication that you agree with them.

b. Discuss how you think you learned these stereotypes and from what sources.

c. Then, describe how these stereotypes may hypothetically influence communication with an individual from the culture you are discussing.

5. Identity Model Exercise: This exercise is designed to help students gain a clearer understanding of their identities and how they are negotiated, co-created, and reinforced depending on a particular situation or context. Ask students to draw a picture or model that depicts their various identities. Students may think of a particular situation when they develop their model, as some may need to place their identities within a context. Let the students know that the models will be posted on the classroom walls and that they will be asked to describe them to the class. Allow ample time for presentations and discussion.

6. Avowed and Ascribed Identities Exercise: This exercise will help students understand the concepts of ascribed and avowed identities and how people resist ascribed identities. Invite students to compile a list of their avowed identities and another list

of their ascribed identities. Then, have them indicate how they got their ascribed identities by identifying who or what group was responsible for placing this identity on them or their group. The last step in this exercise is to ask students to indicate any actions they or others may have taken to resist any of their ascribed identities. This activity may be assigned as homework or done during class time.

7. Video Identity Exercise: The goal of this exercise is to have students think about and explore their cultural identities (ascribed and avowed) by showing the video *Skin Deep*, which is about college students who spend a weekend exploring racial, power, and privilege issues. Ask the students to write a paper or discuss in dyads the character in the video that they best identified with and why. You may also want to ask students to discuss how their chosen person in the video communicated his/her avowed and ascribed identities during interactions with the other students. (*Skin Deep: College Students Confront Racism*, [1995], 60 min. Distributed by Iris Films)

8. Identity Awareness Activity: This activity is designed to help students think about situations in which they become conscious of their identities. As the instructor, you may choose which identity or identities you want to work with in this exercise. Instruct students to write down the answers to the questions below, but tell them they will not be required to hand them in or show them to anyone. The questions focus on racial identity, but other identities (gender, regional, and so forth) could be substituted.

   a. What is your racial identity?
   b. How did you learn that having your racial identity was different from having another racial identity?
   c. When you learned this, how did you feel?
   d. What are the advantages and disadvantages of having this racial identity for you personally?
   e. How does your racial identity influence you in school or at work?
   f. How does your racial identity influence the way you communicate with people from your own and other races?

When the students are finished, invite them to share general observations about when they feel people learn what it means to have a racial identity, how that identity influences them in different contexts, how people feel about their racial identities, and how they influence communication with their own and other racial groups.

SUGGESTED VIDEOS

1. *Bill Cosby on Prejudice*. Distributed by Santa Monica, CA: Pyramid Film & Video, 1971. In this video Bill Cosby discusses the use of labels and describes feelings of prejudice that people have for many of the cultural groups in the United States. (24 minutes)

2. *A-M-E-R-I-C-A-N-S*. Distributed by Los Angeles, CA: Churchill Films, 1977. This film shows interviews with foreign-born U.S. American children who describe what they think it means to be American and some of the racial biases they have encountered. (12 minutes)

3. *Color Adjustment*. Distributed by San Francisco, CA: California Newsreel, 1991. This is a two-part video that explores race relations in the United States as portrayed on television. (Part I is 48 minutes, and Part II is 39 minutes)

4. *Eye of the Storm.* Distributed by Washington, DC: PBS Video Distributer, 1986. This video reports the exercise in racism conducted by a third grade teacher in her classroom. It is a good illustration of some of the effects of racism and some of the strategies people use to adapt to being victims of racist attitudes and actions. (25 minutes)

5. *When Billy Broke His Head ... and Other Tales of Wonder.* Distributed by Fanlight Productions. This video by Billy Golfus and David Simpson is about Billy Golfus, an award winning journalist who sustained a brain injury. Golfus meets disabled people around the country and witnesses firsthand the strength and anger that is forging a new civil rights movement for disabled Americans. (57 minutes)

6. *My America ... or Honk if You Love Buddah.* Distributed by Ho-ho-kus, NJ: Sai Communications, 1999. This video documents the experiences and history of the diverse Asian American cultural groups in the United States. (87 minutes)

CHAPTER 6

LANGUAGE AND INTERCULTURAL COMMUNICATION

LEARNING OBJECTIVES

After studying the material in this chapter, students should be able to:

Understand the difference between language and discourse.

Identify and explain the components of language.

Identify cultural universals of language.

Explain how past research supports a qualified relativist position.

Describe some cultural variations in communication style.

Discuss the role of context in cultural variations of communication style.

Understand the role of power in discourse.

List some communication challenges faced by bilingual and multilingual communicators.

Define translation and interpretation and describe the equivalency challenges.

Explain the role of and challenges faced by an interpreter.

KEY WORDS

activity dimension
bilingual
co-cultural groups
communication style
creole
discourse
equivalency
evaluative dimension
high-context
  communication
honorific
International Phonetic
  Alphabet
interpretation
la langue

language acquisition
language policies
la parole
low-context
  communication
metamessage
multilingual
myths
nominalist position
phonetics
pidgin
potency dimension
pragmatics
qualified relativist
  position

relativist position
semantic differential
semantics
semiosis
semiotics
signified
signifiers
signs
social positions
source text
syntactics
target text
tonal coloring
translation

EXTENDED CHAPTER OUTLINE

This chapter focuses on verbal aspects of intercultural communication. The social science approach generally focuses on language and its relation to intercultural communication. The interpretive approach focuses on contextual uses of linguistic codes, and the critical approach emphasizes relationships between discourse and power. The dialectical perspective will explore how language works dynamically in intercultural contexts using the personal–contextual dialectic and the static–dynamic dialectic.

I. The Study of Language
  A. Language Versus Discourse
    1. French theorists laid the early foundation for the structural study of language and distinguished *la langue*, "language," from *la parole*, or "**discourse**."
    2. *La langue* referred to the entire language system; its theoretical conceptualization.
    3. In the case of English this could include the various forms of English spoken around the world including **pidgin** and **creole**.
    4. *La parole* referred to language in use or how language is actively used by particular communities of people, in particular contexts, for particular purposes.
  B. The Components of Language: Language is usually divided into four components.
    1. Semantics: **Semantics** is the study of how words communicate the intended meaning in our communication.
    2. Syntactics: **Syntactics** is the study of language structure/grammar or the rules for combining words into meaningful sentences.
    3. Pragmatics: **Pragmatics** is the study of the way meaning is constructed in relation to receivers and how language is actually used in particular contexts in language communities.
    4. Phonetics: **Phonetics** is the study of the sound system of language, the way words are pronounced, which units of sound (phonemes) are meaningful in a specific language, and which sounds are universal.
    5. The **International Phonetic Alphabet** (IPA) helps linguists transcribe the pronunciation of words in different languages.
  C. Language and Meaning
    1. Universal Dimensions of Meaning
      a. Intercultural communication scholars are interested in what issues of language are universal.
      b. Intercultural scholars are interested in the role of translation and interpretation.
      c. Intercultural scholars are concerned with the power of language and how language can be used to oppress or hurt individuals or groups of people.
      d. There are a variety of cultural variations in language.
      e. The system of difference in any language influences how we classify the entire world, including peoples and cultures.

f. Osgood (psychologist), after years of investigating cross-cultural universals of meaning, found that every person could reflect on a word and characterize its meaning with three dimensions: evaluation, potency, and activity.
  i. His research led to the formation of the **semantic differential,** a way of measuring attitudes or affective meaning.
  ii. The **evaluative dimension** is the degree to which one feels a word has a good or bad meaning.
  iii. The **potency dimension** is the degree to which a word evokes a strong or weak reaction.
  iv. The **activity dimension** is the amount of energy (fast or slow) a word evokes.
  v. These dimensions may be related to core perceptions and survival reactions, and the most powerful dimension is the evaluative dimension.
2. Cross-Cultural Comparisons of Meaning: Osgood's dimensions are useful in making cross-cultural comparisons and helping us to understand that expressions may not communicate the same meanings in different cultures.
D. Language and Perception: How much of our perception is shaped by the language we speak? The debate over this question has spawned two different points of view: the **nominalist position** and the **relativist position**.
  1. The Nominalist Position: This position assumes that perception is not shaped by the particular language we speak.
  2. The Relativist Position: This position assumes that language is powerful and that the particular language we speak determines our thinking and perception of reality and is best represented by the Sapir-Whorf hypothesis.
    a. This hypothesis suggests that our language is the shaper of our ideas and guides our mental activity.
    b. According to this hypothesis, language shapes our experience.
    c. It questions the basic assumption that we all inhabit the same perceptual world.
    d. The **qualified relativist** takes a more moderate view of the relation between language and perception, recognizing language as a tool rather than a mirror of perception.
E. Recent Research Findings
  1. **Language Acquisition** in Children: If language structures thought, then language should be acquired before and should influence thought. Psychologists who have wrestled with this issue have found that language and thought are so closely interrelated that it is difficult to speak of one influencing the other; their work does not support a strong relativist position.
  2. Cross-Cultural Differences in Language
  Research suggests that groups with different languages do not perceive their world in different ways. Hence, they do not support the nominalist position, nor provide strong evidence to support the relativist position.

3. Cognition of Children Who Are Deaf
Researchers have found that the deaf have the same semantic or categorizing competence and higher cognitive skills as the hearing. Their worldviews do not seem to differ from hearing students.

II. Cultural Variations in Language: Language is powerful, and the particular language we use may predispose us to think in particular ways and not in others. For example, the use of the **honorific** may affect the way speakers of some languages think about formality and informality in their communication.

A. Variations in Communication Style: **Communication style** combines both language and nonverbal communication.

1. It is the **tonal coloring** or the **metamessage** that contexualizes how listeners accept and interpret verbal messages.

2. Some cultural groups prefer **high-context communication** over **low-context communication** styles.

3. High-context communicators find most of the information communicated in the physical context or internalized in the person, whereas low-context communicators depend on the coded, explicit, transmitted part of the message (verbal code) for information.

4. People in the United States tend to value low-context communication in many settings, whereas some other cultural groups value high-context communication.
Note: The following four dimensions of communication style difference were identified by Gudykunst and Ting-Toomey (1988).

5. Direct/Indirect Styles: This dimension refers to the extent to which speakers reveal their intentions through explicit verbal communication and emphasizes low-context communication.
a. Direct: Verbal messages reveal the speaker's true intentions, needs, wants, and desires.
b. Indirect: The verbal message is often designed to camouflage the speaker's true intentions.
c. Individuals or groups do not stick with one style but determine their degree of directness by the context.
d. English speakers in the United States tend to prefer the direct style.
e. Other groups prefer the indirect style because preserving relationships is valued more than being totally honest.
f. Misunderstandings sometimes occur between people who have different priorities for truth, honesty, harmony, and conflict-avoidance in relationships.

6. Elaborate/Exact/Succinct Styles: Refers to the quantity of talk that is valued.
a. Elaborate: Use of rich, expressive language in everyday talk.
b. Succinct: Values understatement, simple assertions, and silence.
c. Exact: Values giving only the amount of information that is required; it is between the elaborate and succinct styles.
d. These different uses of language communicate different things to various audiences.

7. Personal/Contextual: Refers to the emphasis placed on the speaker as an individual or the speaker as a role.
   a. Personal: Characterized by the use of linguistic devices to enhance the sense of "I."
   b. Contextual: Language emphasizes prescribed role relationships, stresses status and formality.
8. Instrumental/Affective: Closely related to the direct/indirect style.
   a. Instrumental: Sender-oriented and goal-oriented.
      i. The burden is on the speaker to make the meaning clear.
      ii. Assertiveness is valued and persuasive skills are important.
   b. Affective: Receiver-oriented and process-oriented; the burden for identifying the meaning is on the receiver.
   c. A dialectical perspective can help people avoid stereotyping groups based on their communication styles.
B. Variations in Contextual Rules: The dialectical perspective recognizes that communication styles vary by context.
   1. People communicate differently in different speech communities.
   2. Communication styles are frequently adapted for the contexts we communicate in.
III. Discourse: Language and Power: Discourse refers to language in use; all discourse is social. In discourse, the language that is used is dependent not only on the context but on social relations (and power differential) as well.
A. Co-cultural Communication: Orbe's co-cultural communication theory suggests that groups with the most power consciously or unconsciously develop a communication system to support their perceptions of the world. Hence, groups without power, **co-cultural groups**, must function in communication systems that may not represent their experiences.
   1. This causes a dialectical struggle as they have to decide when to adapt to the dominant group's style and when not to.
   2. Orbe has identified three general co-cultural group orientations (nonassertive, assertive, aggressive) with three different emphases (assimilation, accommodation, separation) toward the dominant group for a total of nine strategies; strategy choice depends on preferred outcome, perceived costs and rewards, and context.
      a. Nonassertive
         i. Separation: Avoiding, maintaining interpersonal barriers.
         ii. Accommodation: Increasing visibility, dispelling stereotypes.
         iii. Assimilation: Emphasizing commonalities, developing positive face, censoring self.
      b. Assertive
         i. Separation: Communicating self, intragroup networking, exemplifying strengths, embracing stereotypes.
         ii. Accommodation: Communicating self, intragroup networking, using liaisons, educating others.
         iii. Assimilation: Extensive preparation, overcompensating, manipulating stereotypes, bargaining.

        c. Aggressive
           i. Separation: Attacking, sabotaging others.
          ii. Accommodation: Confronting, gaining advantage.
         iii. Assimilation: Dissociating, mirroring, strategic distancing, ridiculing self.

B. Semiotics: The study of **semiotics** is the study of how different discursive units communicate meaning.
1. **Semiosis** is the process of producing meaning.
2. Barthes' (1980) framework suggests that meaning is constructed through the interpretation of **signs**—combinations of signifiers and signifieds.
3. **Signifiers** are culturally constructed, arbitrary words or symbols we use to refer to something else, the **signified**.
4. The meaning or the relationship between the signfier and the signified depends on how the signifier is used.
5. Signifiers may possess multiple layers of meaning or **myths**.
6. Semiotics can be useful for helping unpack the ways that cultural codes regulate verbal and nonverbal communication systems.
7. Our interest is in the ways that signifiers are combined and configured.
8. Semiotic systems rely on many codes taken from a variety of places: economic institutions, history, politics, religion, and so forth.
9. Cultural contexts regulate semiotic frameworks and transform communication situations.
10. Nation-states have multiple cultural contexts within their borders that are regulated by their own semiotic systems.

C. Discourse and Social Structure: Societies are structured so that individuals occupy specific **social positions**.
1. Not all positions are equivalent.
2. Power is the central element of the focus on social position.
3. When people communicate their group membership and social position, they inform us about how communication functions and the meaning of what is being communicated.

D. The "Power" Effects of Labels
1. The use of labels, as signifiers, acknowledges particular aspects of our social identity.
2. Context affects the intensity of our feelings about a label.
3. Concern over labels occurs when people feel trapped or mislabeled.
4. Without labels it would be almost impossible to communicate; the problems occur when people disagree with or dislike the labels.
5. Labels communicate various levels of meaning and establish relationships between the communicators.
6. Sometimes people offend others with the labels they use because they are not aware of what the labels mean to them.
7. The messages communicated by the labels vary by the social position of the speaker; labels used by people in power positions may have a greater impact.

IV. Moving Between Languages
  A. Multilingualism
     1. A **bilingual** person speaks two languages.
     2. People who speak more than two languages are **multilingual**.
     3. They rarely speak the different languages with the same fluency, and it is common for them to prefer one language over another depending on the context and topic.
     4. Entire nations may be bilingual or multilingual.
     5. Bilinguals negotiate which language will be used, and these decisions are sometimes motivated by power and sometimes by courtesy to others.
     6. Bilingualism results from the same imperatives as the need for intercultural communication (for example, mobility, business opportunities, and so forth).
     7. Some are motivated to become bilingual for personal imperatives (for example, "growth, freedom, a liberation from the ugliness of our received ideas and mentalities").
     8. People may use foreign languages to escape the history of oppression in their own languages.
     9. Language may be thought of as a "prison house"; the semantic, syntactic, pragmatic, and phonetic systems are enmeshed in a social system from which the only escape may be learning another language.
     10. Learning languages is not easy, but the rewards are great.
     11. Dialectical tensions arise over different languages and different meaning systems around the world.
  B. Translation and Interpretation
     1. **Translation** refers to the process of producing a written text that refers to something said or written in another language.
        a. The **source text** is in the original language.
        b. The translated text is the **target text**.
     2. **Interpretation** refers to the process of verbally expressing what is said or written in another language.
        a. Simultaneous interpretation occurs when the interpreter is speaking at the same time as the original speaker.
        b. Consecutive interpretation occurs when the interpreter speaks during breaks provided by the original speaker.
     3. Equivalent meanings are not easily transferred from one language to the next, due to linguistic differences.
     4. Issues of Equivalency and Accuracy
        a. Languages differ in their flexibility of expression for different topics, which makes accuracy in translation even more difficult.
        b. Translation studies have focused on **equivalency** and accuracy, comparing the translated meaning to the original meaning.
        c. The intercultural communication focus has been on the bridges that are built to cross from one language to another.
     5. Role of the Translator or Interpreter
        a. Although some assume that translators and interpreters are "invisible," they play an intermediary role and often regulate what is said.

b. Sometimes we assume that anyone who knows both languages can be a translator or interpreter, but high levels of fluency in two languages are not enough.
   c. The task requires far more than language equivalency; it also requires greater insight into the wide variety of ways meanings may be communicated in differing social contexts and relations.
   d. The field of translation studies is becoming more central to academic inquiry.
V. Language Politics and Policies
   A. Nations vary in their number of official languages.
   B. **Language policies** are laws or customs that determine which language is spoken where and when.
   C. Language policies are embedded in the politics of class, culture, ethnicity, and economics—not language quality.

DISCUSSION QUESTIONS

Questions from the Text

1. Why is it important for intercultural communication scholars to study both language and discourse?

2. What is the relationship between our language and the way we perceive reality?

3. What are some cross-cultural variations in language use and communication style?

4. What aspects of context influence the choice of communication style?

5. What does a translator or an interpreter need to know to be effective?

6. Why is it important to know the social positions of individuals or groups involved in intercultural communication?

7. Why do some people say that we should not use labels to refer to people but should treat everybody as individuals? Do you agree?

8. Why do people have such strong reactions to language policies, as in the "English only" movement?

Additional Questions

1. What are some advantages to being bilingual or multilingual?

2. What are some of the challenges to speaking more than one language?

3. How do language policies affect intercultural relationships within nations?

4. What are the responsibilities of an effective translator?

5. What is the relationship between the signified and the signifier?

6. What are some of the ways co-cultures adapt to dominant group communication styles?

CLASS EXERCISES AND CHAPTER ASSIGNMENTS

1. Specialized Discourse Exercise: Ask students to form small groups and try to identify different communities that use discourse in distinct and specialized ways that limit the access other groups have to those communities (for example, medical doctors, computer specialists, and so forth). Ask students to present their examples to the class and discuss the role of discourse in creating exclusions and inclusions.

2. Symbol Perception Exercise: Pick a common noun (for example, the name of an animal or object). Tell your students that you are going to say a word and ask them to write a description of the word using adjectives to describe the first mental picture they received when they heard the word. Say the word and give students 3 to 5 minutes to write their descriptions. Invite students to read their descriptions and discuss the variations of their ideas. Consider the potential for misunderstandings if people communicated about the word from their different mental pictures. This exercise could lead to a discussion of the relationship between the signifier and the signified.

3. Nuts and Bolts of Second Language Acquisition Assignment: The purpose of this assignment is to familiarize students who have not experienced learning a second language with the challenges and benefits of this process. Instruct students to select someone they know who has learned to speak another language fluently (this could be someone who has lived in another country or someone from another country who is living here) and interview the person about what it was like to learn the second language, why he or she was motivated to learn it, and the process he or she went through. Students should then write a brief report about what they learned to answer the question, "What you should know about learning _____."

4. Current Language Issues Assignment: This assignment is designed to increase students awareness of current debates over language usage. Choose a language-related issue (for example, English only or bilingual education) and assign each student a context/role to focus their exploration of the topic. For example, if you chose the English only debate, one student team could represent the federal government, one team could represent the group of non-English speaking immigrants, another could represent the police department or health system, and one could represent English-speaking tax payers. Instruct each team to split into two pairs. One pair is assigned to debate the positive benefits of the proposed language issue, and the other pair is assigned to debate its drawbacks for people in their role/context. Students should work as pairs to research their side of the issue. Each student should write a three- to four-page brief of his or her position to turn in as part of the assignment. You should probably give them two weeks to prepare for a class debate on the issue. Students will probably need part of the class period before the scheduled debate to coordinate efforts with their partners. On the day you split the students into teams, you should briefly discuss the history of the issue with your students and describe the format for the debate. On the day the debate is scheduled, arrange the desks in a large circle and instruct the student teams to sit together. You may want to make place cards for each team so that the other teams will be able to remember from which perspective they are speaking. Start the debate by choosing one team to present the issue from their context/role perspective. Give each pair three minutes to present their side of the debate. After each team is finished, all the students are allowed to question the teams or to challenge their positions in a 5-minute cross-examination. This process continues until all of the teams have presented on the issue.

To debrief the debate you could discuss the following questions:

a. What do you know about this issue that you did not know before the debate?

b. Is it easier for you to take a stand on this issue now than it was before the debate? Why?

c. What do you think will have to happen in society for the conflict over this issue to be resolved?

d. What are the possible solutions?

e. What will be the outcomes for intercultural communication and relationships between cultural groups?

f. How does the debate over this issue in society affect intercultural communication and intercultural relationships today?

g. What is the role of power in the debates over this issue?

5. Variations in Language Style Assignment: This assignment is designed to help students differentiate between the three communication styles of elaborate, exact, and succinct. Assign or have students locate and read a speech written in one of the three communication styles. During class, students will read an excerpt from their speech that they believe best exemplifies that style of speech. Students then discuss which style they preferred, why they preferred it, and how each style can be both negatively and positively evaluated by others simply based on personal and cultural preferences.

6. Regional Language Variations: Show students the video *American Tongues* prior to asking the students to form small groups. Discuss the many examples of regional variations in language portrayed in this video.

SUGGESTED VIDEOS

1. *Bilingual Americans.* Distributed by New York, NY: Video Knowledge: Bennu, 1990. This two-part video explores languages issues and the impact of culture on U.S. American society. (55 minutes)

2. *Dialects.* Distributed by Indiana University, 1959. This video demonstrates some of the different dialects found in the United States and describes the geographical areas where the dialects are found. (29 minutes)

3. *American Tongues.* Distributed by Facets Multimedia, 1988. This video examines the regional diversity of American accents, dialects, and slang, as well as attitudes toward language use (specifically southern and Black English dialects). (56 minutes)

CHAPTER 7

NONVERBAL CODES AND CULTURAL SPACE

LEARNING OBJECTIVES

After studying the material in this chapter, students should be able to:

Understand how verbal and nonverbal communication differ.

Discuss the types of messages that are communicated nonverbally.

Identify cultural universals in nonverbal communication.

Explain the limitations of some cross-cultural research findings.

Define and give an example of cross-cultural differences in proxemics, eye contact, facial expressions, chronemics, and silence.

Discuss the relationship between nonverbal communication and power.

Define cultural space.

Describe how cultural spaces are formed.

Explain why it is important to understand cultural spaces in intercultural communication.

Understand the differences between the modernist and postmodern views of cultural spaces.

KEY WORDS

chronemics	eye contact	regionalism
contact cultures	facial expressions	relational messages
cultural space	noncontact cultures	status
deception		

EXTENDED CHAPTER OUTLINE

Nonverbal elements play an important role in understanding intercultural communication. Learning to read nonverbal communication and to use appropriate nonverbal communication in a variety of cultural spaces is key to successful intercultural interactions. In this chapter nonverbal communication will be examined through the personal–contextual and the static–dynamic dialectics.

    I.   Defining Nonverbal Communication: Thinking Dialectically
        Two forms of communication will be discussed, nonverbal codes (facial expression, personal space, eye contact, use of time, and conversational silence) and cultural spaces. Some nonverbal behaviors are cultural, and others are idiosyncratic.

A. Comparing Verbal and Nonverbal Communication

Both are symbolic, communicate meaning, and are patterned. Different societies have different nonverbal languages. Some of the differences between verbal and nonverbal communication have implications for intercultural interaction. Rules for nonverbal communication vary by culture; nonverbal communication includes more than gestures, and most nonverbal communication is subconscious.

1. Nonverbal behavior operates at a subconscious level: Because our nonverbal behavior is more subconscious than our verbal behavior when there are misunderstandings, it is not easy to figure out why.

2. Learning nonverbal behavior: The rules and meanings for language are taught directly; however, most of our nonverbal meanings and behaviors are learned through implicit socialization.

3. Coordinating nonverbal and verbal behaviors: Nonverbal behaviors can reinforce, substitute, or contradict verbal behaviors. We generally believe that people have less control over their nonverbal behavior and so we perceive the nonverbals as indicating the "real" message.

B. What Nonverbal Behavior Communicates

1. Our nonverbal communication often conveys **relational messages** (our feelings about the person).

2. Nonverbal behaviors communicate **status** and power.

3. Nonverbal behavior also communicates **deception**.

a. Earlier researchers believed that certain nonverbals indicated lying.

b. Now researchers believe that deception is communicated by idiosyncratic behaviors and probably as much by verbal communication.

c. Only a few nonverbal behaviors seem consistently indicative of deception (pupil dilation, blinking, higher pitch).

4. Nonverbal communication is pervasive, unconscious, and communicates how we feel about each other and the other's cultural group.

II. The Universality of Nonverbal Behavior: Traditional intercultural communication research has focused on identifying cross-cultural differences in nonverbal behavior.

A. Recent Research Findings: Recent research has focused on three areas.

1. The relationship of human behavior to that of primates: There are some similarities between nonverbal behaviors of chimpanzees and humans (for example, eyebrow flash, some facial expressions). However, animal communication appears to be less complex, with fewer facial blends.

2. Nonverbal communication of sensory-deprived children who are blind or deaf: Blind children's facial expressions have many similarities to those of seeing children, suggesting an innate, genetic basis for these behaviors.

3. Cross-cultural studies on facial expression: Many cross cultural studies support the universality of some **facial expressions**.

a. Specifically, six or seven basic emotions (happiness, sadness, disgust, fear, anger, surprise) communicated through facial expressions appear to be recognized by most cultural groups as having the same meaning.

4. These are variations in nonverbal behaviors and the contexts in which nonverbal communication takes place.
5. It is more important to learn about larger cultural patterns of nonverbal behaviors than to try to identify and memorize all of the cultural differences.

B. Nonverbal Codes
1. Proxemics: The study of how people use personal space.
    a. Studies show that cultures vary in their rules concerning personal space.
    b. E. T. Hall made a distinction between **contact cultures** and **noncontact cultures**. Contact cultures are societies where people stand closer together while talking, engage in more direct eye contact and more face-to-face body orientation while talking, touch more frequently, and speak in louder voices.
    c. Other factors also influence personal space decisions: gender, age, topic discussed, ethnicity, and context.
    d. Some studies suggest that regional culture is the least important factor.
2. **Eye contact** is often included in proxemics because it regulates interpersonal distance.
    a. Eye contact communicates meanings about respect, status, and often regulates turn taking.
    b. Patterns of eye contact vary by culture.
3. Facial Expression
    a. Eckman and Friesen (1987) conducted studies by having people in different cultures identify facial expressions from photographs of U.S. Americans.
    b. Conclusions from these studies have been criticized because they do not tap into universality: people may be able to recognize the expressions because of previous media exposure, and participants were given a limited number of responses to choose from in identifying the emotions.
    c. Later studies tried to overcome these limitations and support the notion of the universality of facial expression.
4. **Chronemics** concerns concepts of time and the rules that govern its use.
    a. There are several aspects of time on which cultures vary.
    b. E. T. Hall distinguished cultures on two orientations:
        i. Monochronic: Time is viewed as a commodity; time is linear, with one event happening at a time; punctuality, completing tasks, and keeping schedules are valued, sometimes regardless of any relational emergency.
        ii. Polychronic: Time is viewed as more holistic and circular; many events can happen at once; and things get done because of personal relationships, not in spite of them.
        iii. Many international business negotiations and technical assistance projects have failed because of differences in time orientations.

5. Silence: Cultures vary in the emphasis placed on speaking and silence.
    a. In the United States silence is not highly valued, and people reduce uncertainty in initial interactions by using active strategies (asking questions).
    b. In other cultures more passive strategies may be used to reduce uncertainty, including silence, observing, and asking for information from third parties (for example, Basso's study of the Western Apache in Arizona).
    c. Braithwaite's (1990) studies suggested that in some cultures silence may be associated with social situations in which a known and unequal distribution of power existed among participants.
C. Cultural Variation or Stereotype?
    1. The cultural patterns in nonverbal codes should not be used as stereotypes for all members of cultures but as tentative guidelines and, more important, as examples to help us understand the great deal of variation in nonverbal behavior.
    2. Prejudice is often based on nonverbal aspects of behavior.
D. Semiotics and Nonverbal Communication
    1. Semiotics has been useful in examining the way meaning is created in advertisements, clothing, tattoos, and other cultural practices.
    2. Semioticians examine the context in which signifiers are used to understand what meanings they communicate.
    3. Cultural contexts are dynamic and fleeting; to understand them think about how they change and in whose interests they change.
III. Defining Cultural Space: The discourses that construct the meanings of **cultural spaces** are dynamic. The relationship between cultural spaces and our identities is negotiated in complex ways. Cultural space is the particular configuration of the communication (discourse) that constructs meanings of various places. A cultural space is not just a particular location that has culturally constructed meanings, it can also be a metaphorical place from which we communicate.
A. Cultural Identity and Cultural Space
    1. Home: Cultural spaces influence how we think about ourselves and others; the earliest of these are our homes.
        a. Nonverbal communication often involves issues of status, and the appearance of a home often signals social class status.
        b. Home is a place of identification, and people often model their lives on the patterns of their childhood homes.
        c. Home may be a place of safety and security.
        d. Home is not the same as the physical location it occupies nor the building.
        e. The relationship between place and cultural identity varies and is very complex.
    2. Neighborhood: A significant type of cultural space that emerged in the latter part of the 19th and early part of the 20th centuries was the ethnic or racial neighborhood.
        a. Different political pressures caused some cities to develop segregated neighborhoods.

       b. As a result, neighborhoods exemplify how power influences intercultural contact.

       c. Power relations and historical forces influenced settlement patterns of various cultural groups, contributing to various kinds of ethnic enclaves in the United States.

       d. The key to understanding the complex relationships among culture, power, people, and cultural spaces is to think dialectically about these issues.

   3. Regionalism

       a. Regional conflicts throughout the world exemplify struggles to determine who gets to define whom.

       b. People may identify strongly with particular regions.

       c. **Regionalism** can be expressed in many forms, from symbolic expressions to armed conflict.

       d. National borders may appear to be simple, but they often conceal conflicting regional identities.

       e. To understand the effect of borders on intercultural communication, one must consider how history, power, identity, culture, and context come into play.

  B. Changing Cultural Space

    1. Traveling: Traveling changes cultural spaces in a way that often transforms the traveler.

    2. Migration: People change cultural spaces when they relocate, and whether it is forced or not, some people have difficulty adjusting.

  C. Postmodern Cultural Spaces

    1. A postmodern cultural space is unmarked by boundaries or ethnic ties and remains fluid.

    2. The dynamic nature of postmodern cultural spaces underscores their responses to changing cultural needs—they exist only while they are used.

    3. They are created within existing places by people who feel they need a cultural space to engage in a particular aspect of their identity.

    4. Postmodern urban space is dynamic and allows people to participate in the communication of identity in new ways.

DISCUSSION QUESTIONS

Questions from the Text

1. How is nonverbal communication different from verbal communication?

2. What are some of the messages that we communicate through our nonverbal behaviors?

3. Which nonverbal behaviors, if any, are universal?

4. How do our cultural spaces affect our identities?

5. What role does power play in determining our cultural spaces?

6. What is the importance of cultural spaces to intercultural communication?

7. How do postmodern cultural spaces differ from modernistic notions of cultural space?

Additional Questions

1. What do we know about how nonverbal behavior communicates deception?

2. What is the difference between contact and noncontact cultures?

3. How do semiotics help increase our understanding of nonverbal communication?

4. How does regionalism affect intercultural communication?

CLASSROOM EXERCISES AND CHAPTER ASSIGNMENTS

1. Role of Nonverbal Communication Exercise: This exercise may be used to help students understand that nonverbal communication is present in all of our communication interactions and to help them recognize some of the functions of nonverbal communication. Ask for four student volunteers to participate in a class contest. Explain to them that they are to choose an experience to tell the class that was either very funny, scary, exciting, or that made them mad. The object of the contest is to tell the story without using any nonverbal communication other than paralanguage (characteristics and elements of the voice). As such, the only allowable movement is their mouths so that they can formulate the words coherently. Give the four volunteers a few minutes to think of their stories. Meanwhile, instruct the rest of the class that they are to be the judges of the contest. As soon as they notice any nonverbal behaviors they are to shout, "Stop." One student should be selected to keep time. Ask the four volunteers to come to the front of the class. Instruct them to take turns telling their stories and to stop when they hear the word, "Stop." You will probably want to sit where you can see the faces of the volunteers because the students are sometimes hesitant to yell stop on the first one or two, so you will probably have to catch them. Stop the story as soon as you see even the slightest changes in facial expressions, eye movement, swaying, and so forth. Students seldom last more than 4 to 6 seconds. After the student is stopped, tell the student what movement he or she made and ask the student to remain standing in front of the class. When all four students have finished, ask the class whether it is possible to communicate without using nonverbal behaviors.

   Then invite the students to relax and tell the stories as they normally would, using whatever nonverbal behaviors they like. After they finish, let them sit down, and ask the students whether they thought the stories were more or less interesting with the nonverbal communication behaviors. Ask students what functions the nonverbal behaviors of these students played in the telling of their stories. Elicit specific examples.

2. Nonverbal Variations Assignment I: This assignment focuses on nonverbal differences in other cultures. Assign students to choose a culture and research it to discover differences in nonverbal behaviors. Have them write a brief paper (1) outlining the differences, (2) comparing them with general behaviors typically found in the United States, and (3) suggesting implications for intercultural communication when people from both cultures interact without knowing of the potential differences.

3. Nonverbal Variations Assignment II: A variation to the previous assignment is to have the students research the nonverbal behaviors of another culture in small groups (3–4 people) and present their research findings in role-play form instead of as a written report. Suggest that they not only show differences in the nonverbal behaviors but variations for the different contexts within the culture they researched.

4. Cultural Space Assignment: Assign your students to choose a cultural space they are interested in studying. Then instruct them to visit it on four different occasions to observe how the people interact. Students should attempt to determine the rules that govern these behaviors. When their observations are complete, they should turn in their field notes (notes they took of their observations) and write a brief paper summarizing their ideas about proper nonverbal behavior in this cultural space but exercising care about generalizing or overestimating the influence of culture.

5. Ambiguity of Nonverbal Messages Assignment: This assignment is designed to help students express the ease with which nonverbal messages can be misinterpreted. Ask the students to write a one- to two-page essay about an interpersonal situation where the student misread or misinterpreted someone's nonverbal message. Students should describe the nature of the nonverbal message, how it was misinterpreted, and what happened as a result of the misinterpretation. Students can choose any interaction for this assignment, or the instructor may ask students to focus on an intercultural interaction that caused the misinterpretation.

6. Proxemics Exercise: This exercise illustrates the various distances people use in everyday interactions and helps students find their "bubble" or comfort zone. The exercise also points out how our "bubbles" vary depending on our culture and personal preferences. The instructor asks students to select a partner and stand facing each other at a variety of distances apart from one another and have a conversation. Ask students to pay attention to their own and the other person's posture while doing these exercises.

   a. Ask students to stand with toes touching.

   b. Ask students to stand one arm's length away from each other (have them put an arm on each other's shoulder to determine this distance, then drop the arms).

   c. Ask students to stand finger tip to finger tip (again dropping the arms after measuring the distance).

   d. Ask one person to move to his or her comfortable conversational distance while the other does not move.

   e. Ask the person who did not move to find his or her comfortable conversational distance while the other person does not move.

   Debrief this exercise by asking students to describe which of the distances were most comfortable for them. Did they notice any differences between themselves and their partner's "bubble"? When they were uncomfortable, what did they do with their bodies to "create" distance (such as not look at each other, bend backward as far as they could go, turn shoulder to shoulder rather than face each other, and so on). What did this exercise illustrate for them about proximics generally? What did this exercise illustrate for them about proximics based on cultural differences?

7. Chronemics Activity: This exercise is designed to help students think about their cultural norms for time. Ask students to help you create a list on the chalkboard of the different places that they have to go during the week (for example, class, church, a party, dinner with a friend, study groups). Then suggest a meeting time for each event, and ask the students to write on a piece of paper the time that he or she would most likely arrive. After students have finished, have them share the times that they would arrive and keep track of these on the board. Then examine these with the students to identify behavioral patterns using the following questions:

   a. For which activities are we most likely to arrive nearest the suggested meeting time?

b. For which activities are we most likely to arrive late?

c. For which activities do the arrival times vary the most?

d. For which activities is it most socially acceptable to be late? Why? (Note: Here it is a good idea to discuss which reasons are cultural ideas and which are idiosyncratic.)

e. What is the acceptable time to be late for each of these activities? (Note: If there is a lot of variation between students' responses, ask them why they think they have different ideas about when it is acceptable to be late.)

f. How do we learn these rules for being late?

g. What does this exercise tell us about the relationship between culture and time?

SUGGESTED VIDEOS

1. *Communication: The Nonverbal Agenda.* Distributed by Carlsbad, CA: CRM Films, 1988. This video provides a general introduction to nonverbal communication. The relationship between verbal and nonverbal communication is explored, and some elements of nonverbal communication that are important in contemporary business environments are discussed. (20 minutes)

2. *Without Words: An Introduction to Nonverbal Communication.* Distributed by Prentice-Hall Publishing Company, 1977. In this video several examples of nonverbal communication are given, including a discussion of clothing as nonverbal communication. There is also a discussion of contrasts in nonverbal communication between Arab and U.S. American cultures. (23 minutes)

3. *Architecture: Why Man Builds.* Distributed by McGraw Hill Publishing Company, 1971. This video describes how architecture communicates about forces influencing civilizations and the people that design and use buildings. The video posits that architecture should be thought of as "a part of, rather than a backdrop for, life." (18 minutes)

4. *A World of Gestures: Culture & Nonverbal Communication.* Distributed by Berkeley, CA: University of California Extension Media Center, 1991. This video shows some of the cultural variations in gestures and explores the origin and function of gestures. (27 minutes)

CHAPTER 8

UNDERSTANDING INTERCULTURAL TRANSITIONS

LEARNING OBJECTIVES

After studying the material in this chapter, students should be able to:

Understand the complexity of cultural transitions.

Identify four types of migrant groups.

Define and describe the occurrence of culture shock.

Define cultural adaptation.

Explain the four models of cultural adaptation.

Discuss the role of communication in the process of cultural adaptation.

Identify individual characteristics that may influence how one adapts.

Describe how the adaptation process is influenced by context elements.

List outcomes of the adaptation process.

Explain how different approaches to adaptation are related to cultural identity.

Describe the reentry process and how it differs from adaptation to a "host" culture.

Discuss the effect on the identity of living on the border and making multiple returns.

KEY WORDS

assimilation	intercultural identity	separation
cultural adaptation	long-term refugee	short-term refugee
culture shock	marginalization	sojourners
explanatory uncertainty	migrant	transnationalism
fight approach	multicultural identity	U-curve theory
flight approach	predictive uncertainty	uncertainty reduction
functional fitness	psychological health	W-curve theory
integration	segregation	

EXTENDED CHAPTER OUTLINE

This chapter focuses more on the experience of moving between cultural contexts. People travel across cultural boundaries for different reasons: work, study, adventure, or because they are forced.

I.   Types of Migrant Groups: A dialectical perspective requires that we examine intercultural transitions on both a personal and a contextual level. To understand intercultural transitions, we need to examine the personal experiences of the individuals and the larger social, historical, economic, and political contexts in which the transitions occur.

A. A **migrant** is a person who leaves the primary cultural context in which he or she was raised and moves to a new cultural context for an extended period of time.

B. Cultural transitions can vary in length and degree of voluntariness.

C. Four types of migrant groups:

    1. Voluntary: There are two types of voluntary migrant groups.

        a. **Sojourners**: Those who move into new cultural contexts for a limited period of time for a specific purpose (for example, study, work).

        b. Immigrants: Those who voluntarily settle in a new culture.

        c. There are various reasons for immigration, and there are fluctuations in the relationships between countries that send and receive immigrants.

        d. Countries often restrict immigration during economic downturns.

        e. Most of the international immigration does not occur from developing countries to industrialized countries; most is from one developing country to another.

    2. Involuntary travelers: There are two types of involuntary travelers.

        a. **Long-term refugees**: People who are permanently forced to relocate because of war, famine, and oppression.

        b. **Short-term refugees**: People who are forced to move for short or indefinite periods of time within a country.

        c. Reports indicate that there are more refugees than ever before. In 1979, 13 million people left their home countries because of superpower struggles.

        d. The large number of refugees presents complex issues for intercultural communication, suggesting the importance of context.

II. Culture Shock

A. **Culture shock** is a relatively short-term feeling of disorientation and discomfort due to the unfamiliarity of surroundings or the lack of familiar cues in the environment.

B. Oberg (1960) coined the term *culture shock* and suggested that it was like a disease with symptoms and that sojourners could recover/adapt if they treated it properly.

C. People are less likely to experience culture shock if they separate themselves from the new environment because culture shock presumes cultural contact.

D. Most migrants experience culture shock regardless of their motivations for moving.

E. Long-term adaptation is difficult for most people, and people generally resist it in the short term. Some groups choose to actively resist it by not participating in U.S. popular culture.

F. Some people adjust to just some parts of the culture.

G. Some people want to assimilate but are not allowed to because of their relationship with the host culture.

III. Migrant-Host Relationships: There are four different types of migrant-host relationships.

A. Assimilation: In an **assimilation** mode, the migrant does not want to maintain an isolated cultural identity but wants relationships with other groups.

1. The migrant is more or less welcome in the host culture.
2. This is the archetypal "melting pot" because the focus is not on retaining one's cultural heritage.
3. Conflicts may arise if this type of relationship is forced on migrants by the dominant culture.
4. Doses of discrimination over time could discourage or eliminate cultural maintenance of one's native cultural heritage.

B. Separation: There are two forms of **separation**.
1. In the first, migrants willingly choose to maintain interactions within their own cultural groups and avoid interacting with others (for example, Amish).
2. In the second, migrants are forced by the dominant society to separate themselves; this is called **segregation**.
3. Defacto segregation includes practices like redlining—banks refusing loans to people who want to live outside "their" area.
4. If migrants realize that they have been excluded from opportunities, they may promote another mode of relating to the host culture and demand group rights and recognition, but not assimilation.

C. Integration: **Integration** occurs when migrants have an interest in maintaining their original cultures and maintaining daily interactions with other groups.
1. This approach demands a greater degree of interest in maintaining one's own cultural identity.
2. Resistance to assimilation can take different forms, such as celebrating ethnic holidays and avoiding popular culture products or fashion.
3. This approach assumes that the dominant society is open and accepting of others' cultures.

D. Marginalization: **Marginalization** occurs when there is little interest in maintaining cultural ties with either the dominant culture or the migrant culture.
1. This situation may be the result of actions by the dominant culture such as when Native Americans were forced to live away from members of their own nation.
2. Generally, however, individuals are marginalized, not fully able to participate in political and social life, as a result of cultural differences.

E. Combined Modes of Relating: Sometimes immigrants and their families combine the four modes.
1. They may integrate in some areas of life and assimilate in others.
2. Migrants generally have to adapt to some extent in the new culture.
3. Adaptation is a process.
4. It occurs in context.
5. It varies with each individual.
6. It is circumscribed by relations of dominance and power.

IV. Cultural Adaptation: **Cultural adaptation** is the long-term process of adjusting and finally feeling comfortable in a new environment.
A. Models of Cultural Adaptation
1. The Anxiety and Uncertainty Management Model
    a. Gudykunst (1995) stresses that ambiguity is the primary characteristic of relationships in intercultural adaptation.

b. The goal of effective communication is met by information seeking (reducing uncertainty) and anxiety reduction. This is known as **uncertainty reduction**.

c. Types of uncertainty:

    i. **predictive uncertainty**: the inability to predict what someone will say or do.

    ii. **explanatory uncertainty**: the inability to explain why someone behaves the way they do.

d. In most interactions we explain and predict people's behavior using prior knowledge or by gathering more information.

e. Migrants may need to reduce the anxiety that accompanies most intercultural contexts, although some level of anxiety is optimal during interaction because it conveys that we care about the person.

f. Too much anxiety may cause us to focus on the anxiety and not on the interaction.

g. The model is complicated, with 94 axioms; however, some general characteristics of effective communicators include:

    i. having a solid self-concept and self-esteem.

    ii. having flexible attitudes and behaviors.

    iii. being complex and flexible in their categorization of others.

h. The situation in which communication occurs is important to the model with the most conducive environments being those that are informal, supportive, and with equal representation of different groups.

i. The model requires that people be open to new information and recognize alternative ways of interpret information.

j. The theory also predicts cultural variablity between indivdiualists and collectivists.

2. The U-Curve Model

a. The most common theory of adaptation is the **U-curve theory**.

b. Lysgaard constructed it based on results of interviews with Norwegian students studying in the United States.

c. The main idea is that migrants go through predictable phases of adaptation.

d. The model is simple and does not represent every migrant's experience, but the general phases seem to be experienced at one time or another.

    i. Stage 1: Excitement and anticipation.

    ii. Stage 2: Culture shock (bottom of curve): During this phase, migrants often experience disorientation and a crisis of identity (culture shock).

    iii. Stage 3: Adaptation: Gradually, migrants learn the rules and customs, possibly the language, and figure out how much to change. This phase may be a different experience for people if the social/political context is not conducive to their adaptation.

e. The model may be too simplistic, and a more accurate model represents long-term adaptation as a series of U-curves.

3. The Transition Model
    a. Recently, the adaptation process has been viewed as a normal part of human experience, a subcategory of transition shock.
    b. All transition experiences involve loss and change for individuals.
    c. Cultural change depends on the individual and how he or she prefers to deal with new situations; most use one of two strategies:
        i. **Flight approach**: The migrant tends to hang back and observe before becoming involved. This is not necessarily bad. Small periods of flight may rest the sojourner from adjustment pressures, but long-term flights may be very unproductive.
        ii. **Fight approach**: The migrant gets right in and participates using the trial-and-error method. In the productive mode, the migrant tries the language and does not mind making mistakes. Staying in the fight mode may be unproductive if the migrant consistently reacts in an inflexible way.
    d. Neither approach is right or wrong.
    e. An alternative to flight or fight is the flex approach in which migrants use a combination of the productive flight and fight responses.
4. The Communication-System Model: Kim's (1977, 1995) model describes the role of communication in cultural adaptation.
    a. Kim suggests that adaptation is a process of stress, adaptation, and growth.
    b. This model is very conducive to the dialectical approach, showing the interconnectedness between the individual and the context in the adaptation.
    c. Adaptation occurs through communication.
    d. Migrants communicate with individuals in the new culture and develop new ways of thinking and behaving. In the process, they grow to a new level of functioning.
    e. Not everyone grows in the migrant experience; people may choose one of three options: rejecting the new idea, incorporating it into their existing framework, or changing their framework.
    f. Communication may have a double edge in adaptation; those who communicate frequently adapt better but have more culture shock.
    g. Research suggests that the most important characteristics in adaptation are workers' interpersonal communication competencies.
    h. There seem to be three stages in the process of adaptation that communication can aid:
        i. Taking for granted and surprise: In this phase migrants realize that their assumptions are wrong and need to be altered.
        ii. Making sense: Migrants slowly begin to make sense of new patterns through communication experiences.
        iii. Coming to understand: Once migrants get more information they begin to understand and make sense of their experiences, and they come to understand the new culture in a more holistic way.
    i. The mass media also help sojourners adapt.

B. Individual Influences on Adaptation: Several individual characteristics may influence adaptation: age, gender, preparation, and expectations.
   1. Age: The evidence on age and adaptation is contradictory. Younger people may adapt more easily and completely but have a difficult return adjustment. Older people may not adapt as well but have an easier time with their return adjustment.
   2. Preparation may influence how one adapts and is related to expectations. Research suggests that it is best to have positive (realistic) or slightly negative expectations prior to the sojourn.
C. Context and Adaptation
   1. Some contexts are easier to adapt in than others.
   2. Kim (1988) notes that cultures differ in receptivity and welcome. She suggests that in countries where there is an emphasis on homogeneity people may be less welcoming than in some contexts of the United States.
   3. The nature of the status and power difference between the sojourner and the host group may affect the adaptation process.
   4. Class issues may affect the adaptation process.
D. Outcomes of Adaptation: Recent research (Kim, 1988) suggests there are at least three dimensions to adaptation:
   1. **Psychological health** is the most common definition of adaptation and concentrates on the emotional feeling of the migrant.
      a. Migrants who are made to feel welcome will feel more comfortable faster.
      b. It generally occurs more quickly than the second outcome.
   2. **Functional fitness** is the ability to function in daily life in different contexts.
      a. Furnham and Bochner (1986) emphasize that learning skills is more important than psychological well-being.
      b. They suggest that the most important skills are local rules for politeness, rules of verbal communication style, and typical use of nonverbal communication.
      c. Newcomers can become more functionally fit if host members are willing to communicate and interact with them.
   3. **Intercultural identity** is a complex concept because the multicultural individual is significantly different from the person who is more culturally restricted.
      a. The multicultural person is not a part of nor apart from the culture but someone who acts situationally.
      b. The difficulties of a multicultural life are the risks of not knowing what to believe or how to develop ethics or values.
      c. Multicultural people face life with little grounding and lack the basic personal, social, and cultural guidelines that cultural identities provide.
V. Identity and Adaptation
   A. Migrants develop multicultural identities based on three issues:
      1. The extent to which they want to maintain their own identity, language, and way of life compared to how much they want to become part of the larger society.

2. The extent to which migrants want to have day-to-day interactions with others in the new culture.
3. The ownership of political power.

B. Adapting on Reentry
1. When sojourners return to their original cultural contexts, they may experience the adaptation process anew, including culture shock (reentry shock).
2. Sometimes this adaptation is more difficult because it is unexpected.
3. Scholars depict this process as the **W-curve theory** of adaptation because the sojourners seem to experience a second U-curve.
4. There are two fundamental differences between the first and second U-curve of adaptation:
   a. Personal change: In the second U-curve the individual has changed because of the adaptation experience and is not the same person as before he or she left.
   b. Expectations: The sojourner does not expect to experience culture shock in returning home, and family and friends do not expect the sojourner to have difficulties. The sojourner also may encounter cultural and political changes he or she did not expect.

C. Living on the Border: Due to increased international travel and migration, the lines between adaptation and reentry become less clear.
1. **Transnationalism** calls into question notions like nation-states, national languages, and coherent cultural communities.
2. When people frequently go back and forth between cultures, they may develop a **multicultural identity**.
3. The swinging trapeze is a metaphor used by Hegde (1998) to describe the movement back and forth between cultural patterns of the homeland and the new country.
4. Though technology makes it seem easy, movement between cultures is not as simple as getting on a plane.
5. To understand global movements, we have to consider history, identity, language, nonverbal communication, and cultural spaces.

VI. Thinking Dialectically About Intercultural Transitions: Dialectical differences (privilege–disadvantage) shape the intercultural migrant's identity and the changes that this identity undergoes.

DISCUSSION QUESTIONS

Questions from the Text

1. Why does culture shock occur to people who make cultural transitions?

2. Why are adaptations to cultures difficult for some people and easier for others?

3. What is the role of communication in the cultural adaptation process?

4. How do relations of power and dominance affect adaptation?

5. What factors affect migration patterns?

6. What dialectical tensions can you identify in the process of adapting to intercultural transitions?

Additional Questions

1. What contextual variables influence communicative interactions during intercultural transitions?

2. What are some of the different types of relationships that migrants may develop with the new culture?

3. How does the anxiety and uncertainty management model describe the challenge of cultural adaptation?

4. How does the communication–system model describe the role of communication in the cultural adaptation process?

5. What are some of the outcomes of cultural adaptation?

6. What are some of the challenges that may make reentry adaptation a more difficult experience than culture shock?

7. What are the identity challenges that may face people who live on the border?

CLASS EXERCISES AND CHAPTER ASSIGNMENTS

1. Guest Lecture Exercise: Invite two individuals from the college/university or the community who are immigrants to the United States or who are from the United States but have lived abroad to share their experiences of adapting to another culture. During the class period prior to their lectures, ask students to spend 5 minutes writing down questions about the sojourn process that interest them. Have them save these for the guest lecturers.

2. Simulation Exercise: One of the most effective ways to help students identify with the challenges faced by sojourners is to involve them in a simulation that puts them in the position of interacting without knowing the proper rules for communicating and accomplishing tasks. Two popular simulations that have been used in a variety of orientation programs, intercultural communication classes, and cross-cultural training are BaFa BaFa and Barnga. The distributors of these simulations are listed below:

"Barnga." Created by Sivasailam Thiagarajan, distributed by Intercultural Press., P. O. Box 700, Yarmouth, ME 04096; Tel: (800) 370-2665; fax: (207) 846-5181.

"BaFa BaFa: A Cross Culture Simulation." Created by R. Garry Shirts, distributed by Simulation Training Systems., P.O. Box 910, Del Mar, CA 92014; Tel: (800) 942-2900; fax: (619) 792-9743.

3. "I Heard the Owl Call My Name" Assignment: This project is designed to familiarize students with the stages of intercultural adjustment and how people feel about and respond to the experience by reading the account of someone's cultural adjustment. In the book *I Heard the Owl Call My Name*, Margaret Craven tells the story of a young priest, Mark, who must adjust to the culture of an Indian tribe living in a remote area (based on a true life experience). As students read the story, they should identify the different stages of adjustment Mark goes through (using one of the frameworks described in this chapter) and the turning points of his adjustment experience. When they have completed the book, instruct them to write a brief book report that summarizes the story and identifies the adjustment framework they feel fits Mark's

experience and the turning point events that helped him adjust. You could also ask them to write their own conclusions about what they think a person needs to do to adjust to another culture, based on ideas they learned while reading about Mark's adjustment.

Craven, M. (1973). *I Heard the Owl Call My Name*. Garden City, NY: Doubleday.

Note: This is not the only book that could be used for this assignment but is given as an example. A way to shorten the assignment would be to use *The Ugly American* a book of stories based on real experiences of different Americans who lived abroad in Southeast Asia. Each chapter stands by itself as an incident about a person's adjustment, although the characters of some chapters appear in more than one story. Students could be assigned to look at one or two chapters and make a report similar to the one described above.

Lederer, W. J. & Burdick, E. (1958). *The Ugly American*. New York: Norton.

4. Intercultural Interview Assignment: The purpose of this assignment is to provide the opportunity for students to gain an understanding of the challenges faced by people from other cultures who come to live in the United States. This assignment also gives students the opportunity to interact one on one with people from other cultures. Assign students to find someone from a culture outside the United States who has come to live here at least temporarily. The person should have been in the United States for more than one year and less than five years. Tell them their interview should focus on learning about the process of adjusting to living in another culture from that person. After completing the interview, they should write a report that:

   a. Summarizes the information they gained from the interview.

   b. Suggests what in *the student's* opinion seems to be the greatest challenge(s) faced by people adjusting to life in the United States.

   c. Identifies variables that seem to help ease the adjustment process.

   d. Suggests behaviors people in the United States might adopt that could help ease the adjustment process for those who come to live here.

The following suggestions may help students set up and conduct their interview.

Preparing for the Interview

   a. Plan the interview several weeks before the due date.

   b. Decide who you want to interview.

   c. Think of an appropriate place to conduct the interview where both you and the interviewee will be comfortable, able to easily hear each other, and have few distractions.

   d. Call or contact them in person to set up a future appointment for the interview. When you contact them, make sure to first explain the project and purpose of the interview. Ask if they are willing to help. If they agree, set the date, time, and place for the interview. Give them an idea of how much time it will take and ask if they would mind if you took notes or tape recorded the interview.

   e. Prepare your questions so that you are comfortable with how they are worded and are sure that they are clear and easy to understand. Short questions work better than detailed questions. Avoid using clichés or slang in the questions.

f. Prepare any note-taking equipment. (Remember to take extra batteries for a tape recorder if you are using one.)

During the Interview

a. Be professional. Dress comfortably but nicely to show respect for your interviewee. Ask ethical and thoughtful questions that demonstrate your sensitivity to cultural issues and respect for the interviewee.

b. Before you begin the interview, establish rapport with your interviewee by spending a few minutes sharing information about each other, the class, or other issues that will break the ice and create a comfortable atmosphere.

c. Start the interview by explaining the purpose of the interview and verifying that the person is comfortable with the method you have chosen for recording the information you get from the interview.

d. As you ask the questions you have prepared, be sure to listen carefully to the answers and ask follow-up questions if the interviewee does not provide the information you are seeking or gets off track of the question. Be flexible in asking the questions, but try to keep the interviewee from going off on a tangent.

e. Stick to the agreed time limit unless the interviewee seems offended that the time is so short. Avoid being abrupt in ending the interview, but at the same time be respectful of the interviewee's schedule.

f. When the interview is finished, thank the interviewee for his/her time and help. It is always appropriate to send a thank-you note, and it may be appropriate to send a small gift to show your appreciation.

Ideas for Interview Questions

a. For what reason(s) did you come to the United States?

b. Before you came, what did you know about the United States?

c. What were the strangest things you noticed about the United States when you arrived here?

d. What were the most surprising things you found when you arrived in the United States?

e. Did you come by yourself or with family or friends?

f. What were your toughest challenges in adjusting to life in the United States?

g. Who helped you the most in your adjustment?

h. What things made it easier to adjust to living in the United States?

i. What do you like best about living in the United States?

j. Was it easy to make friends here? Why or why not?

k. What can people in the United States do to make it easier for people from other countries to adjust to living here?

5. Marginalization Exercise: This exercise will give students the opportunity to learn (at least in part) what it feels like to be included and excluded in certain interactions. Begin this exercise by discussing how it feels to be part of an "ingroup" (included) and how it feels to be excluded or part of an "outgroup." Then ask students to:

a. Write down examples of when they felt excluded; such as one man working with all women, being the only minority or female, being the only person with a visible disability in a class, and so on.

b. Describe how it felt to be excluded.

c. Write down examples of when they were members of an "ingroup."

d. Describe their feelings as part of the "ingroup."

e. Reflect on whether they made any attempts to be included or excluded. In other words, how did they react to being included or excluded? Did they try to change the situation?

f. In small groups or dyads, ask students to share their answers to these questions.

In the larger group debriefing, refer students to the textbook's discussion on modes of adaptation and encourage them to apply their experiences to the four basic ways people adapt to new cultures.

6. Variation on the Marginalization Exercise: Show the students a video that highlights the concept of ingroup/outgroup and then use examples from the video to answer the questions in the above exercise. Suggested videos are:

Tale of O. Distributed by Goodmeasure, Inc. This video explores group dynamics and demonstrates methods of effectively managing difference.

Rainbow War. Distributed by Pyramid Films. This is an allegorical fairy tale that looks at the concepts of ethnocentrism, fear of difference, and the potential for peaceful synergy.

7. Cultural Adaptation Assignment: This two- to three-page assignment helps students apply their own experience of adaptation to one of the models of cultural adaptation offered in the textbook. Ask students to write about a major transition they have experienced such as moving away to college, being an international student, moving to a different community, getting married, and so on. Have the students describe the transition they experienced, and then ask them to compare their experience to one or more of the models presented in the textbook (Anxiety and Uncertainty Management Model, the U-curve Model, the Transition Model, or the Communication System Model). Ask them to explain how their experience "fits" the model(s) they have chosen by being as specific as possible and using examples from their experiences to illustrate the concepts presented in the textbook.

SUGGESTED VIDEOS

1. *Overture: Linh from Vietnam.* Distributed by LCA, 1981. This video relates the experiences of two immigrants, Linh from Vietnam and José from Mexico, as they cope with the challenges of adapting to life in the United States. (26 minutes)

2. *The Way of the Willow.* Produced by Norwood, MA: Beacon Films; Distributed by New York, NY: Modern Educational Video Network, 1992. This video tells the story of a Vietnamese boat family who immigrated to Canada. It shows some of the challenges they face and how they have worked to adapt to and overcome them. (29 minutes)

3. *Bridging the Cultural Gap.* Distributed by San Francisco, CA: Griggs Productions, 1983. This video was prepared to help families who are adjusting to living abroad. It focuses on some of the cultural differences that Americans going abroad need to understand. (28 minutes)

4. *Beyond Culture Shock.* Distributed by Chicago, IL: Encyclopedia Britannica Educational Corporation, 1983. This video contains practical advice for Americans who are making adjustments to living abroad from experts and experienced sojourners. (29 minutes)

5. *Welcome Home, Stranger.* Distributed by Chicago, IL: Encyclopedia Britannica Educational Corporation, 1983. This video is designed to help families who are returning to the United States from overseas sojourns. It describes reactions people experience during their return adjustment. (14 minutes)

CHAPTER 9

FOLK CULTURE, POPULAR CULTURE, AND INTERCULTURAL COMMUNICATION

LEARNING OBJECTIVES

After studying the material in this chapter, students should be able to:

Define popular culture.

Identify some types of popular culture.

Describe characteristics of popular culture.

Explain why it is important to understand popular culture in intercultural communication.

Discuss why people consume or resist specific cultural texts.

Understand how cultural texts influence cultural identities.

Explain how the decisions about what forms of popular culture are used influence perspectives of social reality.

Describe the relationship between social roles and decisions about popular culture consumption.

Discuss how cultural group portrayals in popular culture forms influence intercultural communication.

Suggest effects of the global domination of U.S. popular culture.

KEY WORDS

cultural imperialism	electronic colonialism	media imperialism
cultural industries	folk culture	reader profiles
cultural texts		

EXTENDED CHAPTER OUTLINE

This chapter explores two kinds of cultures (folk cultural and popular culture) that are often overlooked by intercultural communication scholars but that play an important role in the construction, maintenance, and experience of culture, particularly in intercultural interactions.

    I. Learning About Cultures Without Personal Experience
        A. Much of what we know about other cultures comes from popular culture.
        B. The influence of **folk culture** on the development of cultural identity is often overlooked. But many folk traditions are embedded in the history of a cultural group, and their continuance can be very important to group members.

C. Popular culture has wider audience appeal, and in many ways it is helpful to view popular culture as contrary to and complementary to folk culture.
D. The complexity of these two kinds of culture is unappreciated.
  1. People are concerned about the social effects of pop culture, but they look down on the study of folk and popular culture.
  2. People tend to be interested in folk traditions only if they are members of the specific cultural group that holds them.
  3. These contradictions make them difficult to investigate.
E. Products of U.S. popular culture are widely circulated internationally.
  1. These seem to cross cultural and linguistic boundaries with relative ease, so much so that hardly any systematic research has been done to find out why they are so successful.
  2. However, U.S. Americans are very rarely exposed to popular culture from other nations.
  3. The imbalance of cultural texts globally renders U.S. Americans more dependent on U.S.-produced popular culture and can lead to **cultural imperialism**.
F. What Is Folk Culture?
  1. Folk culture is not the national culture of a nation-state.
  2. It is neither high nor low culture.
  3. Folklorists look to the past to study traditional culture, and they are interested in how traditions are played out in contemporary society to form cultural group identities.
  4. Folk culture "has reminded the nation of social worlds beneath its surface" (Bronner, 1986, p. 129).
  5. Participation in folk culture is usually unrelated to profit, and no one industry controls it.
  6. The social functions of folk culture are different from those of popular culture. Because folk culture is not packaged and exported to other cultures, there is little attempt to sell it.
  7. Folk culture and folk rituals are not evidenced everywhere and cannot be practiced by everyone.
  8. Even celebrations of the same event may vary across different cultural groups, and groups may carry their traditions into new locations with them.
  9. Increasingly, many popular culture products use folk culture to situate their products as different.
    a. Folk culture may be exaggerated to serve the needs of advertisers such as making places seem more unique.
    b. When this happens, it blurs the distinctions between popular and folk culture.
G. What Is "Popular Culture"? Popular culture is a reconceptualized notion of low culture.
  1. Brummett (1994) defines popular culture as "those systems or artifacts that most people share and that most people know about" (p. 21).
    a. Using this definition, television, music videos, and popular magazines would be systems of popular culture.
    b. Popular culture consists of forms of contemporary culture made popular by and for the people.

    c. "The popular speaks to—and resonates from—the people, but it speaks to them through a multiplicity of cultural voices" (Lipsitz, 1990, p. 140).

  2. Intercultural contact and intercultural communication influence the creation and maintenance of popular culture.

  3. Four significant characteristics of popular culture are:
    a. It is produced by culture industries.
    b. It is different from folk culture.
    c. It is everywhere.
    d. It fills a social function.

  4. Popular culture is nearly always produced within capitalist systems by **culture industries** that see products of popular culture as economically profitable commodities.

  5. We are bombarded with popular culture, and it is difficult to avoid.

  6. Popular culture serves as a forum for the discussion of social issues.

  7. The ways people negotiate their relationships to popular culture are complex, making it difficult to understand the role of popular culture in intercultural communication.

  8. People do not passively consume popular culture; they are quite active consumers or resisters of popular culture.

II. Consuming and Resisting Popular Culture
  A. Consuming Popular Culture: Faced with so many **cultural texts**, people negotiate their way through popular culture in quite different ways.

    1. Popular culture does not have to win over the majority of the people to be considered popular.

    2. People seek out or avoid certain forms of popular culture.

    3. Although there is some unpredictability about people's popular culture choices, certain profiles emerge.

    4. Popular magazines even make their **reader profiles** available to advertisers.

    5. Each magazine targets a particular readership and sells this readership to advertisers.

    6. How Magazines Respond to the Needs of Cultural Identities: Magazines respond to the cultural and political needs of cultural identities in these ways:
      a. They may offer information and points of view unavailable in other magazines.
      b. They may serve as a forum to discuss specific cultural concerns.
      c. They tend to affirm cultural identities that are sometimes invisible or silenced by mainstream culture.
      d. Non-English newspapers serve similar functions but with lower production costs, so they survive more easily and reach their limited readerships.

    7. How Individuals Negotiate Consumption: Readers choose from among all of the available magazines those cultural texts to consume and resist those that do not fulfill important cultural needs.

    8. Cultural Texts Versus Cultural Identities: Readers must be careful not to conflate the magazines with the cultural identities they are targeting.
      a. Many viewpoints are expressed, and there is no one unified position that represents members of a single cultural group.

   b. Other cultural populations can participate in different cultural forums, with different discussions and information, than readers of mainstream texts.

   c. Cultural magazines and newspapers function like cultural spaces because people use them to affirm and negotiate their relationships with their cultural identities.

  B. Resisting Popular Culture: Sometimes people actively resist cultural texts.

   1. Sometimes a conflict in culture values and cultural identities is the impetus for resisting certain popular culture texts.

   2. People resist popular culture texts by refusing to participate in them.

   3. Social roles may motivate people to resist popular culture.

   4. Much of the resistance stems from concerns about the representation of various social groups.

   5. Popular culture plays a powerful role in affecting the ways we think about and understand other groups.

III. Representing Cultural Groups: Popular culture is a lens for introducing other cultural groups, and it does so in more intimate ways than tourists experience because it permits us to see the private lives of people. Because some people use popular culture forms as a source for their information about a particular culture, the question of how the cultural groups are portrayed becomes important.

  A. Migrants' Perceptions of Mainstream Culture

   1. Ethnographers and other scholars have been successful crossing international and cultural boundaries to examine the influence of popular culture.

   2. People use popular culture to learn about other cultures.

   3. Some people perceive life in the United States to be similar to how it is portrayed in the television show *Dallas* and other popular U.S. television shows.

   4. Sometimes people use U.S. popular culture to learn about U.S. Americans and watch their own shows to reaffirm their cultural identities.

   5. In this way, migrants may both resist and consume U.S. popular culture.

  B. Popular Culture and Stereotyping: Our knowledge of places, even those we have been to, is largely influenced by popular culture.

   1. For people with limited experience with other cultures, the impact of popular culture may be greater.

   2. Many familiar stereotypes of ethnic groups are represented in the media.

   3. It appears from Manusov and Hegda's (1993) study that having some cultural information and positive expectations may lead to more in-depth conversations and positive outcomes than having no information.

   4. How do negative stereotypes affect interactions?

   5. When Whites interviewed Black and White job candidates, their behavior changed when interviewing Black applicants. Their speech deteriorated, they made more grammatical errors, they spent less time and were less friendly and outgoing with Black candidates.

   6. In short, racial stereotypes appear to constrain the behavior of both Blacks and Whites.

IV. U.S. Popular Culture and Power: It is important to consider the power relationships that are embedded in popular culture.
   A. Global Circulation of Images/Commodities
      1. A high percentage of international circulation of popular culture is U.S. popular culture.
      2. Many U.S. films make more money outside of the United States, which ensures that Hollywood will continue to export media.
      3. Other forms of popular culture are also exported.
      4. The implications of the dominance of U.S. popular culture are unknown.
   B. Cultural Imperialism: It is important to think about the impact of U.S. media on the rest of the world.
      1. Initially, in the 1920s, U.S. media was exported to boost sales of U.S. products.
      2. Discussions about **media imperialism**, **electronic colonialism**, and cultural imperialism began in the 1920s and continue today.
      3. The close interrelationship between economics, nationalism, and culture makes it difficult to determine with much certainty how significant cultural imperialism might be.
      4. Tomlinson (1991) identifies five ways to think about cultural imperialism.
         a. As cultural domination.
         b. As media imperialism.
         c. As nationalist discourse.
         d. As a critique of global capitalism.
         e. As a critique of modernity.
      5. There is no easy way to measure the impact of popular culture, but we should be sensitive to its influences.
      6. Popular culture plays a big role in understanding relations around the globe.
      7. Though the presentations are problematic, we rely on popular culture to understand world issues and events.
      8. For many of us, the world exists through popular culture.

DISCUSSION QUESTIONS

Questions from the Text

1. Why do people select some popular culture forms over others?

2. How do the choices you make about what forms of popular culture to consume influence the formation of your cultural identity?

3. What factors influence the cultural industries to portray cultural groups as they do?

4. How does the portrayal of different cultural groups by the media influence intercultural interactions with those groups?

5. What stereotypes are perpetuated by U.S. popular culture that are exported to other countries?

6. How do our social roles affect our consumption of popular culture?

7. What strategies can people apply to resist popular culture?

Additional Questions

1. What are some differences between folk culture and popular culture?

2. What can intercultural scholars learn from studying folk culture?

3. What are some reasons it is difficult to determine the impact of U.S. popular culture?

4. What are some ways to think about cultural imperialism?

5. Why is it possible for some forms of popular culture to serve as cultural spaces?

CLASSROOM EXERCISES AND CHAPTER ASSIGNMENTS

1. Attraction and Popular Culture Exercise: This exercise is designed to help students explore the relationship between culture and notions of attractiveness. Prior to class, prepare examples of different popular culture images, including pictures of males and females that have been identified as attractive and alternative images that are not viewed as highly attractive. After showing these to the students, lead them in a class discussion using the following questions:

   a. Which images do you consider attractive? Why?

   b. What physical characteristics are considered to be attractive in the United States and why?

   c. What features are considered attractive in other cultures?

   d. How does the perceived attractiveness of an individual influence communication with that person?

   Next, you might point out that most images of "beautiful" people are images of Whites. For example, most models are White, especially on the covers of magazines (editors of women's magazines say that if they put a picture of a woman of color on the cover sales go down), and models of color often have features closely resembling European American features and the color of their skin is light, for example, Naomi Campbell.

2. Cultural Perceptions Exercise: This exercise is designed to encourage students to think about the information they receive about other cultures from different forms of print media. Prior to class, collect examples from the U.S. media portraying people from other cultures (for example, Polish babushka as a representation of Polish people/women) and images of the United States in foreign newspapers and magazines (most libraries have an international section). You might ask students:

   a. Do they tend to accept images of other cultures in the U.S. media as true representations?

   b. Do they want other people to accept images of the United States in foreign media as representatives of the whole country? Why?

   c. Why do the media choose to portray people as they do?

   d. What effect do particular portrayals have on intercultural communication?

3. Defining "Popular" Exercise: The purpose of this class discussion is to explore with students the notion of what popular is. To explore these ideas, you might ask students the following questions:

   a. What is popular today in movies, magazines, and music?

   b. What makes a film, video, or magazine popular?

c. Who decides what is and is not popular?

d. Why do people differ in their perceptions of what is popular?

e. How does contemporary popular culture influence us today?

4. Video Assignment: This project is designed to encourage students to explore how popular culture provides us with information about other cultures. Instruct students to pick a video that portrays a specific cultural group or interactions between two cultural groups. A few suggestions follow. Assign students to view the video and write a brief report on it. In the report, they could address the following questions:

a. What did you learn about the culture(s) portrayed in this video? What are their norms, values, and beliefs?

b. How accurately do you think the directors portrayed the cultures? Why?

c. How could the portrayal of this culture negatively or positively affect people's perceptions of them?

d. How could this video potentially influence people's intercultural communication with members of this culture?

Suggested Videos

Rising Sun	*The Joy Luck Club*
Moscow on the Hudson	*Thunderheart*
Dances With Wolves	*City of Joy*
Sounder	*The Color Purple*

5. Foreign Video Assignment: Using instructions similar to those in assignment 4, assign students to find and view a foreign video with English translations or subtitles. In addition to the questions listed above, ask them to write an evaluation of the video exploring similarities and differences to films/videos made in the United States. Ask them to describe what they liked or disliked about the video.

6. Exported Popular Culture Assignment: Identify for students examples of television programs that are popular exports in other countries. Assign students to watch one of them and write a critique addressing the following ideas:

a. How are U.S. Americans portrayed in this show?

b. Which cultural groups are portrayed?

c. Imagine that this show was your first introduction to the culture of the people in the United States. What would you think about them? What norms, values, and beliefs would you think they had?

d. How could the portrayal of U.S. Americans in this show influence intercultural communication with the people who have seen the show but had no other experience with U.S. Americans?

7. Cultural Perspectives on Current Issues: Assign students to choose a current social/political issue or news story that appears with frequency in the print media. Instruct them to compare two magazine articles that portray the perspective of mainstream U.S. Americans versus a particular co-cultural group. For example, students could compare an article from *U.S. News & World Report* on the issue of gay marriages and an article from a magazine that is targeted toward a gay audience. In their comparison, they should discuss:

a. Differences in the perspectives displayed in the article.

b. Examples of how these perspectives are written to appeal to the audiences reading the magazines.

c. How the perspectives support/reject and voice/ignore the opinions of the particular co-cultural group.

d. How the perspective of the other group is explained in the magazine targeted for the mainstream U.S. audience.

e. How the mainstream U.S. perspective is portrayed in the magazine targeted for the co-cultural group.

8. Folk Culture or Art Exercise: This exercise will help students explore the differences and similarities between folk art and other forms of art. Divide the class in two groups and have one group bring to class either an object or a picture of an example of folk culture and the other group an example of "art." Guide the students to look for examples they can use for this assignment in magazines, on the Internet, in local stores, galleries, books, and at things around their homes. Instruct the students to attempt to find out as much as possible about the object, the artist, the artist's culture, and so on to aid them in their discussion of the object. On the day of the assignment, pair one student from each group with a student from the other group, and in these dyads ask them to compare their pictures or objects and answer the following questions:

a. Who made the objects (to what cultural or gender group does the artist belong, where did the artist live when it was created)?

b. How much might the objects be worth?

c. Where might you find these objects (museums, galleries, small specialty stores)?

d. How are they similar?

e. How are they different?

f. Why is the distinction made to classify one as art and the other as folk art?

g. Who or what group makes this distinction?

h. Is it necessary to make this distinction?

9. Consuming Pop Culture Assignment: This exercise will help students analyze their relationship to pop culture and help them determine to what extent they are influenced by pop culture. Ask the students to be detectives in their own homes by examining the labels on their clothes, the product labels on their home decorations (for example, a poster of a movie, a candy dish with Mickey Mouse on it), and the magazines and newspapers they buy. In a one- to two-page paper, students should identify those items they believe are examples of pop culture. Then, students should discuss the level of influence these items hold for them and whether they could resist any of these items. For instance, if most of the clothes the student owns display the Nike swoosh, the student may feel highly influenced by this form of pop culture. However, the student may also write that he/she could easily live without Nike products, thereby indicating this is a form of pop culture that he/she could resist.

10. Folk Culture Assignment: This assignment is designed to encourage students to think about the functions folk culture serves for different groups. Instruct students to choose an example of folk culture to research. Encourage them to try to find people who participate in this form of folk culture to use as resources in addition to books and articles on this type of folk culture. Students should write a two- to three-page paper that contains information including:

a. A description of the folk culture form and information about where, how, and who can participate. Do different groups participate together?

b. What are the reasons people are motivated to participate?

c. What are the origins of this form of folk culture?

d. What original or contemporary cultural values are reflected in this folk culture form?

e. What can participants learn by participating in this folk culture form?

f. What role does it play for participants in the culture(s) who participate?

CHAPTER 10

CULTURE, COMMUNICATION, AND INTERCULTURAL RELATIONSHIPS

LEARNING OBJECTIVES

After studying the material in this chapter, students should be able to:

Explain how relationships develop.

Identify some differences in how intercultural relationships develop.

Describe the stages of relational development.

Discuss how cultural differences influence the initial stages of relational development.

Describe cultural differences in romantic relationships.

Understand relational differences between gay and heterosexual relationships.

List some of the characteristics of intercultural relationships.

Identify some of the benefits and challenges in intercultural relationships.

Suggest reasons people give for and against intercultural dating and marriage.

Describe some of the approaches partners take to dealing with differences in intercultural marriages.

Explain how contexts influence intercultural relationships.

KEY WORDS

cognitive consistency
complementarity
  principle
compromise style
consensus style
exploratory phase

intercultural relationships
intimacy
obliteration style
orientation phase
proximity principle

romantic relationships
self-disclosure
similarity principle
stability phase
submission style

EXTENDED CHAPTER OUTLINE

This chapter explores the role of communication in the development of **intercultural relationships** with others who are culturally different across class, race, gender, age, and sexual orientation. The influence of context (social, historical, political) on these relationships is also investigated.

I. Benefits and Challenges of Intercultural Relationships
   A. Benefits: Most people have a variety of intercultural relationships that may include differences in age, physical ability, gender, ethnicity, class, religion, race, or nationality.
      1. Rewards of intercultural relationships are great, and the key to these relationships is an interesting balance of differences and similarities.
      2. Benefits include:
         a. Acquiring knowledge about the world
         b. Breaking stereotypes
         c. Acquiring new skills
      3. In intercultural relationships we often learn about the partner's language, cultural patterns, and history.
      4. Building intercultural relationships provides information and experiences that may challenge previously held stereotypes.
      5. We may learn how to do new things (new games, new recipes, new sports).
      6. These benefits lead to a sense of interconnectedness to others and establish a lifelong pattern of communication across differences.
   B. Challenges: There are several ways in which intercultural relationships are unique, and these present particular challenges.
      1. Dissimilarities may be more obvious during early stages of the relationship and then have less impact as commonalities are established and the relationship develops.
      2. There seems to be an interplay between differences and similarities in intercultural relationships.
      3. Because differences are a given, the challenge is to discover and build on similarities.
      4. Negative stereotypes often affect intercultural relationships.
      5. People often experience anxiety initially in intercultural relationships.
         a. It is greater in intercultural relationships than intracultural relationships.
         b. It comes from being worried about possible negative consequences.
         c. Once someone has developed a close intercultural relationship, that person is more inclined to have others.
         d. The level of anxiety will be higher if one or both parties has negative expectations because of negative stereotypes or negative previous experiences.
      6. Intercultural relationships often present us with the challenge to explain to ourselves, to each other, and to our communities.
      7. The biggest obstacles come from majority communities because they have less to gain from boundary-crossing friendships.
      8. In intercultural relationships, individuals recognize and respect differences.
      9. They require "[m]utual respect, acceptance, tolerance for the faux pas and the occasional closed door, open discussion and patient mutual education, all this gives crossing friendships—when they work at all—a special kind of depth" (Pogrebin, quoted in Gudykunst & Kim, 1992, p. 318).

II. Stages and Cultural Differences in Relational Development: Relationships develop in phases: initial attraction, the **orientation phase**, the **exploratory phase**, and the **stability phase**. Cultural differences affect relational development at each of these four stages.

   A. Differences in Initial Attraction: There are four principles of relational attraction:

      1. Proximity: One of the most powerful principles of relational attraction in the United States is the **proximity principle**.

         a. People form relationships with people they are in close proximity to.

         b. We tend to be attracted to individuals from similar social, economic, and cultural backgrounds.

         c. Proximity is not as important in other cultural contexts. In some cultures, a person's background (family, ethnicity, religion, and so on) is more important than who he or she is as an individual.

         d. The structures of society often determine whom we come in contact with.

         e. The more diverse your daily contacts, the more opportunities you have to develop intercultural relationships.

      2. Physical Attraction: We are attracted to specific people because we like the way they look.

         a. In the United States physical attraction may be the most important aspect in the beginning of a relationship.

         b. Standards for physical attractiveness are culturally based.

         c. Everyone wants to believe that relational partners are chosen outside the influences of social discourses; however, our relationships are strongly influenced by social and cultural ideas about interracial, intercultural, heterosexual, gay, lesbian, and intergenerational romance.

         d. Other people are influential in the development of our relationships through their support, silence, denial, or hostility.

      3. Similarity: According to the **similarity principle**, we tend to be attracted to people whom we perceive to be similar to ourselves.

         a. Finding that people agree with our beliefs confirms that they are right and provides us with **cognitive consistency**.

         b. People may seek partners with the same beliefs and values due to deep spiritual, moral, or religious convictions.

         c. Also, it is easier to successfully predict people's behavior who are like us.

         d. The research is less conclusive, but there is some evidence that we may be attracted to people who appear similar to us in personality.

         e. We may perceive greater similarity with people whom we like.

         f. Similarity is based not on whether people are actually similar but on the discovery of a similar trait.

         g. When people think they are similar, they have higher expectations about future interactions.

      4. Complementarity: In intercultural relationships, we are attracted to persons who are somewhat different from ourselves.

         a. The **complementarity principle** suggests that the differences that form the basis for attraction may involve personality traits and may contribute to complementarity, or balance, in a relationship.

      b.   Some individuals are attracted to people simply because they have a different cultural background.

      c.   Most people seek a balance between novelty and predictability in their relationships.

      d.   Most people are attracted to certain differences and not to others.

      e.   Society accepts some relationships of complementarity better than others.

      f.   This similarity–difference dialectical may operate differently in Eastern countries where levels of hierarchy shape interpersonal relations.

      g.   It seems likely that both the similarity and complementarity principles operate at the some time in intercultural relationships.

B.   Differences in Orientation Interactions: Cultural differences may come into play at the very beginning stages of relational development.

    1.   There are different cultural rules for how to address strangers.

    2.   Barnlund (1989) and colleagues found many differences in Japanese and U.S. American students' relational development.

    3.   These differences may be due to different cultural patterns, such as preferences for high- or low-context communication.

    4.   In high-context cultures, relationships will not easily develop without background or contextual information.

C.   Differences in the Exploratory Phase: The term *friend* may have different meanings for different cultural groups.

    1.   In the United States *friend* is given a broad meaning and can be applied to many different kinds of relationships.

    2.   In most parts of the world, a friend is what a U.S. American would consider a "close friend."

    3.   Barnlund's (1989) study and Collier's (1996) study suggest that there are both similarities and differences in the characteristics people feel are important in friendships.

D.   Differences in the Stability Phase

    1.   Friendships: As relationships develop more **intimacy** in this phase, friends share more personal and private information.

      a.   Lewin (1948) suggests that there are three areas of information we self-disclose.

        i.   The outer boundary includes superficial information about ourselves and our lives.

        ii.   The middle circle includes more personal information—life history, family background.

        iii.   The inner core includes very personal and private information, some of which we never share.

      b.   These areas may correspond with relational phases:

        i.   In the orientation phase, superficial information is shared.

        ii.   In the exploratory phase, personal information is exchanged.

        iii.   In the stability phase, more intimate information is disclosed.

      c.   The most cross-cultural variation in Lewin's studies was in the degree to which the outer area was more or less permeable.

      d.   There are also cultural variations in how much nonverbal expression is encouraged.

2. Romantic Relationships: Some intimate relationships develop into **romantic relationships**.
    a. Cross-cultural studies suggest some cultural differences in romantic relationships.
    b. Studies suggest that people with extremely individualistic orientations experienced less love, care, trust, and physical attraction with partners in romantic relationships and that these problems were less common in collectively oriented societies.
3. Gay Relationships: Little information is available about cultural differences in gay relationships.
    a. Homosexuality has existed in every society and in every era, and Chesbro (1981) suggests that in the majority of cultures outside the United States homosexuality is not considered problematic behavior.
    b. There are several areas where gay and straight relationships differ: the role of same-sex friendships, the role of cross-sex friendships, and the relative importance of friendships.
    c. Same-sex friendships may play different roles for gay and straight males in the United States because typically U.S. heterosexual men turn to women for their social support and emotional intimacy.
    d. Earlier in the United States and in many countries male friendships have often closely paralleled romantic love.
    e. This also seems to be true for gay men who tend to seek emotional support in same-sex friendships.
    f. The same pattern does not hold true for women because both gay and heterosexual women seek more intimacy in same-sex friendships.
    g. Sexuality may play a different role in heterosexual and gay friendships.
    h. In heterosexual relationships, friendship and sexual involvement sometimes seem mutually exclusive.
    i. In gay relationships, friendships often start with sexual attraction and involvement but last after sexual involvement is terminated.
    j. There is a clear distinction between "lover" and "friend" for both gay men and women.
    k. Close relationships may play a more important role for gay people than for straight people because of the social discrimination and strained family relationships.
    l. Many romantic relationship issues are the same for both heterosexual and gay couples; however, some issues (permanent relationships, relational dissolution) are unique to gay partners.
    m. Same-sex relationships, like heterosexual relationships, are very much influenced by the cultural contexts in which they occur.
III. Relationships Across Differences:
    A. Intercultural Relationship Dialectics: A dialectical way of thinking about relationships will help us avoid stereotyping relational differences. Martin, Nakayama, and Flores (1998) have extended Baxter's (1993) relational dialectics to include:

1. Differences–Similarities Dialectic: Real, important differences do exist between various cultural groups, and these affect intercultural relationships. Similarities also exist, and successful relationships occur, when both these notions are considered at the same time.
2. Cultural–Individual Dialectic: Communication in relationships is both cultural and idiosyncratic.
3. Privilege–Disadvantage Dialectic: Being sensitive to power differentials is important and usually less obvious to those in more powerful positions.
4. Personal–Contextual Dialectic: We frequently use different communication styles with people in different contexts.
5. Static–Dynamic Dialectic: People and relationships are constantly in flux, responding to various personal and contextual dynamics.
6. History/Past–Present/Future Dialectic: To understand relationships, it is important to consider the contexts in which they occur, including the historical context.

B. Communicating in Intercultural Relationships: Although intracultural and intercultural relationships share some similarities, they have some unique characteristics that can guide our thinking about communicating in these relationships.
1. In the research of Sudweeks (1990) and colleagues, several themes emerged as important to intercultural relationships: competence, similarity, involvement, and turning points.
2. Language is important and may challenge intercultural relationships even when people speak the same language.
3. Although dissimilarity may account for initial attraction, it is important to find similarities in relationships that transcend cultural differences.
4. Time has to be made for the relationship.
5. Intimacy of interaction is important, and so are shared friendship networks.
6. Turning points were important to intercultural friendship development, such as doing favors for each other, **self-disclosure**, and so on.

C. Intercultural Dating and Marriage
1. Lampe's (1982) study showed that people gave similar reasons for dating within and outside of their ethnic groups: they were attracted to each other physically and/or sexually.
2. The variations occurred in reasons for not dating.
   a. Reasons given for not dating within one's group were lack of attraction and so forth.
   b. Reasons given for not dating outside of one's group were no opportunity and never thought about it.
3. Other studies suggest that negative attitudes from families influence one's decision not to date outside one's own ethnic group.
4. The results of replications of Lampe's study suggest that this trend continues today.

D. Permanent Relationships
1. Studies in Canada and the United States suggest that more women than men, older more than younger, and more educated individuals marry outside their ethnic groups.

2. Major concerns of intercultural relationships include pressures from family and society and issues around raising children.
   a. Sometimes these concerns are intertwined.
   b. People in intercultural marriages tend to have more disagreements about how to raise children and are more likely to encounter opposition and resistance from their families about the marriage.
3. Romantic love is also influenced by society, and certain groups have been made to seem as if they are more attractive and acceptable as partners. How else can the high rates of outmarriage for some groups be explained?
4. Romano's interviews of people who had married spouses from other countries found 17 challenges in these marriages.
   a. Challenges they shared with intracultural couples were friends, politics, finances, sex, in-laws, illness and suffering, and raising children.
   b. Challenges that seemed exacerbated in intercultural marriages were values, eating and drinking habits, gender roles, time, religion, place of residence, dealing with stress, and ethnocentrism.
5. Romano also found that most intercultural couples have their own systems for working out the power balance in their relationships, which can be categorized into four styles:
   a. **Submission style**: The most common style, with one partner submitting to the culture of the other and abandoning or denying his/her own. This model rarely works because people cannot erase their cultural backgrounds.
   b. **Compromise style**: Each partner gives up certain parts of his or her cultural beliefs and norms to accommodate the other.
   c. **Obliteration style**: Both partners deal with the differences by attempting to abandon their own cultures and forming a new third culture with new beliefs. This is difficult because it is hard to be completely cut off from your own cultural background.
   d. **Consensus style**: The most desirable model; it is based on agreement and negotiation. Neither person permanently tries to abandon his/her cultural ways but may temporarily suspend them to adapt to the context. This requires flexibility and negotiation.
6. She suggests that couples planning intercultural relationships should prepare carefully for the commitment.
IV. Contexts of Intercultural Relationships: It is important to consider intercultural relationships in the contexts in which they emerge.
   A. History is an important context for understanding intercultural relationships.
   B. The dialectical tension rests, on the one hand, between the social, political, and economic contexts that make some kinds of intercultural relationships possible and, on the other hand, the desires and motives of the partners involved.

DISCUSSION QUESTIONS

Questions from the Text

1. What are some of the benefits of intercultural relationships?

2. What factors contribute to our forming relationships with some people and not with others?

3. How is the development of intercultural relationships different from that of intracultural relationships?

4. What challenges do intercultural couples face when they decide to make their relationships permanent?

5. What are the advantages of taking a dialectical perspective on intercultural relationships?

Additional Questions

1. How do social and cultural influences affect decisions about who you will form relationships with?

2. How are gay relationships different from and similar to heterosexual relationships?

3. How do media influence the formation of intercultural romantic relationships?

4. What challenges are different for intracultural and intercultural married couples?

5. What are some reasons for choosing not to date interculturally?

6. How do cultural differences influence the formation of friendships?

CLASSROOM EXERCISES AND CHAPTER ASSIGNMENTS

1. Relationship Formation Exercise: The purpose of this exercise is to help students explore how and with whom they tend to form relationships. Form groups of four to six students and ask them to identify and record responses to the following questions:

   a. Why do we develop relationships with other people?

   b. How did you get to know your friends and romantic partners?

   c. How do we form relationships with people with whom we want to become friends?

   d. How do you get to know people who are different from you? Are these relationships different from those characterized by similarity?

   e. What are some of the criteria we use to determine who we want to form friendships with and with whom we don't want to be associated?

   Students should keep track of their answers, and after 15 minutes instruct each group to report back to the class. You might write different types of responses on the board and ask students to identify the main patterns.

2. Defining Friendship Exercise: This exercise helps students explore the definition and characteristics of friendship. Instruct students to form groups of four to six students and come up with a definition of friendship. Explain to them that this definition needs to be broad enough to distinguish a friendship from an acquaintanceship. Suggest that before they form their definition they should identify differences between friendships and acquaintanceships and generate a list of characteristics found in

friendships. After the students have identified their definitions, they should share them with other groups in the class. This may motivate a class discussion on characteristics important to friendships and some cultural differences in how friendships are defined.

3. Physical Attraction Exercise: The object of this exercise is to encourage students to explore what characteristics constitute physical attractiveness and where their notions of physical attractiveness come from. You will need six to eight pictures of males and females from magazines or catalogues per group. Divide your students into groups of four to six individuals (mixed males and females). Give each group a set of pictures and ask them to work as a group to rate the attractiveness of each person in the pictures on a scale of 1 to 10 and to explain their rating by listing the characteristics of the person they consider to be attractive/unattractive. Instruct the students to think about these characteristics and where they got the idea that these characteristics were considered to be positive/negative. At the end of this activity, lead a class discussion exploring the following questions:

   a. Did everyone in the group agree about what characteristics were considered attractive? If there were differences/similarities, why do you think they existed?

   b. Did male and female members of the group have the same ideas about what characteristics made men/women attractive?

   c. What are some of the sources that inform our notions of attractiveness?

4. Cultural Variations in Relationships Assignment: The purpose of this assignment is to encourage students to become familiar with relationship differences in a specific culture. The assignment may be modified to work as a term or chapter assignment depending on the number of issues you assign students to investigate. The assignment could also be given as a group project. Instruct the students to choose a national or cultural group they are interested in studying. Then suggest they investigate the following questions to study relationships in the culture:

   a. Who do members of the culture consider to be part of their family?

   b. What are some differences in the roles and responsibilities of specific family members as compared with your culture?

   c. Are family members encouraged to stay in the same house/area as their family after adolescence?

   d. What are the cultural norms and taboos regarding dating and meeting people of the opposite sex?

   e. How are marriage proposals conducted in the culture?

   f. What is a typical wedding like in the culture?

   g. How do members of the culture view divorce?

   h. If divorce occurs, what are the rights of each partner?

   i. What is the general opinion of the culture toward homosexuality?

   j. How are the general perspectives of this culture the same/different from yours regarding gender roles?

5. Intercultural Relationships Interview Assignment: This assignment focuses on exploring the challenges of forming intercultural relationships. Assign students to interview someone from their own culture who has lived for an extended period of time (minimum of 4 months) in a foreign country or someone from another country living in the United States. Advise them to follow the suggestions and guidelines given for the Cultural Adjustment Interview Assignment in Chapter 8 and use the following questions as a basis for the interview:

a. How did you feel about meeting members of the culture for the first time?

b. What information best prepared you to interact with them, and where did you get it?

c. Before you met members of the culture, what did you expect them to be like?

d. Did you encounter any surprises when you began interacting with members of the culture?

e. How would you describe the experience of forming relationships with members of this culture? Was your experience different or similar to forming relationships with members of your own culture?

f. Did you notice differences or similarities to your own culture in how friendships were formed with members of the opposite sex?

g. Did you notice differences or similarities to your own culture in the expectations and norms for friendships with members of the same sex?

h. What advice would you give to people unfamiliar with the culture about forming relationships with members of this culture?

6. Intercultural Relationships Interview Assignment Variation: This assignment is similar to the previous assignment in that it focuses on the challenges of intercultural relationships. However, this assignment asks students to interview a person who is in an intercultural romantic relationship such as marriage, going steady, or some other form of a committed relationship. Encourage the students to view "intercultural" broadly to include persons of different religions, different class or economic groups, persons with and without disabilities, gay/lesbian/bisexual couples, and so on. Have the students summarize the interview data in a two- to three-page paper. Advise them to follow the suggestions and guidelines given for the Intercultural Interview Assignment in Chapter 8 and use the following questions as a basis for the interview:

a. What cultures/religions are they members of?

b. How did they meet?

c. How long have they been in the relationship?

d. What attracted them to each other?

e. What role did culture/religion play in their attraction to each other, if any?

f. What are the strengths of their intercultural relationship?

g. What are the challenges of their relationship?

h. Do they see the strengths and challenges as different from those found in same-culture relationships?

i. How have friends and family displayed their support or lack of support for the relationship?

7. Intercultural Relationships Video Assignment: The idea of this assignment is to encourage students to explore the unique challenges and rewards of intercultural relationships. The video for this assignment can be shown during class time or students can choose from a list of popular videos that highlight intercultural relationships. After viewing the video, students should be assigned to write a one- to two-page paper answering the questions from the previous assignment. Some suggested videos are:

Suggested Videos

Jungle Fever   *Fools Rush In*
Mississippi Masala   *The Joy Luck Club*

SUGGESTED VIDEOS

1. *Halmani.* Distributed by Chicago, IL: California Newsreel, 1988. This video tells the story of a Korean grandmother who comes to the United States to visit her daughter, American son-in-law, and granddaughter. It recounts the generational and cultural differences she encounters. (30 minutes)

2. *Hot Water: Intercultural Issues Between Women and Men.* Distributed by Washington, DC: NAFSA Association of International Educators, 1996. This video examines cultural differences in the relationships between women and men. Cultural variations discussed include perceptions of dating, intercultural marriage, and homosexual relationships, as well as nonverbal differences. The video also suggests some safety issues for men and women who sojourn in other countries. (27 minutes)

3. *The Politics of Love in Black and White.* Distributed by San Francisco, CA: California Newsreel, 1993. This is a documentary video in which college students discuss interracial relationships and their experiences with and feelings about interracial dating and marriage. (32 minutes)

4. *In My Country: Gender Perspectives on Gender.* Distributed by Orem, UT: Utah Valley State College, Behavioral Science Department. This is a two-part video that explores dating, marriage, and other relationship issues and cultural influences.

CHAPTER 11

CULTURE, COMMUNICATION, AND CONFLICT

LEARNING OBJECTIVES

After studying the material in this chapter, students should be able to:

Describe the conflict as opportunity and conflict as destructive orientations to conflict.

Define interpersonal conflict and its characteristics.

List the basic principles of nonviolence.

Suggest some ways in which cultures differ in their views toward conflict.

Identify five different types of conflict.

Identify and describe strategies for dealing with interpersonal conflict.

Understand how people come by their conflict strategies.

Discuss the relationship between ethnicity, gender, and conflict communication.

Describe how conflict styles vary in individualistic and collectivistic societies.

Define social movements.

Explain why it is important to understand the role of the social and historical contexts in intercultural conflicts.

List the characteristics of intercultural conflict.

Discuss some suggestions for dealing with intercultural conflicts.

KEY WORDS

avoiding style	integrating style	mediation
compromising style	intercultural conflict	obliging style
conflict	interdependent	pacifism
confrontation	intermediary	social conflict
dominating style	international conflicts	social movements
incompatibility		

EXTENDED CHAPTER OUTLINE

The significance of peace crosses many cultures and religions; it is hardly unique to Christianity. However, conflict is unavoidable. World wide, conflicts occur at many different levels: interpersonal, social, national, and international. Three broad, complementary approaches to understanding conflict are the interpersonal approach, which focuses on how cultural differences cause conflict and influence the management of the conflict, the interpretive approach, and the critical approach, which both focus more on intergroup relationships, cultural, historical and structural elements as the primary sources of conflict. These three approaches emphasize different aspects of the individual–contextual dialectic. Understanding intercultural conflict seems important because of the relationship between culture and conflict. Cultural differences can cause conflict, and once conflict occurs, cultural backgrounds and experiences influence how individuals deal with conflict. Unfortunately little is known about how to deal effectively with intercultural conflict because most of the research to date in the United States applies exclusively to majority culture members. This chapter reviews this information and identifies what can be applied in intercultural contexts and suggests some new ways to think about conflict.

I. Characteristics of Intercultural Conflict
   A. The dialectical perspective is useful in thinking about **intercultural conflict**.
      1. Intercultural conflicts can be viewed as both individual and cultural.
      2. They can be seen as both personal and social.
      3. The history/past–present/future dialectic can also be useful.
   B. Ambiguity is a typical characteristic of intercultural conflicts and causes people to resort to their default conflict style, which sometimes exacerbates the conflict.
   C. Language issues are also significant in intercultural conflict; when you do not know the language well, it is difficult to effectively handle the conflict.
   D. Different orientations to conflict and conflict management styles also complicate intercultural conflict.
II. Two Orientations to Conflict
   A. Conflict as Opportunity: This view is the one most commonly advocated in U.S. interpersonal communication texts.
      1. **Conflict** is defined as involving a perceived or real **incompatibility** of goals, values, expectations, process, or outcomes between two or more **interdependent** individuals or groups.
      2. This perspective is shared by many Western cultural groups, and Augsburger (1992) suggests that it is based on four assumptions:
         a. Conflict is a normal, useful process.
         b. All issues are subject to change through negotiation.
         c. Direct **confrontation** and conciliation are valued.
         d. Conflict is a necessary renegotiation of contract, a redistribution of opportunity, a release of tensions, and a renewal of relationships.
      3. The main idea is that working through conflicts constructively results in stronger, healthier, and more satisfying relationships.
      4. Some of the benefits for groups who work through conflicts are:
         a. Gaining new information about people or other groups.
         b. Diffusing more serious conflict.
         c. Increasing cohesiveness.
      5. Individuals should be encouraged to think of creative, even far-reaching solutions to conflict resolution.
      6. The most desirable conflict response is to recognize and work through it in an open, productive way.
      7. Relationships without conflict may mean that partners are not resolving issues that need to be dealt with.
      8. Conflict is a renegotiation of contract, so it is worthy of celebration.

B. Conflict as Destructive: Many cultural groups view conflict as ultimately unproductive for relationships, sometimes related to spiritual and/or cultural values (for example, many Asian cultures, Quakers, Amish).

1. Augsburger (1992) notes that this approach has four assumptions:

   a. Conflict is a destructive disturbance of the peace.

   b. The social system should not be adjusted to the needs of members; rather, members should adapt to established values.

   c. Confrontations are destructive and ineffective.

   d. Disputants should be disciplined.

2. The Amish, for example, see conflict not as an opportunity for personal growth but as certain destruction of their interpersonal and community harmony.

   a. When conflict does arise, the strong spiritual value of **pacifism** dictates a nonresistant response—often avoidance.

   b. This nonresistant stance prohibits the use of force in human relations, and legal and personal confrontation is avoided.

   c. This extends to refusal to participate in military confrontation and in personal and business relations; they would prefer to lose face or money than escalate a conflict.

3. Cultural groups that view conflict as destructive often avoid low-level conflict and sometimes seek intervention from a third party, or **intermediary**.

   a. Informal intervention: a colleague or friend is asked to intervene.

   b. Formal intervention: professional help is used to intervene (for example, lawyers, real estate agents, counselors/therapists).

4. Discipline is seen as a means for censuring conflict.

5. The approach does not suggest the absence of conflict and is not just an objection to fighting but is a difficult (possibly risky) orientation to interpersonal relationships.

6. The "peacemaking" approach:

   a. Strongly values the other person and encourages his or her growth.

   b. Attempts to de-escalate or keep conflicts from escalating once they start.

   c. Attempts to find creative negotiation to resolve conflicts when they arise.

7. Ting-Toomey (1991) suggests that these two orientations are based on different cultural values for identity and face saving.

   a. The conflict as opportunity orientation stems from a concern for saving individual dignity.

   b. The conflict as destructive orientation stems from a value for maintaining harmony in interpersonal relationships and saving the dignity of others.

III. The Interpersonal Approach to Conflict: Different orientations to conflict may result in more conflict.

A. Types of Conflict: There are many different types of conflict and different styles to deal with them. In Cole's (1996) study, he found that Japanese students use most of the same categories as those identified in the United States:

1. Affective Conflict: This type of conflict occurs when individuals become aware that their feelings and emotions are incompatible.
2. Conflict of Interest: This occurs when people have incompatible preferences for courses of action or plans.
3. Value Conflict: This is a more serious conflict type and occurs when people differ in ideologies.
4. Cognitive Conflict: A situation in which people become aware that their thought processes or perceptions are incongruent.
5. Goal Conflict: This occurs when people disagree about a preferred outcome or end state.

B. Strategies and Tactics: The ways people deal with conflict are influenced by their cultural backgrounds, and they usually are defined by how people manage self-image in relational settings.
   1. Although people may have a general disposition toward conflict, they may choose different tactics in different situations.
   2. There are at least five styles of conflict management.
      a. **Dominating style**: This win-lose style reflects high concern for self and low concern for others and uses forcing behaviors to win one's position.
      b. **Integrating style**: High concern for both self and others are reflected in an open and direct exchange of information in an attempt to reach a solution acceptable to both parties. It is seen as the most effective style for most conflicts, but it requires a lot of time and energy.
      c. **Compromising style**: Reflects a moderate degree of concern for self and others. It involves sharing and exchanging information to the end that both individuals give up something to find a mutually acceptable decision.
      d. **Obliging style**: In this style, one person plays down the differences and incompatibilities while emphasizing commonalities that satisfy the other.
      e. **Avoiding style**: Reflects low concern for self and others in U.S. cultural contexts, but in some cultural contexts this may be viewed as an appropriate style leading to harmonious relationships.
   3. There are many reasons one style may be preferred over another, and the primary influence on style choice is family background.

C. Gender, Ethnicity, and Conflict: In this section ideas concerning the effect of gender and ethnicity on handling conflict are investigated.
   1. Gender differences: Sometimes the clash of communication styles between men and women seem like cross-cultural differences and can both lead to conflict and influence how it is handled. These differences include:
      a. How they show support.
      b. How they talk about difficulties.
      c. How they tell stories.
      d. How they talk about relationships.
   2. The relationship between ethnicity, gender, and conflict is more complex.
      a. Studies suggest contradictory evidence for how males and females of different ethnic backgrounds prefer to deal with conflict.

b. Although some differences appear to exist, it is important to remember that it is inappropriate to assume that a person will behave a particular way because of his/her ethnicity and/or gender.

D. Value Differences and Conflict Styles
1. Cultural variations in intercultural conflict resolution may be understood by looking at how cultural values influence conflict management.
   a. Contrasting value differences, such as individualism and collectivism, influence communication patterns during conflict.
   b. Studies suggest that people from individualist societies tend to be more concerned about their own self-esteem during conflict; more direct in their communication; and use more controlling, confrontational, and solution-oriented conflict styles.
   c. People from collectivist societies tend to be more concerned with preserving group harmony and with saving the other person's dignity during conflict so they may use a less direct conversational style and may use avoiding and obliging conflict styles instead.
2. The way one chooses to deal with conflict in any situation depends on the type of conflict and the relationship one has with the other person.
3. For example, Cole's (1996) study suggests that Japanese college students use more dominating or avoiding styles with outgroup members where harmony is not as important.

IV. Interpretive and Critical Approaches to Social Conflict: Both approaches have tended to emphasize the social and cultural aspects of conflict.
A. Conflict from these perspectives is more complex than the ways interpersonal conflict is enacted.
B. It is deeply rooted in cultural differences in the context of social, economic, and historical conflict.
1. **Social conflict** arises from unequal or unjust social relationships between groups.
   a. These conflicts may be motivated by the desire for social change.
   b. In **social movements** people band together to create social change.
   c. Sometimes social movements use confrontation to highlight system injustices.
2. Historical and political contexts are sources of conflict.
   a. Many **international conflicts** have centered on border disputes.
   b. Historical reasons for conflicts help us understand the claims of both sides.
C. Social Contexts
1. The context makes a difference in how people handle conflict.
2. Many conflicts arise and must be understood against the backdrop of existing social movements.
3. Social movements are large-scale efforts designed to accomplish change in contemporary society (for example, women's suffrage movement).
4. Confrontation from this perspective is seen as an opportunity for change.
5. Some social movements use a nonviolent confrontation strategy whereas others choose violence.
6. Social movements highlight issues related to intercultural interaction.

D. Economic Contexts: Many conflicts are fueled by economic problems.
    1. Economic problems are often expressed in terms of cultural differences and blaming.
    2. Kivel (1996) suggests that blaming immigrants, people of color, and Jews for economic problems diverts our attention from the decision makers who are responsible for the problem.
    3. As economic contexts change, more cultural conflict occurs.
    4. Prejudice and stereotyping that lead to conflict are often due to perceived economic threat and competition.
    5. This is an important context for understanding intercultural conflict.
E. Historical and Political Contexts: Derogatory words can be a source of conflict, and the force they carry comes from their historical usage and the history of oppression to which they refer.
    1. Since much of our identity comes from history, it is only by understanding the past that we can understand what it means to be a member of a particular cultural group.
    2. Some identities are constructed in opposition or in conflict with other identities.
    3. The act of identifying with particular groups marks them as different from others and can lead, if fueled by historical antagonism, to future conflicts (for example, conflicts in Bosnia-Herzegovina).
    4. Historical antagonisms become part of cultural identities and cultural practices that place people in positions of conflict.
    5. When conflict occurs, it is important to avoid assuming it is caused by personal conflicts and to view it in terms of the context as well.
V. Managing Intercultural Conflict
    A. Productive Versus Destructive Conflict
        1. One way of dealing with conflict management in intercultural interaction is to get a handle on what is more or less successful conflict management or resolution.
        2. Augsburger (1992) suggests there are four ways in which productive conflict is different from destructive conflict:
            a. In productive conflict individuals narrow the conflict in definition, focus, and issues.
            b. In productive conflict individuals limit conflict to the original issue.
            c. In productive conflict individuals direct the conflict toward cooperative problem solving.
            d. In productive conflict individuals trust leadership that stresses mutually satisfactory outcomes.
    B. Competition Versus Cooperation: The general theme in destructive conflict is competitive escalation.
        1. Competitive relational atmospheres promote coercion, deception, and poor communication.
        2. Cooperative atmospheres promote perceived similarity, trust, flexibility, and open communication.

3.   The key is that the atmosphere must be introduced in the beginning stages of relationships or group interaction because it is difficult to turn a competitive relationship into a cooperative one once the conflict starts to escalate.
   a.   Exploration is essential to setting a cooperative atmosphere.
   b.   Exploration consists of putting the conflict issue on hold, exploring other options, or delegating the problem to a third party.
   c.   Blaming must be suspended so that it is possible to generate new ideas or positions.
   d.   If all parties are committed to the process, they will share joint ownership in the solution.
   e.   Exploration can encourage people to think of innovative and interesting solutions to conflicts.
C.   Dealing With Conflict: There are no easy answers for dealing with intercultural conflict.
   1.   Sometimes looking at conflict dialectically can help.
   2.   Sometimes stepping back and showing self-restraint is the answer.
   3.   Sometimes it is appropriate to be assertive and show strong emotion.
   4.   The authors' suggestions for dealing with intercultural conflict are:
      a.   Stay centered and do not polarize: It is important to practice self-restraint and avoid either-or thinking.
      b.   Maintain contact: People may take a break from the conflict but not the relationship—continued dialogue is important for better understanding the conflict.
      c.   Recognize the existence of different styles: Conflict may be exacerbated when people fail to recognize style differences.
      d.   Identify your preferred style: It is important to recognize your own preferred styles and which styles are difficult for you to deal with.
      e.   Be creative and expand your conflict style repertoire: If the conflict approach you are using is not working, be willing to try a different style.
      f.   Recognize the importance of conflict context: The social, economic, political, and historical contexts need to be considered in understanding conflict in addition to the interpersonal issues.
      g.   Be willing to forgive: Genuine forgiveness is particularly important for long-term relationships.
D.   Mediation: When individuals or groups cannot work through conflict on their own, they may get help from an intermediary.
   1.   In Western societies, lawyers may act as mediators to settle community or family disputes, but the contemporary Western **mediation** models often ignore cultural variations in conflict processes.
   2.   Augsberg suggests that culturally sensitive mediators engage in conflict transformation (not conflict resolution or conflict management).
   3.   Conflict transformers help disputants to think in new ways about the conflict, but this requires a commitment by both parties to regard each other with goodwill and mutual respect.

4. Traditional societies often use mediation based on nondirect means.
5. Meditation is advantageous because disputants are actively involved and tend to buy-in to the resolution.
6. It is also more creative and integrative, and it is cheaper than legal resolution.

DISCUSSION QUESTIONS

Questions from the Text

1. How does the "conflict as opportunity" orientation differ from the "conflict as destructive" orientation?

2. Why is it important to understand the context in which an intercultural conflict occurs?

3. How are conflict strategies used in social movements?

4. How does an attitude of forgiveness facilitate conflict resolution?

5. What are some general suggestions for dealing with intercultural conflict?

Additional Questions

1. What are some gender and ethnic group conflict style differences?

2. Describe some reasons mediation may be an effective approach to conflict resolution?

3. Why is it important to understand your own conflict style preference?

4. How does the economic context influence conflict?

5. What are the characteristics of productive versus destructive conflict?

6. How do intercultural conflicts differ from intracultural conflicts?

7. How do value differences influence intercultural conflict?

CLASSROOM EXERCISES AND CHAPTER ASSIGNMENTS

1. Guest Speaker on Cultures in Conflict Exercise: The purpose of this exercise is to acquaint students with a cultural conflict and the history of that conflict. You should invite a speaker who has studied a particular cultural conflict between national or local cultural groups and who can provide students not only with an update of the current situation but also explain the history of the conflict and relations between the two groups. For example, you may invite a professor from the political science department who has studied the political conflict in Kosovo. Motivate your students to take notes and ask questions at the end of the presentation by requiring them to hand in a two- to three-paragraph response at the beginning of the next class period. In the response they should describe what they feel each side will need to do to work toward resolving the conflict, including differences that must be negotiated.

2. Conflict Styles Activity: The purpose of this activity is to familiarize students with the way conflict is conceptualized and dealt with by a specific cultural group. Students should form groups of three to four individuals and select a culture they are not familiar with. Ask them to conduct a research project in which they attempt to identify the communication styles preferred by this group, specifying which conflict strategies members of this group might be most likely to use, and which conflict

strategies might be most useful in conflict situations with this group. Suggested strategies must be culturally appropriate for each group. Students should also suggest, using available resources, cultural values that may be antecedents of conflict style preferences (such as, individualism) or political and historical contexts that encourage these preferences. This report may be given in oral (see assignment 3) or written form.

3. Conflict Styles Exercise: This exercise is an extension of the Conflict Styles Activity, which may be used in class to stimulate thinking about how cultures vary in conflict styles. Assign the students to prepare a one-page summary describing the major conflict style differences for the cultures on which they wrote their reports. Ask them to present this orally and then suggest a hypothetical example of how these differences may affect the outcome of a conflict between a member of that culture and their own. You may want to assign students to role-play the hypothetical example.

4. Intercultural Conflict Exercise: The focus of this exercise is to encourage students to think more critically about previous intercultural conflict situations that they have been involved in or observed. (Note: If your students have had limited interaction with people from other cultures, you may modify this assignment by choosing examples of intercultural conflicts from newspaper stories or literature for them to read and discuss.) Instruct the students to form groups of three to four individuals. Students should take turns describing an intercultural conflict, and then the group should critically discuss the situation to understand why the conflict occurred, taking into account personal and intercultural as well as historical factors. Next, as a group, they should try to identify possibilities for resolving the conflict positively. If some students are embarrassed to share a personal experience, encourage them to frame the account as though they observed the conflict rather than participated in it.

5. Cultures in Conflict Exercise: This exercise is an extension of the Cultures in Conflict Group Assignment found in the text on page 313. Its purpose is to familiarize students with some current cultural conflicts. Instruct the group of students who prepared the report for the Cultures in Conflict Group Assignment to work in two teams to present a 10 minute (5 minutes for each team) oral report summarizing the position of each culture in the conflict. After both groups have presented their reports, conduct a brief class discussion in which you work with students to identify the major conflict issues and their roots. (Note: A more elaborate modification of this exercise could include an actual debate between the two teams discussing the conflict.)

6. Intercultural Conflict Role Plays: This exercise encourages students to practice various strategies that can be employed to manage or resolve intercultural conflicts. Students form groups of about four to five members. Each group develops a scenario that depicts an intercultural conflict, which they then resolve using one of the strategies discussed in the textbook. Each group performs their role play in front of the class. The class then tries to "guess" which conflict strategy the group enacted. After each role play the actors remain at the front of the class to answer any questions or offer any comments they may have about their role play.

7. An alternative to the above exercise may be that the students enact their role plays, without offering a strategy or resolution to their scenario. The "audience" then answers questions about the scenario such as:

a. Is this productive or destructive conflict?

b. Is this competitive or cooperative conflict?

c. What strategies could the persons in the role play employ to manage the conflict? (Students could even "try out" the suggested strategy to test its appropriateness.)

8. Identifying One's Preferred Style of Managing Conflict Exercise: Frequently the preferred style of dealing with conflicts is based (often unconsciously) on the style individuals may have seen modeled as children. This exercise is designed to help students identify their preferred style of dealing with conflict by reflecting on the style(s) they grew up with or the style that stands out for them. Begin this exercise by asking students to think back and reflect on the style of conflict they were most exposed to as children. They may need to be coached to think about specific instances where a conflict in their family arose and how the conflict was handled. For instance, in one family, every time there was a conflict, a loud shouting match ensued, and then everybody went to their rooms for a nap. When they all awoke, the family members acted as if the conflict had never happened.

    After the student identifies the preferred style(s) of handling conflict that they were exposed to, ask them to reflect on whether this is their preferred style as adults, or whether they have consciously or unconsciously changed their preferred style of managing conflict. Debrief this exercise by asking students to share their answers. This sharing will expose students to various styles. The discussion that follows should be respectful of the different styles of dealing with conflict, and the instructor should urge students to think more about the implications of the styles rather than polarizing them in terms of right or wrong.

9. Attitudes Toward Conflict Exercise: As a first step to understanding and managing conflict, students need to become aware of their personal feelings toward conflict. In this simple exercise, ask students to write down the first words that come into their minds when they think of "conflict." Then ask students to share some of their words with the class and record them on the board. After a few minutes, ask the students to reflect on the words you've recorded and to share any of their observations. One of the most powerful observations that comes out of this exercise is the negative feelings people have about conflict. Another important observation the instructor could make is that often the behaviors that are expressed about managing conflict are negative or destructive behaviors such as war, hate, yelling, hit, and so on. Once students have had an opportunity to explore their attitudes toward conflict, the instructor will be able to introduce alternate and more positive views of conflict.

SUGGESTED VIDEOS

1. *Arab and Jew: Wounded Spirits in a Promised Land.* Distributed by Alexandria, VA: PBS Video, 1989. The video explores the cultural tensions between Arabs and Jews in Israeli territories. (118 minutes)

2. *A Conflict of Cultures.* Distributed by Annenberg/CPB Project, 1986. This video shows the conflicts that emerge from the mixing of cultures in Africa. (60 minutes)

CHAPTER 12

THE OUTLOOK FOR
INTERCULTURAL COMMUNICATION

LEARNING OBJECTIVES

After studying the material in this chapter, students should be able to:

Identify components of intercultural competence.

Describe important attitudes for competent intercultural communicators.

Make the distinction between descriptive, interpretive, and evaluative statements.

List behaviors that are important for competent intercultural communicators to display.

Identify four levels of intercultural competence.

Explain the relationship between context and intercultural competence.

Define ethics and discuss the universality of ethics.

Discuss the role of self-reflexivity in intercultural competence.

List guidelines for becoming an ethical intercultural communicator.

Describe the dialectical approach to thinking about intercultural communication and suggest some examples of intercultural dialectics.

KEY WORDS

attitudes	intercultural alliances	self-knowledge
conscious competence	knowledge	tolerance for ambiguity
conscious incompetence	linguistic knowledge	transpection
D.I.E. exercise	motivation	unconscious competence
empathy	nonjudgmental	unconscious incompetence

EXTENDED CHAPTER OUTLINE

To learn how to become a good intercultural communicator, experience is often the best teacher; reading books is not enough. This chapter will provide ideas and suggestions for improving intercultural communication skills.

I. The Components of Competence
    Knowledge, attitudes, behaviors, and motivation are traditional building blocks of intercultural communication competence. Although these represent a starting point, they are just a starting point. Further, they are related in such a way that it is difficult to separate them.

A. Individual Components
   1. Motivation: **Motivation** is perhaps the most important dimension of communication competence.
      a. If one is not motivated to communicate, skill level is not important.
      b. We can't assume people always want to communicate.
      c. Historical and political contexts sometimes create an absence of motivation to communicate.
   2. Knowledge: The **knowledge** component comprises what we know about ourselves, others, and various aspects of communication.
      a. **Self-knowledge** includes knowing how you may be perceived as a communicator and your strengths and weaknesses.
         i. We gain this information by listening to others and seeing how they perceive us.
         ii. Acquiring self-knowledge is a long and sometimes complicated process because it involves being open to information coming in many different ways.
         iii. Sometimes we do not get this information because we do not search for it or have a relationship with enough trust to reveal such information.
      b. Knowledge about how others think and behave is important.
         i. Learning about others in an abstract way often leads to stereotyping.
         ii. It is often better to learn through relational experience, however this is not always possible.
         iii. To avoid stereotyping, it is important to be aware of the range in thought and behavior across cultures and not to assume that since a person belongs to a particular group that he or she will behave in a particular way.
         iv. Expanding one's mental "category width" is also important.
      c. **Linguistic knowledge** is another important aspect of intercultural communication.
         i. Understanding the challenges of learning a second language helps us appreciate the challenges of sojourners and immigrants.
         ii. Knowing a second or third language expands one's communication repertoire and empathy for culturally different individuals.
   3. Attitudes: Many **attitudes** contribute to intercultural communication competence.
      a. **Tolerance for ambiguity** refers to ease in dealing with situations where there is much unknown and is one of the most difficult things to attain.
      b. **Empathy** is the ability to know what it is like to "walk in another person's shoes."
         i. Since our empathic skills are tied to our cultures, we cannot be empathetic without knowing something about others' experiences and lives.
         ii. Howell suggests that empathy is the capacity to imagine oneself in another role, within the context of one's cultural identity.
         iii. Empathy across cultures has also been described as **transpection** or trying to see the world exactly as the other person sees it.

   iv. Bennett suggests a "Platinum Rule": "Do unto others as they themselves would have done unto them"(1998, p. 213).

  c. Being **nonjudgmental** is not easy because we do not like to recognize that we judge using our own cultural frames of reference.

   i. The **D.I.E. exercise** is helpful in developing nonjudgmental attitudes.

   ii. It involves learning to distinguish between description, interpretation, and evaluation in processing information.

   iii. Descriptive statements (nonjudgmental) contain factual information that is verified through the senses (for example, "It is five o'clock and the bus is not here.").

   iv. Interpretive statements attach meaning to the description (for example, "The bus is late.").

   v. Evaluative statements clarify how we feel about something (for example, "I am angry that the bus is not here.").

   vi. This device may enable us to recognize the level at which we are processing information.

   vii. Confusing the levels in our communication can lead to misunderstandings and ineffectiveness.

4. Behaviors and Skills: This is another component of intercultural competence.

  a. Ruben (1976, 1977) devised the following list of universal behaviors, which includes some attitudes:

   i. Display of respect

   ii. Interaction management

   iii. Ambiguity tolerance

   iv. Empathy

   v. Relational rather than task behavior

   vi. Interaction posture

  b. Some general behaviors may work well in all cultural groups and contexts, however they can become problematic when we try to apply them in very specific ways.

  c. There are also culturally specific rules and expectations for behavior. For example, respect may be an important behavior in all cultures, but the way respect is displayed may be different in specific cultures.

  d. There appear to be two levels of behavioral competencies: at the macro level are culture-general behaviors, and at the micro level are behaviors that are implemented in culture-specific ways.

  e. It is important to know behaviors at both levels and to be able to adapt them.

  f. Intercultural communication competence means being able to exhibit or adapt different kinds of behaviors, depending on the other person's cultural background.

  g. Howell (1982) emphasized that intercultural communication required a combination of holistic and analytic thinking and identified four levels of intercultural communication competence:

     i. **Unconscious incompetence**: The "be yourself" level where there is no consciousness of differences or need to act in any particular way. During intercultural communication, being ourselves may mean being incompetent and not realizing it.

     ii. **Conscious incompetence**: We may realize that we are not having success but not be able to figure out why.

     iii. **Conscious competence**: This is the level that intercultural communication courses try to motivate students to reach by focusing on analytic thinking and learning.

     iv. **Unconscious competence**: Communication at this level is successful, but not conscious, and occurs when the analytic and holistic parts are functioning together. It occurs when one is attitudinally and cognitively prepared but lets go of conscious thought and relies on holistic cognitive processing.

B. Contextual Components: Competence requires an understanding of the context in which the communication occurs.

    1. An interpretive perspective reminds us that a good communicator is sensitive to the many contexts in which intercultural communication occurs.

    2. It is important to recognize the social position from which one is communicating in relation to the speech community and the contexts.

    3. A critical perspective reminds us that an individual's competence may be constrained by political, economic, and historical contexts.

II. Applying Knowledge About Intercultural Communication: Some specific suggestions for becoming better intercultural communicators that recognize both the importance of individual skills and contextual constraints in improving intercultural relations include:

A. Becoming Interpersonal Allies: The dialectical approach involves becoming allies with others, all working for better intergroup relationships.

    1. We need to think about multiculturalism and cultural diversity in a new way that recognizes the complexities of communication across cultures and power issues.

    2. The goal is to find a way in which people can work toward equitable unity that holds many different and contradictory truths, a unity based on conscious coalition, of affinity, of political kinship, in which we all win.

    3. Collier (1998a) suggests **intercultural alliances** are characterized by three issues:

       a. Power and unearned privilege: Intercultural friends recognize and try to understand issues of ethnic, gender, and class differences and how these determine power and then try to manage these power issues.

       b. Impact of history: Intercultural friends recognize that people in power interpret the importance of history differently from those who have less power.

       c. Orientations of affirmation: Intercultural friends value and appreciate differences and are committed to the relationship even during difficulties and misunderstandings.

4. Dace (1994) suggests that European Americans often have difficulty wanting to hear about examples of prejudice from African Americans; they want affirmation that they are not racist; they want to be absolved of history. African Americans learn this expectation in communication and respond by fulfilling European American expectations.
5. Dace concludes that for any real interracial communication and learning to occur, Whites must make a commitment to really listening.
6. Kivel's (1996) list of suggestions given by people of color to White people who want to be allies includes (Note: Some of these are contradictory, which underscores the need for the dialectical perspective.):
   a. Find out about us.
   b. Don't take over.
   c. Speak up.
   d. Provide information.
   e. Take risks.
   f. Don't take it personally.
   g. Be understanding.
   h. Don't make assumptions.
   i. Don't assume you know what's best for me.
   j. Talk to other White people.
   k. Interrupt jokes and comments.
   l. Don't ask me to speak for my people.
B. Building Coalitions: There are specific ways to build coalitions.
   1. Coalitions can arise from multiple identities.
   2. As people strive to build better intercultural relations, they may need to transcend some of their identities or reinforce other identities.
   3. Shifting identities allow people to build coalitions across seemingly different peoples, to foster positive intercultural relationships for a better world.
   4. Coalitions built of multiple identities are never easy, and in the process people may find that some of their own identities feel neglected or injured. To achieve success, they have to work through emotional injuries.
III. What the Future Holds: The world is rapidly changing, but not all of the changes are good for intercultural relations.
   A. It is important to think dialectically about these changes.
   B. Seeing the complexities of life is an important step toward successful intercultural communication.
   C. Have the confidence to engage in intercultural communication, but know that there is always more to learn.

DISCUSSION QUESTIONS

Questions from the Text

1. In what ways is the notion of intercultural competence helpful? In what ways is it limiting?

2. How can you be an ally? How do you know if you are being an ally?

3. How might you better assess your unconscious competence and unconscious incompetence?

4. How might the European Union affect the United States?

5. How does your own social position (gender, class, age, and so on) influence your intercultural communication competence? Does this competence change from one context to another?

Additional Questions

1. What are the characteristics of a competent intercultural communicator?

2. How is self-reflexivity important to intercultural competence?

3. Why should we think about intercultural communication in terms of dialectics?

4. How can the D.I.E. exercise help increase our intercultural communication competence?

5. What does it mean to be a competent intercultural communicator?

CLASSROOM EXERCISES AND CHAPTER ASSIGNMENTS

1. Course Closure Exercise: This exercise is designed to be both a course summary and an opportunity to articulate individual learning experiences in the course. Conduct this exercise as a roundtable session by instructing students to sit in a large circle and discuss what they have learned in class, what they found most useful, and what significant experiences they have had during the course that helped them to understand some of the theoretical issues. You may conduct these discussions in small groups first and then with the class as a whole.

2. D.I.E. Exercise: The focus of this exercise is to familiarize students with description, interpretation, and evaluation statements. For this exercise you will need either a blank overhead transparency and an overhead marker or chalk for each of the groups. Instruct students to form groups of four to six individuals. Assign them to come up with a mixture of five descriptive, interpretive, or evaluative statements. Ask them to write these statements on the board or overhead transparency without labeling their type. When they are finished, each group is to take turns testing the class to determine whether they can label each statement as the correct type.

3. Cultural Specific Competence Assignment: This assignment is designed to encourage students to explore competent behaviors for a specific culture. Instruct students to choose a culture to research and one or more contexts (school classroom, initial interactions, bartering, and so on), depending on the desired length of the report. Assign them to use the library as well as people in the community familiar with the culture as resources in completing an oral or written report detailing the behaviors that would generally be considered appropriate to use in the context(s) for this culture.

4. Variations in Ethics Assignment: This assignment is designed to increase students' awareness of some of the ethical variations that exist between cultures. Assign students to select a national culture they are interested in and to identify a context within the culture where cultural ethics contrast with ethics in the United States (business practices, law enforcement, moral codes). Instruct them to research the differences and write a report that contrasts the ethics of the culture with those of the United States and then suggests a hypothetical situation in which conflicts may occur in intercultural interaction because of these differences. Ask them to suggest how they would resolve this situation if they were involved; that is, would they "Do as the Romans do" or not?

5. Plan of Action Assignment: The focus of this assignment is to encourage students to think about how they can continue to improve their intercultural communication skills after the class has ended. Introduce the assignment by suggesting to students that with the end of the course there will be fewer reminders for them of the importance of intercultural communication and opportunities to identify and practice intercultural skills. Ask them to write a thought paper in which they briefly identify the most important things they feel they have learned about intercultural communication, evaluate their intercultural communication expertise, and suggest a plan detailing ways in which they can continue to develop intercultural skills on their own after the course ends. Encourage them to research opportunities for continued intercultural training and information provided in their communities, the university/college, and their workplaces that they could take advantage of as part of creating their plans.

6. Cultural Competence Assignment: This last assignment will enable students to review what they've learned in this class by asking them to write a two- to three-page self-analysis paper. Refer students to the section in this chapter on the Components of Competence and ask them to evaluate themselves on each of the competencies (motivation, knowledge, attitudes, behaviors and skills). Students should end their paper with a plan outlining how they will continue increasing their competence in each or all of the competency areas. If time allows, the students could present their plans to the entire class as an end-of-class closure activity.

7. Competence Skills Exercise: This exercise is designed to give students a chance to apply competence skills and attitudes to a "real" intercultural issue. Show students the video, *In Whose Honor? American Indian Mascots in Sports*. Instruct each of them to take a few minutes and answer the following questions on their own. (Note: You may want to make a handout or overhead with the questions for them.) Tell them that they will not be turning in their answers for grading so that they will not feel pressured to answer the questions the way they think the instructor might want them to.

   a. How do you personally feel about the issue of using Native American names and symbols in sports?

   b. What are the reasons alumni and others want to continue to use their traditional symbols and mascot? How do you feel about their reasons?

   c. What are the reasons Native Americans are opposed to this? How do you feel about their reasons?

   d. What solution to this conflict would you suggest?

   Then organize students into groups of five to six people. Instruct them to work together to come up with a plan for how a competent intercultural communicator might respond to this situation if he or she were a participant in a debate over this conflict. After about 10 minutes ask students to share their ideas with the class. Then ask students what kind of a solution a competent intercultural communicator would work toward. After this discussion, ask students to look back over their responses and evaluate their responses for elements of intercultural competence. Finally, ask students to identify some of the barriers that make it difficult to resolve this particular conflict.

   In Whose Honor? American Indian Mascots in Sports. Distributed by Champaign, IL: Rosenstien Productions, 1996. This video documents the conflict between Native Americans and the University of Illinois over the use of Native Americans and Native American symbols for sports teams. (46 minutes)

SUGGESTED VIDEOS

1. *Managing a Diverse Workplace: Understanding Different Cultural Values and Styles*. Distributed by Princeton, NJ: Films for the Humanities and Sciences, 1991. This video is a rebuttal to the "melting pot" theory, suggesting that employees should not be expected to change their cultural values when they work in organizations. It focuses on the views of African Americans, Hispanics, Asians, and Native Americans and suggests that the most successful organizations are those that understand diversity and how to benefit from it. (56 minutes)

2. *Crosstalk*. A BBC-TV Production distributed by New York, NY: Films Inc., 1979. This video explores some cultural differences in language use that have the potential to create misunderstandings in social contexts such as job interviews. (25 minutes)

PART IV
TEST BANK

CHAPTER 1

WHY STUDY INTERCULTURAL COMMUNICATION?

MULTIPLE-CHOICE QUESTIONS

1. To what does McLuhan's term "global village" refer?
   a. It refers to the political environment created by the formation of the United Nations.
   b. It refers to the ease with which modern transportation enables us to visit other nations.
   c. It refers to a collection of nation-states unified by political alliances.
   *d. It refers to a world of people closely connected by communication technology.

2. Which of the following is a factor in the increased mobility of families in the United States?
   a. increased electronic technology
   b. inexpensive travel opportunities
   *c. increasing divorce rates
   d. increasing intercultural interest

3. From what areas of the world do most of today's immigrants to the United States come?
   *a. Asia and Latin America
   b. Mexico and eastern Europe
   c. Haiti and China
   d. eastern Europe and the Middle East

4. Which of the following statements about the immigration history in the United States is true?
   a. After the European immigrants became firmly established in the United States, they welcomed other immigrants by providing them employment and allowing them to retain cultural characteristics.
   b. Throughout the history of immigration in the United States, the government has worked to develop policies that provide equal immigration opportunities to people from all nations.
   c. Relationships between groups who have immigrated to the United States have generally been positive and peaceful.
   *d. When the economy is bad in the United States, people's attitudes toward new immigrants have generally been negative.

5. Which of the following factors may have increased tensions between African Americans and Korean immigrants during the Los Angeles riots?
   a. The Korean immigrants rebelled against assimilating into the United States.
   *b. African Americans resented the success of the more recently arrived Koreans.
   c. African Americans felt that the Korean immigrants were causing declining property values in the area.
   d. Korean immigrants wanted their children to go to the same schools as the African American children.

6. Which of the following has occurred due to advances in technology?
   a. People are beginning to spend more time with family members.
   b. The number of relationships we have with people have decreased.
   *c. People have more frequent contact with people from other cultures.
   d. People are gaining a clearer sense of themselves.

7. Why is the number of international executives from U.S. companies decreasing?
   *a. It is less expensive to hire a local executive than to send a U.S. executive overseas.
   b. The number of U.S. business offices overseas is decreasing.
   c. Fewer U.S. executives want to deal with the challenges of working in another country.
   d. U.S. government policies discourage businesses from sending their employees overseas for extended time periods.

8. Immigration affects the economic conditions of U.S. cities by
   a. taking jobs away from native minorities.
   b. increasing the national debt.
   c. decreasing the government tax base.
   *d. eventually providing benefits to the economy.

9. Colonialism occurs when
   a. groups of immigrants band together with a specific goal and move to a geographic region where they can accomplish the goal.
   *b. groups with different languages, cultures, and religions are forced together by outside powers.
   c. people from one nation decide to take over the political system of another nation.
   d. people establish themselves in one geographic region and begin expanding their boundaries as a result of growth and the need for more natural resources.

10. What is the greatest individual and societal challenge resulting from increasing diversity in the United States?
   a. convincing the government to provide more economic incentives for minority group members
   b. training people to better adapt to foreign business assignments
   c. helping people from other cultures get fair opportunities in jobs, housing, education, and the welfare system
   *d. looking beyond stereotypes and biases to apply what we know about intercultural communication

11. Ethical issues often become salient during intercultural encounters because
    a. in some cultures ethical principles are not as important as they are in others.
    *b. ethical principles are often culture-bound, and notions of what is ethical behavior vary across cultures.
    c. no ethical guidelines can be applied to intercultural interactions because they lead to transformations in individuals' value systems.
    d. individuals of different genders, races, ages, ethnic groups, languages, and cultural backgrounds cannot get along.

12. To effectively compete with other nations, U.S. companies have to
    a. impose their own business conventions on other countries.
    b. emphasize quick returns and short-term goals.
    *c. understand how business is conducted in other countries.
    d. encourage their overseas representatives to complete business deals very quickly.

13. The 1887 U.S. Congressional act, known as the Dawes Severalty Act,
    a. recognized Native Americans' right to self-government.
    b. established a special relationship between Native Americans and the U.S. government.
    c. supported Native Americans' rights to their land.
    *d. paved the way for Native Americans to be removed from their lands.

14. The anti-immigrant nativistic movements
    *a. promoted violence primarily against newly arrived and Asian immigrants.
    b. targeted immigrants of English descent only.
    c. were not supported by the government of the United States.
    d. discriminated against firmly established European immigrants.

15. By the 1930s, the concept of race changed, and many had concluded that
    a. economic and political opportunities should be reserved for native-born Americans.
    *b. only eastern and western Europeans were White and assimilable.
    c. all immigrants had equal opportunities.
    d. discrimination against immigrants based on skin color was illegal.

16. The melting pot metaphor
    a. reflects the cultural diversity of the United States.
    b. describes well the history of cultural groups in the United States.
    *c. was never very accurate because cultural groups retain their distinctiveness.
    d. refers to the process in which cultural groups remain distinct as well as contribute to a whole unified pattern.

17. Communication technology is an important issue in intercultural communication because
    *a. it enables us to come into contact with people who are very different from ourselves in ways we do not always understand.
    b. we are not always able to meet or see people with whom we communicate.
    c. it is not possible to develop cultural understandings with people over E-mail or other such high-tech communication devices.
    d. cultural differences disappear when we are able to communicate with people all over the world.

18. To what does the term *Anglocentrism* refer?
    a. a concern felt by immigrants when they came to the United States that they might lose their cultural identity if they interacted too often with Americans
    b. the modifications to the English language influenced by the languages of immigrants who came to the United States
    c. another label for the ethnocentrism of U.S. Americans
    *d. the desire of European immigrants, mainly British, to protect their culture and language

19. What is one difference between the way Japan and the United States do business with other countries that sometimes gives Japan an advantage?
    a. People generally like the personality of Japanese business executives better than U.S. executives.
    b. Japanese executives generally are more task-oriented and get their negotiations completed faster.
    *c. Japanese business personnel are willing to spend more time and effort studying the countries with which they do business.
    d. People in other countries feel that the bowing of the Japanese shows more respect than the handshakes of U.S. Americans.

20. The metaphor of U.S. cultural diversity that implies that it is desirable for cultural groups to retain their own unique identities and at the same time contribute to the whole is the
    a. melting pot metaphor.
    b. tapestry metaphor.
    c. tributary metaphor.
    *d. garden salad metaphor.

21. One problem with the melting pot metaphor is that it
    a. held true only for European immigrants during the early 1900s.
    b. applies only to African American immigrants.
    *c. was not possible for everyone to assimilate into the dominant U.S. culture.
    d. is too outdated to reflect the welcome experienced by recent immigrants in the United States.

22. One Japanese business practice that contributes to better productivity is the belief
    a. that individuals should receive recognition for individual contributions to the company.
    *b. in effort for its own sake.
    c. that each day may be one's last.
    d. that intergroup harmony takes priority over one's own challenges.

23. Which of the following describes the experience of African American immigrants?
    a. Many wanted to leave Africa because of the population explosion there.
    b. Despite what media have suggested, most arrived safely and in good health.
    c. Slavery happened so long ago that it has little influence on present relationships with White Americans.
    *d. Europe outlawed the slave trade before it was outlawed in the United States.

24. The myth of the classless society
    *a. reinforces middle- and upper-class beliefs in their own superiority.
    b. brings real hope to the lower class of a brighter future.
    c. resulted from the nativistic sentiments of early Europeans.
    d. was created by politicians who wanted the support of middle-class voters.

25. According to the Workforce 2000 study, which of the following changes will occur in the U.S. workforce population?
    *a. Women will represent 48% of the workforce.
    b. Ethnic minorities will decrease in the workforce.
    c. The mean age of workers will decrease.
    d. The United States will have to encourage more immigrants to come to fill lower paying jobs.

MATCHING QUESTIONS

For each of the following terms, select the letter that identifies its definition.

26. colonialism (b)

27. ethnocentrism (d)

28. nativistic (c)

29. Anglocentrism (a)

   a. using White cultural standards as the criteria for judging other people's behaviors and attitudes

   b. the system that forced people with different languages, cultures, religions, and identities to form one state

   c. a form of extreme patriotism to the pint of being anti-immigrant

   d. the tendency to elevate one's own cultural group above other people's cultural groups

TRUE/FALSE QUESTIONS

30. The removal of time and space barriers to forming relationships has increased the number of electronic relationships we have with others. (T)

31. Immigrants from Europe did not experience racial hostilities as they adapted to living in the United States. (F)

32. One reason the United States is an economic super power is that U.S. businesses invest a great deal of time and money in understanding the business practices of other countries. (F)

33. Studies suggest that residents in areas that receive large numbers of immigrants will suffer economically. (F)

34. In the study of intercultural communication, the influence of immigration histories has little significance for current intercultural communication interactions. (F)

35. When people see the differences between their culture and others', they usually gain a better understanding of their own cultural identity. (T)

36. The definition of who was White has changed through history. (T)

37. Ethics are universal principles of conduct guiding the behavior of individuals and groups in all cultures. (F)

38. Intercultural communication is really not more important today than it was in the past because we know more about other cultures now. (F)

40. An extreme universalistic perspective of ethics holds that any cultural behavior should be judged within the cultural context in which it occurs. (F)

41. "Microwave relationships" were short, heated conflicts between immigrant groups in the United States during the 1980s and 1990s. (F)

42. Most people in the United States live their lives in the same economic class into which they were born. (T)

ESSAY QUESTIONS

39. Describe how advances in electronic media have changed the ways we form intercultural relationships.

40. Explain how studying intercultural communication will better prepare you for the demographic changes described in the Workforce 2000 study.

41. Describe the paradox between the individualistic and group perspective of affirmative action.

42. What difference should intercultural communication make in our understanding of ethical issues?

43. Explain why self-reflexivity is an important step in ethical intercultural communication.

44. What are the potential benefits for business organizations that understand cultural differences?

45. What opportunities result from the increase in diversity in the United States?

CHAPTER 2

THE HISTORY OF THE STUDY OF INTERCULTURAL COMMUNICATION

MULTIPLE-CHOICE QUESTIONS

1. How did E. T. Hall contribute to the origins of intercultural communication?
   a. Hall developed technology that increased our ability to communicate with people in other cultures.
   b. Hall explored the relationship between a person's cultural identity and his or her communication.
   c. Hall helped describe the relationship between language and reality.
   *d. Hall identified and wrote about cultural differences in nonverbal communication.

2. Which of the following is true about the development of the intercultural communication area of study?
   *a. It originated with researchers looking for practical answers to help overseas workers.
   b. This area of study differs very little from the research done in the field of anthropology.
   c. It began as a result of people's displeasure over the foreign relations resulting in the Vietnam conflict.
   d. The primary focus of researchers was to develop theories that described intercultural communication processes.

3. Which approach to intercultural communication has the goal of initiating social change?
   a. social science
   b. interpretive
   *c. critical
   d. none of the above

4. Which of the following approaches to intercultural communication views reality as external to humans.
   *a. social science
   b. interpretive
   c. critical
   d. none of the above

5. Which methods are primarily used in the critical approach to intercultural communication?
   a. field studies and observations
   b. questionnaires and observations
   *c. text and media analyses
   d. interviews and experiments

6. Which of these statements is NOT true of the dialectical approach?
   a. Communication is viewed as both individual and social.
   b. The relationship between communication and culture is viewed as being interdependent.
   *c. Cultural reality is viewed as subjective and not objective.
   d. Communication is viewed as an arena where power struggles are played out.

7. Researchers using a critical perspective attempt to explain
   *a. how macrocontexts such as political structures influence communication.
   b. how specific cultural differences might predict communication conflicts.
   c. intercultural communication by providing in-depth descriptions of cultural patterns.
   d. variations in communication strategies used by people from different cultures.

8. One limitation of the social science approach is
   a. the potential to place too much focus on the historical and political contexts while ignoring the relationships between the people being studied.
   b. the lack of empirical measures for assessing communication strategies.
   *c. the possibility that the methods used are not culturally sensitive.
   d. a lack of attention to communication interactions between different cultural groups.

9. The goals for the social science approach are to
   a. understand and describe human behavior.
   b. understand human behavior and change it.
   c. predict and change human behavior.
   *d. describe and predict human behavior.

10. To establish translation equivalence, the researcher's materials should be
    a. translated word for word by a single translator.
    b. distributed to the participants of the research project in the original language.
    c. read by a native speaker.
    *d. translated several times using different sets of translators.

11. Which discipline contributed information about stereotypes and prejudice and how they influence our communication to the study of intercultural communication?
    a. anthropology
    *b. psychology
    c. linguistics
    d. political science

12. Which dialectic of intercultural communication addresses the fact that some of our cultural patterns are constant and some are shifting?
    a. history/past–present/future dialectic
    b. differences–similarities dialectic
    *c. static–dynamic dialectic
    d. privilege–disadvantage dialectic

13. Which of the following might explain why early intercultural researchers paid little attention to intercultural communication in domestic contexts?
    *a. Most of the researchers had international intercultural experience.
    b. They were disinterested in studying conflicts.
    c. Most felt that this research would involve a violation of personal ethics.
    d. There were few research instruments designed to use in domestic studies.

14. One of the contributions of anthropologists to the study of intercultural communication was
    a. information about how variables such as nationality, ethnicity, personality, and gender influence intercultural communication.
    b. information about how learning languages can contribute to intercultural communication.
    c. information about the importance of language in the study of intercultural communication.
    *d. an understanding of the importance of nonverbal behaviors in intercultural communication.

15. Worldviews are
    a. cultural views about relationships between cultures.
    b. political philosophies about the role of government in intercultural contexts.
    *c. assumptions about the nature of reality and human behavior.
    d. the meanings that emerge from the language symbols we use.

16. Gudykunst's studies of differences between individualist and collectivist cultures in how uncertainty is reduced during communication interactions is an example of
    a. critical research.
    b. interpretive research.
    c. macrocontext research.
    *d. social science research.

17. Which of the following is an example of emic research?
    *a. Researching the communication strategies people in India use to show respect.
    b. Researching differences in the management styles of Japanese and German managers.
    c. Researching which emotions are universally understood.
    d. Researching similarities in the child-rearing styles of Samoan and Tongan mothers.

18. Asante's notion of Afrocentricity is an example of the
    a. social science approach.
    *b. interpretive approach.
    c. functionalist approach.
    d. critical approach.

19. Researchers who assume that their research can help people resist forces of power and oppression represent the
    a. social science approach.
    b. interpretive approach.
    c. functionalist approach.
    *d. critical approach.

20. Nakayama's study of the film, *Showdown in Little Tokyo,* which showed how filmmakers favored the European American character over the Asian American character by giving him better camera shot sequences and making him more physically attractive, is an example of research from the
    a. social science approach.
    b. interpretive approach.
    c. functionalist approach.
    *d. critical approach.

21. If we attempted to study intercultural communication without considering the perspective of the critical approach we would miss
   a. understanding how specific cultural differences might predict communication outcomes.
   *b. the role of history in our present intercultural interactions.
   c. knowledge about specific behaviors in a culture that should be used to show respect.
   d. an understanding of how the cultural patterns of a specific culture reflect cultural values.

22. The challenge of using the dialectical approach to study intercultural communication is that it
   a. emphasizes the processual nature of intercultural communication.
   b. makes a simple process seem complex.
   *c. requires people to overcome dichotomous thinking.
   d. emphasizes the organizational aspects of intercultural communication.

MATCHING QUESTIONS

For each discipline below, select the letter that identifies its contribution to the study of intercultural communication.

23. anthropology (b)

24. psychology (a)

25. linguistics (c)

   a. information about stereotypes and prejudice and how they influence our communication

   b. a notion of the meaning of culture, its role in our lives, and its influence on the perspectives of researchers

   c. a conceptualization of the relationship between language and culture

   d. an understanding of how political and social forces influence our cultural identities

TRUE/FALSE QUESTIONS

26. Researchers from the interpretive perspective assume the existence of an external reality that can be described by researchers. (F)

27. Hall suggests that different cultural groups have different rules for personal space and that these affect intercultural communication. (T)

28. The example of researching Euro Disney by exploring what aspects of U.S. culture and history are being exported to represent the American experience illustrates an interpretive approach to intercultural communication. (F)

29. Carbaugh's observation and analysis of the communication rules for talking used by the guests and audience members of the *Donahue* show is an example of research from the social science perspective. (F)

30. Early intercultural communication research was dictated by the needs of middle-class U.S. professionals conducting business overseas. (T)

31. Experiences of U.S government and business personnel working overseas after World War II suggest that language training alone is a sufficient form of preparation for working in foreign countries. (F)

32. Social science, interpretivist, and critical perspectives are contradictory and cannot be connected in ways that help us better understand social reality. (F)

33. Social science research is aimed at the identification of emic behaviors. (F)

34. The dialectical perspective suggests that people are either privileged or disadvantaged depending on the culture to which they belong. (F)

35. The goal of researchers who study human behavior from the interpretive perspective is to explain and predict human behavior. (F)

36. It is possible for cultural members to be simultaneously privileged and disadvantaged. (T)

37. During the civil rights movement, the focus of early intercultural scholars quickly shifted to studying domestic intercultural communication. (F)

38. Researchers are able to prevent their own cultural biases from affecting their intercultural research. (F)

39. Worldviews have little influence on the approach researchers take to studying intercultural communication. (F)

40. One contribution of the anthropologists to the study of intercultural communication was an understanding of the role of culture in our lives. (T)

41. The Sapir-Whorf hypothesis suggests that cultures vary in the meaning they assign to nonverbal behaviors. (F)

42. Ethnography of communication is a quantitative method used to identify cultural patterns of oppression. (F)

43. Taking a dialectical approach to studying intercultural communication is more difficult than viewing intercultural communication from a single approach. (T)

ESSAY QUESTIONS

44. Describe the difference between etic and emic research perspectives.

45. How has the practical focus, from which the field of intercultural communication originated, influenced contemporary approaches to intercultural communication.

46. Choose one of the three approaches to intercultural communication and describe the limitations of this approach.

47. Create an argument advocating the dialectical approach to intercultural communication.

48. What is one of the challenges of using the dialectical approach to intercultural communication?

49. What are some of the contributions to the study of intercultural communication made by anthropologists?

50. Identify and explain two of the dialectics of intercultural communication.

CHAPTER 3

CULTURE, COMMUNICATION, CONTEXT, AND POWER

MULTIPLE-CHOICE QUESTIONS

1. Which of the following would be an example of high culture?
   a. music videos
   b. TV talk shows
   *c. the Nutcracker ballet
   d. fashion shows

2. Which statement describes an outcome of challenging the distinction between high and low culture?
   a. The quality of the education system dwindled as more low culture activities became popularized.
   b. The boundaries between national groups became less distinct as high cultures began to mix more with low cultures.
   c. More racial minorities were given job and education opportunities.
   *d. It spawned the current debates about what the required university curriculum should be.

3. Which is true of traditional definitions of culture in intercultural communication studies?
   *a. They focused on the nation-state or ethnic group level of culture.
   b. They were primarily influenced by definitions proposed by linguists and experts in the English language.
   c. They primarily influenced scholars interested in the critical approach to intercultural communication.
   d. They encouraged researchers to take a very broad focus of culture, observing culture as patterns of communication.

4. What is the limitation of using the cultural value framework?
   a. The relationship between cultural values and communication is complex to the degree that it is overwhelming.
   b. A lack of intercultural information is generated because the research is primarily focused on one cultural group.
   *c. Sometimes people assume that a particular group characteristic is the essential characteristic of a given person at all times and in all contexts.
   d. The political agenda of the researcher may prevent the researcher from observing other more salient cultural patterns.

5. When researchers study culture as performative, what are they examining?
   a. They are studying the way cultural values determine communicative styles and patterns.
   b. They are studying cultural patterns that emerge during specific communication events.
   *c. They are studying the way persons enact and represent their own worldviews.
   d. They are studying how individuals use their own space to resist a dominant society.

6. Which term refers to "those forces that attempt to change or retain existing social structures and relations"?
   a. social context
   b. historical context
   *c. political context
   d. relational context

7. Which of the descriptions below is NOT an accurate representation of the relationship between communication and culture?
   a. Culture influences communication.
   *b. Communication is enacted through culture.
   c. Communication is a way of contesting and resisting dominant culture.
   d. Communication transmits cultural information.

8. Which anthropologist(s) investigated and categorized over 150 definitions for culture from across various disciplines?
   a. Kluckhohn and Strodtbeck
   b. Hofstede
   *c. Kroeber and Kluckhohn
   d. E. T. Hall

9. One difference between the cultural studies approach to culture and the psychological and anthropological approaches to culture is that
   a. psychological and anthropological approaches focus on power relations whereas the cultural studies approach focuses on shared meanings.
   b. the cultural studies approach emphasizes cognitive aspects of culture whereas psychological and anthropological approaches focus on cultural struggles.
   *c. the cultural studies approach is interested in political aspects of culture whereas psychological and anthropological approaches are interested in more neutral aspects of culture.
   d. psychological and anthropological approaches focus on resistance whereas the cultural studies approach focuses on the meanings of social rituals.

10. In what way has cultural studies influenced the study of intercultural communication?
   *a. It has brought attention to the cultural groups that are trying to negotiate their identities in the United States.
   b. It has helped increase researchers awareness of how collectivist and individualist cultures differ in deeply held values.
   c. It has given researchers motivation to better understand how people acquire cultural knowledge.
   d. It has provided researchers with a framework for using communication to identify significant cultural patterns.

11. Symbolic significance can be defined as
    a. the characteristic of a cultural event that is enduring and international in its popularity.
    b. the type of category or talk used by cultural members to communicate ideas that they share.
    c. the quality of culturally shared values that makes them reflect what ought to be in a culture.
    *d. the meaning that most members of a cultural group attach to a communication activity.

12. Which value orientation is found in a culture where emphasis is placed on self-actualization in accomplishing tasks?
    *a. being
    b. growing
    c. masculinity
    d. femininity

13. A culture with less specific gender roles that values the quality of life for all has a
    a. low degree of collectivism.
    *b. low degree of masculinity.
    c. low degree of power distance.
    d. low degree of femininity.

14. Dominance, harmony, and subjectivity are all value orientations that correspond to which of the following cultural problems?
    a. What is the nature of human beings?
    *b. What is the relationship of humans to nature?
    c. What is the orientation of humans to time?
    d. What is the human orientation to activity?

15. A culture in which importance is placed on the family or work teams over the individual has a high degree of
    a. uncertainty avoidance.
    b. femininity.
    c. individualism.
    *d. collectivism.

16. Which time orientation is held by cultures that value living and realizing the potential of today?
    a. past orientation to time
    b. immutable orientation to time
    *c. present orientation to time
    d. mutable orientation to time

17. The uncertainty avoidance and power distance values were identified through the research of
    a. Kluckhohn and Strodtbeck.
    *b. Hofstede.
    c. Kroeber and Kluckhohn.
    d. Hymes.

18. Which of the following value orientations emerged from the Chinese research team?
    *a. long-term versus short-term orientation
    b. masculinity/femininity orientation
    c. preferred form of activity orientation
    d. uncertainty avoidance orientation

19. In Hymes' framework, the "key" is
    a. the setting of the communication event.
    b. the order of the event phases.
    *c. the tone of the conversation.
    d. the goal of the participants.

20. What level of group-related power would include educational background, marital status, and geographic location?
    a. primary
    b. dominant
    c. genre
    *d. secondary

21. Which group of researchers felt that the notion of culture should be reserved for patterns of symbolic action and meaning that are deeply felt, commonly intelligible, and widely accessible?
    a. psychologists
    b. anthropologists
    *c. ethnographers of communication
    d. cultural studies

22. Which of the following is true about power in communicative relationships?
    a. Empowered people tend to find more ways to creatively use power than disempowered people.
    b. In most communication interactions, people share equal power.
    c. Power is negotiated solely through conscious communication tactics and strategies.
    *d. Powerful communication systems will ultimately take over those who do not share them.

MATCHING QUESTIONS

For each intercultural communication approach below, select the letter that describes its approach to defining culture.

23. anthropology (d)

24. cultural studies (c)

25. ethnographers of communication (a)

    a. patterns of symbolic action and meaning that are deeply felt, commonly intelligible, and widely accessible

    b. the interactive aggregate of common characteristics that influence a human group's response to its environment

    c. culture is a contested site or zone where diverse groups struggle to negotiate their relationships, social positions, and well-being in society

    d. culture is learned, shared patterns of beliefs and behavior

TRUE/FALSE QUESTIONS

26. The relationship between communication and culture may be best described by saying that culture has tremendous influence on communication but that communication only moderately affects culture. (F)

27. In intercultural interactions, the status of the communicators has very little affect on their communication. (F)

28. Distinctions between high and low culture reflect prevalent Asian attitudes. (F)

29. For ethnographers of communication to suggest that observed patterns are "deeply felt," the patterns must be sensed collectively by members of the cultural group. (T)

30. The acceptance of multiple perspectives toward defining culture enables a researcher to more narrowly define what culture is. (F)

31. In cultural studies, low culture was renamed popular culture to emphasize that it was of little interest to academic disciplines. (F)

32. Culture primarily functions at a subconscious level. (T)

33. Cultural studies researchers define culture as the "interactive aggregate of common characteristics that influence a human group's response to its environment." (F)

34. Ballet and fine art are examples of pop culture. (F)

35. Cultures that are willing to accept what nature brings hold the value of harmony between humans and nature. (F)

36. People in the United States generally have a being orientation toward activity. (F)

37. Cultures that emphasize quick results in endeavors and social pressure to conform have a long-term orientation. (F)

38. Most people share equal power in communication interactions. (F)

ESSAY QUESTIONS

39. Explain the criteria that ethnographers of communication use to determine what significant cultural patterns are.

40. Describe the contributions by British cultural studies to the way we think about culture in intercultural communication studies.

41. Describe possible relationships between communication and culture.

42. How does one's definition of culture affect the study of intercultural communication?

43. How do cultural values influence intercultural communication?

44. How is understanding culture as a contested zone different from anthropological, psychological, and ethnographic definitions? How does it shift the focus of intercultural communication?

45. Discuss different ways of describing context and its relationship to communication. Use specific examples. What are the sources of power in the different contexts you describe?

46. Why is popular culture an important area of study?

CHAPTER 4

HISTORY

MULTIPLE-CHOICE QUESTIONS

1. What histories trace the development of particular ideas through various thinkers?
    a. political histories
    b. social histories
    *c. intellectual histories
    d. cultural histories

2. Which type of history is most likely to be passed down orally to each generation?
    a. social histories
    b. intellectual histories
    c. cultural histories
    *d. family histories

3. How have colonial histories influenced intercultural interactions?
    a. They have encouraged the unification of peoples and dissolved of national boundaries.
    b. They have promoted an equalization of economic and political powers.
    c. They have engendered positive feelings between national and ethnic cultural groups.
    *d. They have had a significant role in determining what languages we speak.

4. What point do the authors make about "hidden" histories when they recount the example of the suppression of atrocities to homosexuals in Nazi Germany and the attempt by the state of Montana to force gays and lesbians to register with the police?
    a. Histories are never isolated but crisscross and situate various cultural groups in differential positions.
    *b. If we do not know the history of the past, we will miss the significance of historical lessons.
    c. History helps us understand how others have negotiated cultural attitudes of the past that have relevance for the present.
    d. One's identity is difficult to define without understanding the history of one's cultural or social group in relationship to contemporary groups.

5. Which label describes the situation of people who, due to various reasons, are linked to more than one nation?
    a. multicultural
    b. ascribed
    *c. diaspora
    d. postcolonial

6. Which of the following conditions must be present for contact between individuals from different cultural backgrounds to lead to positive attitudes?
   *a. There should be institutional support.
   b. The interactions should be casual.
   c. The contact should be involuntary.
   d. The individuation of members should be repressed.

7. The forced removal of the Cherokees from New Echota on what is called the "Trail of Tears" to Springfield, Illinois and then to Oklahoma is an example of
   a. national histories.
   b. family histories.
   *c. cultural group histories.
   d. social histories.

8. National histories are important to members of particular nations because they
   a. are discussed in textbooks.
   b. give an objective view of history.
   c. discuss social situations of different groups in the nation.
   *d. give them a shared notion of who they are.

9. It is important to understand the role of power in construction of historical accounts because
   a. grand narratives are viewed as the most credible types of historical accounts.
   *b. material and political positions affect individuals' abilities to record history.
   c. we use histories as stories to make sense of who we are.
   d. knowledge of history increases prejudice at the interpersonal level.

10. Strong normative and institutional support for contact
    a. does not decrease prejudice because individuals do not like to feel forced to interact.
    *b. may decrease prejudice because it creates incentives and encouragement.
    c. may decrease prejudice only when members of minorities are in high status positions.
    d. is not one of the elements that reduces prejudice.

11. A diversity program would *not* be effective in reducing prejudice if it
    a. minimized competition and maximized cooperation.
    b. offered institutional and normative support for interaction.
    c. equalized numbers of group members.
    *d. emphasized differences and promoted competition between groups.

12. Rewriting traditional histories to include hidden histories
    a. is not an academic discipline.
    *b. empowers different cultural identities.
    c. introduces chaos to historical accounts.
    d. strengthens grand narratives.

13. Allport and Amir suggest that prejudice might be reduced if members of groups coming into contact are of equal status because
    a. members of the majority should help members of the minority.
    *b. inequalities in material positions contribute to stereotyping.
    c. contact should extend beyond the immediate situation.
    d. it reduces the influence of history on intercultural interactions.

14. Why did Marsha Houston say she did not want the White people who wanted to be her friends to say "I don't notice you're Black" or "I know how you feel."
    a. She felt these comments were condescending.
    b. She felt that White people did not understand her well enough to become friends.
    c. She felt that these comments showed an ignorance of her hidden history.
    *d. She felt that these comments rejected a part of her identity.

15. Even when people do not feel they fit their national narratives, they need to know them
    a. to achieve success in the nation's academic institutions.
    b. to understand how colonialism affects the present political processes.
    c. to more effectively negotiate power in their intercultural interactions.
    *d. to understand references used in communication.

16. A modernist identity is
    a. based on the notion of the "grand narrative."
    b. attributed to people because of their perceived group memberships.
    *c. grounded in the Western tradition of scientific and political beliefs and assumptions.
    d. grounded in the notions that one racial group has superior attributes and traits over others due to evolutionary superiority.

17. One reason it has been difficult to rewrite women's histories is that
    *a. there were restrictions against women's access to public records.
    b. people are concerned that this will exacerbate gender differences.
    c. so few women were interested in writing down their histories.
    d. women in general are interested in using other strategies to gain equality.

18. An example of a history that cannot be suppressed because of its marks on a person's identity is
    a. national history.
    b. intellectual history.
    c. colonial history.
    *d. racial history.

19. Which of the following is true for socioeconomic class histories?
    *a. They are frequently forgotten in explaining U.S. immigration patterns.
    b. They had little effect on immigration histories.
    c. They are the most understood histories in the United States.
    d. They have had the least effect of all histories on intercultural relationships in the United States.

20. The contact hypothesis suggests that
    a. histories of groups that came into contact during colonialism revolve around negotiations over the choice of which language should become dominant.
    *b. better communication between groups is facilitated by simply putting them together in the same place and allowing them to interact.
    c. through diasporic migrations every racial and ethnic group has become interwoven genetically and culturally.
    d. the interactions of cultural groups can be improved by taking careful steps to communicate about the influence of past histories prior to the interaction.

21. What is the first step toward negotiating histories dialectically in our interactions?
    a. acknowledging our position in society as a result of our histories
    b. understanding the role histories play in the identities we bring into our interactions
    *c. recognizing that we have both known and hidden histories
    d. recognizing how the past–present and disadvantaged–privilege dialectics operate together

MATCHING QUESTIONS

For each of the following scholars, select a letter matching their contribution to the study of history.

22. Gordon Allport (d)

23. Mei Nakano (c)

24. Walter Fisher (b)

25. Jean-Francois Lyotard (a)

    a. The grand narrative has lost its credibility.

    b. Telling stories is fundamental to our experience.

    c. Gender histories call for reevaluation of assumptions and principles that govern history.

    d. Contact between members of different cultures will reduce prejudice only under some conditions.

    e. The imposition of language is an example of cultural invasion.

TRUE/FALSE QUESTIONS

26. All people and cultural groups have equal opportunity to record their histories. (F)

27. One of the best ways to reduce prejudice among members of cultural groups is to get them together for a casual meeting where they can just talk out their feelings. (F)

28. History is a collection of unbiased narratives of events. (F)

29. According to Blanchot, people are responsible for history prior to their birth. (T)

30. Contact is likely to reduce prejudice if there are an equal number of each group present when they meet together. (T)

31. In the context of history, groups have either emerged as victims or victimizers but not both. (F)

32. Once solved, racism is a problem that will not reoccur in the United States. (F)

33. People can negotiate history during interpersonal interactions. (T)

34. During World War II, both German and Japanese Americans were placed in internment camps. (F)

35. History is a series of events occurring along a singular time continuum. (F)

36. Postcolonialism is a position that calls for the independence of colonialized states. (T)

37. Diasporic histories are histories that have been hidden because one group prevented another from recording them. (F)

38. If we ignore history in our interactions, it will have less effect on how we interrelate with others. (F)

ESSAY QUESTIONS

39. Why is it important for someone studying the language of a country to also know the history of the country?

40. Describe some reasons histories become "hidden."

41. Why have cultural movements begun to rewrite and restore histories that have been "hidden"?

42. What antecedents do we bring into contact situations with other groups?

43. Why should we use the term *histories* rather than *history* in the study of intercultural communication?

44. What view of social reality do political and intellectual histories encourage?

45. What role does power play in constructing historical accounts? Give some examples.

46. Why is it important to understand history to understand intercultural communication?

47. What are some of the reasons contributing to hidden gender histories?

CHAPTER 5

IDENTITY

MULTIPLE-CHOICE QUESTIONS

1. Which of the following is a characteristic of identity from the communication perspective?
   a. Identity development is culture-bound.
   b. Identity is self-created through crises.
   *c. Identities are emergent.
   d. Identity formation is contextual.

2. The process by which others attribute identities to an individual is
   a. interpellation.
   b. avowal.
   c. normative.
   *d. ascription.

3. Which of the following is a characteristic of identity from the critical perspective?
   *a. Identity formation is contextual.
   b. Identities are emergent.
   c. We have multiple identities.
   d. Identities are ascribed.

4. Which of the following describes how competent intercultural communicators negotiate identities in conversation?
   a. They recognize the identity of the other most like their own.
   *b. They affirm the identity of the other that is most salient in a conversation.
   c. They understand that the identity they portray is the one their partners ascribe to them.
   d. They ignore the salience of noncultural identities so that conflicts are limited to differences in cultural identities rather than gender, age, and so forth.

5. What is a core symbol?
   a. deeply felt zero-order beliefs of what ought to be
   b. symbols/terms we use to refer to particular aspects of our own and another's identity
   *c. an expression of fundamental beliefs/central concepts that define a particular identity
   d. behaviors that are associated with particular identities in specific cultural contexts

6. Which is true concerning the influence of culture on the formation of our identities?
   a. Culture has little effect on how we perceive age and age differences.
   b. Cultures are similar in the emphasis they place on the development of self-identity.
   *c. Cultures are but one influence on a person's self-identity.
   d. Cultures have very little impact on people's notions about gender.

7. How does the concept of racial formation inform our understanding of racial identity?
   a. It suggests that race is a simple concept.
   b. It suggests that identities are fixed and concrete.
   c. It suggests that racial identities are objective.
   *d. It suggests that race has complex social meanings.

8. Which stage in minority identity development is characterized by a blanket endorsement of one's group, values, and attitudes and the rejection of dominant group values and norms?
   a. integration
   b. unexamined identity
   *c. resistance and separatism
   d. conformity

9. In which stage of majority identity development do people begin to blame their own dominant group instead of the minority members as the source of racial problems?
   a. redefinition
   b. unexamined identity
   c. acceptance
   *d. resistance

10. Which of the following does NOT describe a characteristic of whiteness in the United States?
    a. White people may have cultural practices in which only they engage.
    *b. Privilege and White are synonymous.
    c. Some feel that being White is a liability.
    d. Many Whites believe equality has been achieved between Blacks and Whites on the issues that motivated the civil rights movement.

11. Which of the following describe multiracial people?
    a. They represent the majority of the people in the United States.
    b. They develop a clearer sense of their identities because they are more open-minded.
    *c. They may receive criticism from both cultures as they negotiate their identities.
    d. Their identities eventually become defined by their sense of belonging to one or the other race.

12. Intercultural communication competence as described by Collier and Thomas refers to
    *a. communication that affirms the identity that is most salient in any conversation.
    b. the knowledge communicators have about each other's cultural background.
    c. the complexity of topics communicators discuss during an interaction.
    d. the ability of communicators to present different identities to others in an inoffensive way.

13. Encapsulated marginals are persons who
    a. have identities ascribed to them by others.
    *b. feel disintegrated between shifting cultures.
    c. see themselves as choice makers.
    d. are able to make commitments within the relativistic framework.

14. The notions of masculinity and femininity
    a. are universal for every culture across time.
    *b. are not just based on biological differences.
    c. have not changed through the ages.
    d. have well-established and understood meanings.

15. Critical perspectives insist on the dynamic nature of identities because
    a. identities are culture bound and expressed in many core symbols and norms.
    b. identity develops in relation to group membership.
    c. identities are constructed through hard to account for crises.
    *d. identities are shaped by social forces that are constantly fluctuating.

16. Which of the following is true for religious identity?
    *a. People vary in the importance they place on their religious identity.
    b. A person's religious identity is generally very easy to recognize.
    c. Due to a decrease of interest in religion, religious identity has little influence on intercultural communication.
    d. Everyday interactions are more influenced by religious identity than age and gender identities.

17. Which of the following statements represents how class identity is generally understood in the United States?
    a. Race and class identities are synonymous today in the United States.
    b. Most people readily acknowledge that there are class divisions in the United States.
    *c. People in the United States can generally move up in class standing if they work hard enough.
    d. Members of the middle class tend to think about and recognize class differences more readily than do members of the working class.

18. People who demonstrate passive resistance in their majority development
    a. feel embarrassed about how their group has contributed to racial problems.
    *b. show little behavioral change as they recognize their group's contribution to racial problems.
    c. integrate their whiteness into all other facets of their identity and appreciate other groups.
    d. begin to refocus their energy on redefining whiteness in nonracist terms.

19. Multicultural people experience stress because
    a. there are so many demands on them for serving as cultural brokers.
    b. the number of times they move leaves them feeling a strong sense of instability.
    c. they feel responsible for developing a relativistic framework.
    *d. they may suffer the loss of their own authenticity.

MATCHING QUESTIONS

For each perspective, select the letter that describes its approach to the study of identity.

20. communication perspective (d)

21. social psychological perspective (c)

22. critical perspective (a)

a. Identities are formed within contexts of history, economics, politics, and discourse.

b. Identities are formed in relation to the perception individuals have of their physical and psychological selves.

c. Identity is partly created by the self and in relation to group membership.

d. Identities are not created by the self alone but are co-created through communication with others.

Select the letter that provides the best definition for each of these concepts.

23. prejudice (d)

24. stereotyping (b)

25. discrimination (a)

a. overt actions to exclude, avoid, or distance

b. widely held beliefs about a specific group of people

c. the process of organizing people into groups

d. a negative attitude toward a cultural group

TRUE/FALSE QUESTIONS

26. Bounded identities include religion, gender, and ethnicity. (F)

27. During the course of your experiences, you develop a single identity that influences your presentation of self and expectations for others' behaviors toward you. (F)

28. Members of minority groups tend to formulate a sense of identity earlier than majority group members. (T)

29. Gender is the same as the biological sex of an individual. (F)

30. Some of the identities ascribed to us are socially and politically determined. (T)

31. The emphasis on the development of a strong sense of self-identity (independence and autonomy) is a shared value in all cultures. (F)

32. Slang is frequently used to create ingroups within generations. (T)

33. We fully develop our identities in early childhood. (F)

34. In different contexts, one of our multiple identities will be highlighted. (T)

35. Most scholars today view the concept of race as describing biological differences between people. (F)

36. Gender identification usually occurs when a child is 7 to 9 years old. (F)

37. Global nomads are children who grow up in many different cultural contexts. (T)

38. Constructive marginals have difficulty making decisions. (F)

ESSAY QUESTIONS

39. Describe potential communication outcomes when a person's avowed and ascribed identities conflict.

40. How is the formation of our identities influenced by social and political forces?

41. Describe distinctions between one's racial and ethnic identities.

42. Identify arguments against using a physiological basis for determining a person's racial identity.

43. Describe the dimensions included as part of our identities.

44. Explain how different kinds of contexts affect identity formation.

45. Explain why it is often difficult for European Americans to define whiteness as a cultural position.

46. Explain why people in different social positions have different views of social reality.

CHAPTER 6

LANGUAGE AND INTERCULTURAL COMMUNICATION

MULTIPLE-CHOICE QUESTIONS

1. Which component of language is concerned with the way meaning is constructed in relation to the receivers and context?
   a. syntactics
   b. phonetics
   *c. pragmatics
   d. semantics

2. Which component of language is concerned with cultural variations in sounds, such as the difference between the French and English "r"?
   a. semantics
   b. pragmatics
   c. syntactics
   *d. phonetics

3. Which of the following terms denote Osgood's universal dimension of meaning for the strong or weak reactions we have to words?
   *a. potency
   b. evaluation
   c. activity
   d. instrumental

4. Which is true about instrumental/affective communication styles?
   a. They are closely related to personal/contextual communication styles.
   b. The affective communication style is more goal-oriented than the instrumental style.
   *c. The affective communication style is more receiver-oriented than the instrumental style.
   d. The instrumental/affective communication style contributes little to cultural stereotypes.

5. Which of the Gudykunst and Ting-Toomey communication style dimensions refers to the emphasis placed on the self versus the speaker's role?
   a. instrumental/affective
   b. direct/indirect
   *c. personal/contextual
   d. elaborate/exact/succinct

6. Which communication style is more receiver-oriented and process-oriented?
   a. contextual
   b. instrumental
   *c. affective
   d. elaborate

7. Which communication style, frequently used by the Amish, values understatement, simple assertions, and silence?
   *a. succinct
   b. exact
   c. direct
   d. instrumental

8. Which statement best describes labels?
   a. The use of labels is a habitual but unnecessary practice in our communication.
   *b. The message of a label varies by the social position of the speaker.
   c. It is not the label but the sound of the label that is offensive to some people.
   d. People in less powerful groups tend to possess less powerful labels.

9. The term *discourse* refers to
   a. the entire system of language.
   b. the study of structure or grammar of a language.
   *c. the way language is used by particular communities.
   d. the study of universal dimensions of meaning.

10. The personal/contextual dimension of variations in language use refers to
    a. the extent to which the speakers reveal their intentions through explicit verbal communication.
    b. the quality of talk that is valued by persons involved in interactions.
    *c. the emphasis placed on the speaker as individual or the speaker as role.
    d. sender- and goal-oriented communication style.

11. The qualified relativist position suggests that
    *a. language is a tool rather than a mirror of perception.
    b. language shapes our experience.
    c. language does not shape our perceptions.
    d. language forms a mirror of perception.

12. The studies of language acquisition in children
    a. support a strong relativist position.
    *b. lend some support to the nominalist position.
    c. provide strong support for a qualified relativist position.
    d. lend a little support to the Sapir-Whorf hypothesis.

13. Tonal coloring in a message
    a. communicates respect through the use of honorifics.
    b. provides information about the context of the message to the speaker.
    *c. tells others how they should respond to the message based on their relationship with us.
    d. indicates the degree of responsibility the listener has to determine the meaning of the message.

14. Which orientation has a co-cultural group adopted when they begin emphasizing commonalities, developing positive face, and censoring self?
    a. assertive accommodation
    b. assertive assimilation
    c. aggressive separation
    *d. nonassertive assimilation

15. Which orientation has a co-cultural group adopted when they begin communicating self, intragroup networking, using liaisons, and educating others.
    a. aggressive assimilation
    b. aggressive separation
    *c. assertive accommodation
    d. nonassertive assimilation

16. Myths refer to
    a. the information that contextualizes how listeners should interpret verbal messages.
    *b. the multiple layers of meaning possessed by some signifiers.
    c. the arbitrary words or symbols we use to refer to something.
    d. the ways different discursive units create meaning.

17. Which of the following is true concerning translation?
    a. There are two types of translation, simultaneous and consecutive.
    b. Accuracy of translation is more important than equivalency.
    c. Translators are generally "invisible" in intercultural communication interactions.
    *d. Good translators need more than a high level of language fluency.

MATCHING QUESTIONS

For each of the terms below, select the letter identifying its definition.

18. source text (c)

19. consecutive interpretation (a)

20. target text (b)

21. simultaneous interpretation (d)

 a. an interpretation done during the original speaker's breaks

 b. a text that results from a translation effort

 c. an original language text

 d. an interpretation done at the same time that the original speaker is speaking

For each component of language below, select the letter that identifies its definition.

22. semantics (c)

23. syntactics (a)

24. pragmatics (d)

25. phonetics (b)

 a. the study of the rules for combining words into meaningful sentences

 b. the study of how words are pronounced, which sounds have meaning, and which are universal

 c. the study of how words communicate our intended meanings in communication

 d. the study of the way meaning is constructed in relation to receivers and contexts

TRUE/FALSE QUESTIONS

26. The critical approach to intercultural communication has generally focused on the contextual uses of linguistic codes. (F)

27. There are universal dimensions of meaning. (T)

28. Osgood's research suggests that everyone can characterize whether a word is "fast" or "slow" regardless of what language they speak. (T)

29. Studies of cross-cultural differences in language suggest that people cannot perceive concepts when they have no word in their language to identify them. (F)

30. People in all cultures place the burden for intuiting the meaning from what is said on the receiver. (F)

31. The terms we use to refer to other cultural groups have little influence on the way we perceive and feel about them. (F)

32. One of the advantages of becoming bilingual is to escape the prison of your own language. (T)

33. High levels of fluency in two languages ensure good interpretation skills. (F)

34. The indirect communication style is related to the instrumental communication style. (F)

35. *La langua* refers to language in use or how language is actively used by particular speech communities. (F)

36. The activity dimension refers to the amount of energy a word evokes. (T)

37. People with a low-context communication style depend on the verbal code for the meaning of a message. (T)

38. A language policy determines what syntax rules will apply to a specific language during a specific period of time. (F)

ESSAY QUESTIONS

39. Describe the characteristics you would want in an interpreter if you had to choose one to help you negotiate a business deal in a country where you did not speak the language.

40. How does our social status affect our choice and use of labels?

41. What should the goals of an interpreter/translator be with regard to equivalency?

42. Why is it important for us to understand interpretation/translation issues in intercultural communication?

43. Describe some of the principal ways communication styles vary across cultures.

44. Discuss the qualified relativist position in terms of the relationship of language and perception.

45. Discuss why it is important to situate discourse within social structure to understand intercultural communication.

46. Describe how language use affects identity of and relations between speakers and receivers.

CHAPTER 7

NONVERBAL CODES
AND CULTURAL SPACE

MULTIPLE-CHOICE QUESTIONS

1. How does nonverbal communication differ from verbal communication?
   a. People have more control over their nonverbal than their verbal behavior.
   b. We tend to think about our nonverbal behaviors more than about our use of language.
   *c. We learn nonverbal behaviors implicitly.
   d. Nonverbal behavior always complements verbal behavior.

2. Which of the following is NOT typically communicated by nonverbal behaviors?
   a. status
   b. relational messages
   c. deception
   *d. content information

3. Which of the following is true about nonverbal behavior?
   *a. We are rarely conscious of our nonverbal communication behaviors.
   b. The lower a person's status, the more likely the person is to use large, expansive gestures.
   c. There are no nonverbal behaviors that consistently reveal deception.
   d. There is little cultural variation in how nonverbal communication is used.

4. According to Basso's observations of the Western Apache, which of the following is a context in which silence is likely to be used?
   a. to show enthusiasm and excitement
   *b. during courtship
   c. when making tribal decisions
   d. while people are busy accomplishing their tribal tasks

5. What label refers to the way people conceptualize and think about time?
   a. proxemics
   b. semiotics
   *c. chronemics
   d. paralanguage

6. Recent research findings suggest that
   a. all nonverbal behavior is learned, not innate.
   b. blind children use different facial expressions to reveal their emotions than seeing children.
   *c. chimpanzees and humans are similar in some of their facial expressions.
   d. the facial expressions used for all emotions are recognizable by most cultural groups.

7. Which of the following statements is true?
    *a. The gestures used in the United States may have different meanings in other cultures.
    b. There are really no facial expressions that are universally understood.
    c. Cultures with a polychronic orientation to time view time as a commodity.
    d. Eye contact varies only by context, not by culture.

8. Which of the following is generally true for nonverbal communication in the United States?
    a. People in the United States tend to stand closer to each other than Arabs do while talking.
    b. The United States is a higher contact culture than most of the cultures in South America.
    *c. Most people feel it is important to maintain eye contact during communication.
    d. Time is generally viewed as more holistic or circular.

9. Which of the following is true about cultural spaces?
    a. The influence they have on our identities is static.
    *b. We negotiate relationships to the cultural meanings attached to particular spaces we inhabit.
    c. Generally, cultural spaces are designated by physical markers.
    d. Cultural spaces can be accepted or rejected, they are never forced on us.

10. Which of the following describes the influence of cultural space on our identities?
    a. When we travel, we experience new cultural spaces, but they have little influence on us.
    *b. Sometimes people are forced to change to adapt to new cultural spaces.
    c. Once we leave a cultural space, the meaning that space has for our identity becomes static.
    d. The cultural space we presently inhabit is the one that has the most influence on our identity.

11. Which of the following underscores one of the differences between modernist and postmodern cultural spaces?
    *a. A postmodern cultural space exists as long as it is needed in its present form.
    b. The borders of postmodern cultural spaces are closely guarded.
    c. Postmodern cultural spaces are closely tied to a physical location.
    d. Postmodern cultural spaces give rise to fixed notions of ethnic identity.

12. The creation of ethnic/racial neighborhoods was influenced by all of the following *except*
    a. nonverbal codes.
    *b. cultural laws.
    c. economics.
    d. racist discourses.

13. Which orientation to time prevails in the United States?
    a. polychronic
    b. semiotic
    *c. monochronic
    d. subjective

14. Which of the following is true about cultural variations in nonverbal communication?
    a. Most nonverbal communication is universal.
    *b. Although some behaviors are similar, rules differ.
    c. Similar behaviors are governed by the same rule.
    d. Similar behaviors are evoked by the same stimuli.

15. All of the following are true about cultural spaces *except* that
    a. they are framed by cultural discourses.
    b. they overlap with other spaces.
    *c. they are fixed in time and space.
    d. they change as new people move in.

16. Which of the following nonverbal behaviors appears to be consistently indicative of deception?
    *a. higher pitch
    b. sweating
    c. blushing
    d. slight skin tremors

17. What is the difference between primate and human facial expression?
    a. Primates have a greater number of facial expressions because they have more facial muscles.
    *b. Primates have less complex facial expressions.
    c. Primates appear to have more facial blends.
    d. Primates express more intense emotions.

18. Which of the following is NOT a universal facial expression.
    a. disgust
    b. sadness
    *c. frustration
    d. surprise

19. In a noncontact culture people
    *a. speak in softer voices when they communicate.
    b. engage in more direct eye contact during communication.
    c. touch more frequently during communication interaction.
    d. have more face-to-face body orientation during communication.

20. How does the home as a cultural space affect our intercultural communication?
    a. Home is the physical location people return to when they have cultural difficulties.
    b. Home is the place where our cultures least affect our communication patterns.
    c. Home is the cultural space that has the least effect on intercultural communication.
    *d. Home is the place where we form a large portion of our cultural and self-identities.

21. When researchers examine how meaning is created in advertisements, clothing, and other cultural practices, they are studying
    a. chronemics.
    b. proxemics.
    c. regionalism.
    *d. semiotics.

22. When people are loyal to a particular demographic area that holds significant cultural meaning, they are
    a. building postmodern cultural spaces.
    b. studying nonverbal semiotics.
    *c. expressing regionalism.
    d. utilizing a cultural space.

MATCHING QUESTIONS

For each concept below, select the letter that identifies its definition.

23. chronemics (c)

24. proxemics (b)

25. polychronic (a)

  a. A holistic and circular view of time in which many events can happen at once.

  b. The study of how people use personal space in communicative interaction.

  c. The study of time and the rules that groups have to govern its use.

  d. A linear view of time that treats time as a commodity and emphasizes punctuality.

TRUE/FALSE QUESTIONS

26. Prejudice is often based on nonverbal behaviors. (T)

27. Cultures with a polychronic orientation to time prefer to do things one at a time, and time is regulated in small precise units. (F)

28. One of the main challenges facing intercultural communication researchers who study nonverbal communication is the need for more theoretical support to explain cross-cultural differences. (T)

29. Low-contact societies are cultures in which people tend to stand farther apart while communicating and speak in softer voices. (T)

30. Most studies suggest that national culture is the most important factor determining personal space decisions. (F)

31. One general cultural rule is the use of active uncertainty reduction strategies in initial interactions. (F)

32. The areas in which we live have little influence on our identities. (F)

33. When nonverbal behavior contradicts a verbal message, people tend to believe the verbal message more because it happens at a more conscious level. (F)

34. The term *cultural space* refers to a physical location from which an individual speaks. (F)

35. San Francisco's Chinatown is an example of a postmodern cultural space. (F)

36. Blind children's facial expressions are very different from seeing children's facial expressions. (F)

37. Surprise is thought to be a universal facial expression. (T)

38. Age and gender do not influence the way we use our personal space. (F)

ESSAY QUESTIONS

39. Explain the potential intercultural challenges there might be for a person with a polychronic orientation to time and a person with a monochronic orientation to time.

40. Discuss why cultural variations in nonverbal communication might be more difficult to identify than verbal differences.

41. What are some similarities across cultures in nonverbal communication?

42. How does power influence the relationship between the cultural spaces and our identities?

43. Describe the differences between the modernist perspective and the postmodern perspective of cultural space.

44. How does semiotics help intercultural communication scholars understand cross-cultural variations in nonverbal systems?

45. What factors influence how we negotiate our cultural spaces?

46. What factors introduce change into cultural spaces?

47. How does your home influence your intercultural communication?

CHAPTER 8

UNDERSTANDING
INTERCULTURAL TRANSITIONS

MULTIPLE-CHOICE QUESTIONS

1. What type of migrants are people who leave their countries to come to the United States because they want to be close to relatives who have already come?
   a. sojourners
   b. domestic refugees
   *c. immigrants
   d. long-term refugees

2. Which of the following represents a group of domestic refugees?
   a. international students who have come to attend U.S. universities
   b. Vietnamese who relocated to Australia after the Vietnam conflict
   c. a family from Iran who come to the United States because they want their children to have Western educations
   *d. German Jews who were sent to prison camps during World War II

3. What two primary characteristics distinguish different migrant groups?
   a. language and status differences
   *b. length of migration and motivation for migration
   c. gender and status differences
   d. goals for sojourn and ability to adapt

4. The W-curve suggests that
   a. cultural adjustment is a long-term process of ups and downs.
   *b. people may experience cultural adjustment upon returning home.
   c. sojourners experience excitement, shock, and then adaptation to "host" cultures.
   d. cultural adjustment is a growth process.

5. Which of the following is true for culture shock?
   a. Every sojourner will experience culture shock.
   b. There are no benefits to experiencing culture shock.
   *c. Culture shock can result in an identity crisis.
   d. Older people may experience less severe culture shock than younger people.

6. What two types of uncertainty do migrants experience when they begin interacting in the "host" culture?
   a. voluntary and forced uncertainty
   b. long-term and short-term uncertainty
   *c. predictive and explanatory uncertainty
   d. psychological and functional uncertainty

7. Which model has traditionally been the most commonly used to describe cultural adaptation?
   a. anxiety/uncertainty management model
   b. transition model
   c. communication-system model
   *d. U-curve model

8. Which of the following is true about how individual characteristics affect the adaptation process?
   a. Older people adapt better than younger people because they have a broad range of life experiences on which to draw.
   b. Class issues do not appear to affect the adaptation process.
   *c. The amount of preparation one makes before a sojourn may determine how well one adjusts.
   d. The power of positive thought is important for sojourner adaptation; people with highly positive expectations adjust better than those with negative ones.

9. Which of the adaptation dimensions occurs the most quickly?
   *a. psychological health
   b. functional fitness
   c. intercultural identity
   d. assimilation

10. What are two fundamental differences between the first and second U-curve of adaptation?
    a. predictive and explanatory uncertainty
    b. functional fitness and psychological health
    *c. personal change and expectations
    d. assimilation and separation

11. According to the transitional model of adaptation,
    a. individuals experience excitement, culture shock, and adaptation.
    b. adaptation is a process of stress, adaptation, and growth.
    c. adaptation occurs through uncertainty reduction.
    *d. adaptation involves loss and change.

12. Which statement explains why communication is described as having a double edge in the communication-system model?
    a. People who are not competent communicators receive more negative feedback, which aids in their adjustment.
    b. Interpersonal communication helps people with cultural adaptation, whereas mass communication makes their adjustment more difficult.
    *c. Those who communicate frequently adapt better but have more culture shock.
    d. Popular culture may contribute to better cultural adjustment, but at the same time it may segregate migrants from interacting with members of the dominant culture.

13. A multicultural identity can be defined as
    *a. an identity built on the sense of in-betweenness that develops as a result of frequent or multiple cultural border crossings.
    b. an identity that is grounded in the Western tradition of scientific and political beliefs and assumptions.
    c. an identity based on two or more cultural frames of reference.
    d. an identity that has a number of competing dialects that are the result of different cultural influences.

14. Which of the following is true for reentry adaptation?
    a. One of the best things about returning home is that the primary changes are political and cultural, not personal.
    *b. One of the challenges of reentry adaptation is that people do not expect to have difficulties.
    c. The reentry adaptation process is completely different from the cultural adaptation process.
    d. It is easier to go through reentry adaptation because people are already familiar with the norms and attitudes of their home cultures.

15. Transnationalism refers to
    a. the process of adapting to multiple cultural influences simultaneously.
    b. a sense of loyalty to multiple nation-states.
    c. the attitude that one's national culture has an interdependent relationship with other national cultures.
    *d. the activity of migrating across the borders of one or more nation-states.

16. Functional fitness refers to
    a. the emotional well-being of a migrant.
    *b. the ability to accomplish daily life tasks in different contexts.
    c. the physical well-being of a migrant.
    d. the ability to accomplish a variety of relational behaviors in socially appropriate ways.

17. Which of the following information is addressed in the communication-system model?
    a. Ambiguity is the primary characteristic of relationships in intercultural adaptation.
    b. Migrants go through at least three predictable phases of adaptation.
    *c. Adaptation occurs through communication and is preceded by stress.
    d. All transition experiences involve adapting to situations that involve loss and change.

MATCHING QUESTIONS

For each approach to cultural identity listed below, select the letter that best describes/defines the approach.

18. marginalization (b)

19. assimilation (a)

20. separation (d)

21. integration (c)

 a. The migrants give up aspects of their own cultures to establish relationships with members of the "host" culture.

 b. Migrants have little interest in maintaining their original culture and little interest in daily interactions with members of other cultures.

 c. Migrants show interest in maintaining their original culture and in daily interactions with members of other cultures.

 d. Migrants have interest in maintaining interactions with members of their own cultural group but little interest in interactions with members of other cultural groups.

For each cultural adaptation model listed below, select the letter that best explains the model.

22. transition model (b)

23. U-curve model (a)

24. communication-system model (d)

25. anxiety/uncertainty management model (c)

   a. Migrants first experience excitement, then shock/disorientation, and finally adjust to the "host" culture.

   b. The cultural adaptation process is similar to other adjustments in that one must find an effective strategy to adapt to the losses and changes experienced.

   c. To adapt, migrants must reduce ambiguity by seeking information that will help them predict people's behavior.

   d. Adaptation is a process of stress caused by cultural differences, adaptation, and growth.

TRUE/FALSE QUESTIONS

26. Reentry shock is usually less severe than culture shock because the sojourner knows what to expect his/her home culture to be like. (F)

27. The flight approach to cultural adaptation is a completely unproductive strategy. (F)

28. Migrants who observe more and communicate less will experience more culture shock than those who communicate a lot. (F)

29. Countries with an emphasis on heterogeneity may be more welcoming of people from different cultures. (T)

30. The majority of migrants move from Third World countries to Europe and the United States. (F)

31. The social/political context affects individual immigration. (T)

32. A sojourner is a long-term involuntary migrant. (F)

33. Countries generally restrict immigration during economic downturns. (T)

34. People are more likely to experience culture shock when they avoid contact with members of the new culture. (F)

35. Long-term sojourners more actively resist adaptation than short-term sojourners. (F)

36. Even a slight degree of anxiety can be extremely detrimental to intercultural adaptation. (F)

37. One of the main difficulties in a multicultural life is the risk of not knowing how to develop ethics. (T)

38. Today, movement between cultures is as simple as getting on a plane. (F)

ESSAY QUESTIONS

39. Suppose your friend is going on a study abroad trip to Taiwan. What would you tell this friend about culture shock?

40. Describe what happens during the three stages of sojourner adaptation in the communication-system model.

41. Describe why you think some migrants have a more difficult time experiencing reentry shock than others.

42. Describe some of the challenges faced by an individual who makes multiple returns.

43. Describe the double edge of communication in adaptation. What is the most effective communicative strategy in new environments?

44. Describe the three issues that Berry argues affect the relationship migrants have with the host society.

45. How do intercultural transitions affect identity?

46. Describe the four types of contact between migrants and the host society. What kinds of intercultural interactions result from each type of contact?

47. What are some of the general characteristics Gudykunst (1995) suggests are found in effective intercultural communicators?

CHAPTER 9

FOLK CULTURE, POPULAR CULTURE, AND INTERCULTURAL COMMUNICATION

MULTIPLE-CHOICE QUESTIONS

1. Which of the following is true about people's responses to popular culture?
   a. In general people cannot resist popular culture.
   b. The study of popular culture is considered by most people to be worthy of serious attention.
   *c. People are often unaware of the complex nature of popular culture.
   d. The United States imports much of its popular culture from other countries.

2. What initially motivated the exportation of U.S. popular culture?
   a. the desire to share new information and technological advances
   b. requests from countries that did not have high-quality entertainment
   c. a need to help people from other cultures understand the benefits of democracy
   *d. the decision to use it to advertise U.S. products

3. How does popular culture differ from folk culture?
   *a. Folk culture is not driven by financial profit.
   b. Popular culture meets needs not satisfied by dominant culture forms.
   c. Folk culture is considered to be less informative than popular culture.
   d. Popular culture is not really as popular as folk culture.

4. In the study of White and Black job applicants, how did interviewers who were influenced by negative stereotypes of Blacks differ in their behavior?
   a. They spent more time interviewing some applicants.
   b. They showed more immediacy behaviors.
   *c. Their speech deteriorated.
   d. They were more outgoing.

5. To what does cultural imperialism refer?
   a. The idea that many White people have superiority over people of color.
   b. The technological advancement of the United States in media forms.
   c. The resistance of people in the United States to popular culture forms from other countries.
   *d. The dominance of U.S. popular cultural forms throughout the world.

6. What ideas about U.S. cultural imperialism are illustrated by the Michael Fay case?
   *a. The popular culture focus was on the relationship between Singapore and the United States.
   b. Popular culture portrayals focused on the intercultural trauma experienced by Michael Fay and his family.
   c. Popular culture was used to perpetuate the idea that Singapore had more social ills than the United States.
   d. The focus was on the difficulties children experience when they are subjected to another culture's norms and values.

7. Intercultural communication scholars are interested in popular culture because
   a. it gives us true representations of other people.
   *b. most people rely on popular culture for information about others.
   c. people all over the world assign the same meanings to popular culture texts.
   d. there is little cultural variation in the way people negotiate their relationships to popular culture.

8. Magazines that target specific cultural identities do *not* fulfill which of the following functions?
   a. provide a forum for discussing concerns overlooked in other magazines
   *b. provide more objective information about specific cultural groups
   c. affirm identities silenced in the mainstream culture
   d. offer information and points of view unavailable in other magazines

9. Which statement is *not* true about popular culture and information about cultures?
   *a. People tend to think popular culture presents true information about their own culture.
   b. People use popular culture texts to learn about other cultures.
   c. People tend to think popular culture presents true information about other cultures.
   d. People use popular culture texts to negotiate their relationships with cultural identities.

10. According to the study on how interviewers respond to Black and White job applicants, Black job applicants
    a. were less qualified than White applicants.
    b. do not have interviewing skills.
    c. were less immediate than White applicants.
    *d. were reacting to the interviewers.

11. French writer Jean Baudrillard argued that the Gulf War was a media simulation because
    a. there were too many images of the war in the media.
    b. the United States never declared a war with Iraq.
    *c. people had no access to truth.
    d. few people were killed in the war.

12. Which of the following statements is NOT true about the relationship between popular culture and images of different nations?
    a. We receive information about other countries from U.S.-produced media.
    b. We try to understand the dynamics of other cultures and nations through popular culture.
    c. We have to rely on popular culture to understand all kinds of world issues.
    *d. We learn about other countries through popular culture produced in those countries.

13. Which statement is true about popular culture and stereotypes?
    a. Sometimes we unconsciously accept stereotypes presented in the media.
    *b. Popular culture reinforces existing stereotypes.
    c. We resist stereotypes projected by popular culture.
    d. Popular culture is the main reason stereotypes persist.

14. How are U.S. Americans affected by the global imbalance of popular cultural texts?
    a. They get fewer opportunities to learn about how other cultures view them.
    b. They have fewer popular cultural options than people in other nations.
    c. They get exposed to more misinformation than people from other cultural groups.
    *d. They are more dependent on U.S.-produced popular culture.

15. Which of the following is NOT a characteristic of folk culture?
    *a. It is a form of high culture.
    b. No one industry controls it.
    c. There is little attempt to export it.
    d. Participation is unrelated to profit.

16. Which of the following is true about how people resist cultural texts?
    a. A person's preference for popular culture is based more on media sensitivity than on cultural values.
    *b. Refusal to participate in popular culture is one form of showing resistance.
    c. Motivation to participate in popular culture is unrelated to a person's social role.
    d. Resistance may be motivated by displeasure over media representation of certain social issues.

17. Electronic colonialism is
    a. domination by one country through economical, political, and cultural exploitation.
    b. domination through the spread of cultural products.
    *c. domination or exploitation utilizing technological forms.
    d. domination or control through media.

18. Manusov and Hegda found that having some cultural information and positive expectations
    a. motivates migrants to be overconfident about their knowledge of a culture.
    b. leads to more rigid stereotyping than having no information.
    c. leads to greater levels of disappointment and frustration for migrants.
    *d. may lead to more in-depth conversations than having no information.

19. What is the result of folk culture being used to sell popular culture products?
    *a. The distinctions between popular culture and folk culture are becoming blurred.
    b. The relationship between popular culture and folk culture is stronger now.
    c. Folk culture is losing its popularity among traditional participants.
    d. Folk culture and popular culture together are challenging the position of high culture.

20. What advantage do non-English newspapers have over magazines as cultural texts?
    a. They reach a broader readership.
    b. They are more objective.
    *c. They are cheaper to produce.
    d. They transmit more popular culture.

21. Who tends to be most influenced by popular culture portrayals of another cultural group?
    a. People who have been very exposed to the other group.
    b. People who have a tendency toward ethnocentric attitudes.
    c. People who have visited in the culture of the other group.
    *d. People who have limited experience with the other group.

22. Cultural texts, such as magazines, influence consumers' cultural identities by
   *a. functioning as cultural spaces for them.
   b. causing them to question their cultural identities.
   c. forcing dominant culture identities on them.
   d. silencing the aspects of their identities that are incongruent with the dominant culture.

MATCHING QUESTIONS

For each of the following concepts, select the letter that identifies its definition

23. cultural texts (c)

24. cultural industries (b)

25. reader profiles (d)

   a. contrived cultural spaces sold to affirm cultural identities

   b. organizations that produce and sell popular culture products as commodities

   c. cultural artifacts that convey cultural norms, values, and beliefs

   d. portrayals of customer demographic characteristics by magazines

TRUE/FALSE QUESTIONS

26. There is a great deal of research on why U.S. television programs are so successful in other cultures. (F)

27. People resist the use of popular culture as a forum for dealing with social issues. (F)

28. Cultural groups are generally depicted accurately in popular culture. (F)

29. The U.S. film industry makes more money on their films outside the United States than they do inside. (T)

30. One way of thinking about the cultural imperialism of the United States is as nationalist discourse. (T)

31. Popular culture provides very little information to us about other cultures. (F)

32. Popular culture is a uniform product of the capitalist system of production. (F)

33. People in other countries are less likely to perceive U.S. popular culture as representative of life in the United States. (F)

34. People are not able to resist the overwhelming influence of popular culture. (F)

35. Popular culture really has little influence on stereotypes because people recognize that most characters are just fictional. (F)

36. Popular culture has to win over the majority of the people to be considered popular. (F)

37. Magazines targeted toward certain cultural groups may be considered a type of cultural space. (T)

38. For people with limited exposure to other cultures, the impact of popular culture may be greater. (T)

ESSAY QUESTIONS

39. Discuss some of the characteristics of popular culture.

40. Describe some ways in which magazines respond to the needs of members of specific cultural groups.

41. Explain the role popular culture plays in our perceptions of other cultural groups.

42. Discuss how you think the world dominance of U.S. popular culture may affect intercultural communication.

43. What are the dangers of using popular culture as your only source of information about other cultural groups?

44. Are we able to completely resist images propagated by popular culture? Present arguments for and against.

45. What is the relationship between cultural texts and identities?

CHAPTER 10

CULTURE, COMMUNICATION, AND INTERCULTURAL RELATIONSHIPS

MULTIPLE-CHOICE QUESTIONS

1. Which of the following is true about why we form relationships?
   a. Physical attractiveness really has little influence on the initial phases of relationship formation.
   b. People have a tendency to perceive people as less similar to them than they are.
   *c. In some cultures the compatibility of your partner is the major relationship issue.
   d. Social and cultural forces have little influence on our notions of attractiveness.

2. In which phase of relationship development do people try to discover commonalities in the other by seeking information about the other person?
   a. attraction phase
   b. stability phase
   *c. exploratory phase
   d. orientation phase

3. In which relational phase do people find that their conversations have more depth and breadth?
   *a. stability phase
   b. exploratory phase
   c. attraction phase
   d. orientation phase

4. Barnlund suggests that when people meet in high-context cultures
   a. the educational level and degree of attractiveness will determine possible relationship formation.
   *b. the background of the person is important in determining whether to pursue a relationship.
   c. relationships form very quickly as there are more sources of information available about the person (nonverbal and contextual).
   d. relationships outside the culture are viewed as less significant than those within the culture.

5. Which of the following is NOT a pattern generally found in U.S. relationships?
   a. The most important characteristics in friends are understanding, respect, and sincerity.
   b. A friend is someone to occasionally do things with and share problems.
   *c. In romantic relationships, the importance of the partner's connectedness to his or her family is emphasized.
   d. Disclosure of superficial information occurs earlier in relational phases.

6. What do we know about cultural differences in gay relationships?
   a. The majority of cultures outside the United States view them as illegal and antisocial.
   b. In some cultures gay relationships terminate after adolescence and the partners marry heterosexual partners.
   *c. There is little information available on cultural variations in gay relationships.
   d. Gay relationships vary culturally in the degree to which the partners desire permanent as opposed to temporary physical and emotional relationships.

7. In what ways are intercultural relationships similar to intracultural relationships?
   *a. They pass through the same basic developmental phases.
   b. There is a similar amount of anxiety during the early stages of the relationship.
   c. They take the same basic amount of work and effort.
   d. They are based on the same notions of attraction.

8. Which of the following is true of intercultural relationships?
   a. Minority communities will be more opposed to them than majority communities.
   b. They are generally more superficial in the long run than intracultural relationships.
   *c. People may be attracted to each other because they have different cultural backgrounds.
   d. People tend to enter into them more out of sympathy or curiosity than genuine liking.

9. Which of the following are major reasons for people choosing not to date outside their ethnic group?
   a. They perceive people from other ethnic groups as less attractive.
   *b. They just don't think about it.
   c. They seldom have the time to put forth the extra effort to date outside their ethnic group.
   d. They are too busy dating people from their own culture.

10. In studies from the United States and Canada, what is a typical characteristic found in people who have married someone from another culture?
    a. They are less educated.
    *b. They are older.
    c. They have large families.
    d. They have a higher income.

11. What is one of the two major concerns of people in intercultural marriages?
    a. immigration issues
    b. sexual intimacy
    *c. issues around raising children
    d. relational satisfaction

12. During the orientation phase of relational development,
    *a. people use categorical or noninterpersonal information about the other person to guide the interaction.
    b. people try to discover more about the other person by talking about nonintimate topics.
    c. people try to find out what the other person thinks about a variety of different topics to reduce uncertainty.
    d. people rely on idiosyncratic information to guide their actions and expectations.

13. Which of the following statements is NOT true about stereotypes and romantic relationships?
    a. Some stereotypes deter people from forming relationships with those who are different.
    b. Some people are encouraged by stereotypes to form relationships with those who are different.
    c. Some cultural groups are stereotyped as particularly desirable.
    *d. Stereotypes have little influence on our choice romantic partners.

14. According to the proximity principle,
    *a. people form relationships with those with whom they come in close physical contact.
    b. people tend to be attracted to people they think are like them.
    c. people tend to be attracted to people they are different from in ways that complement them.
    d. people tend to be attracted to people they believe have a similar degree of attractiveness.

15. People generally self-disclose more intimate information in the
    a. orientation phase.
    b. initial phase.
    *c. stability phase.
    d. exploratory phase.

16. Which of the following is true of differences between homosexual and heterosexual relationships?
    a. Same-sex relationships play the same roles for gay and straight males in the United States.
    b. Both gay and heterosexual women seek emotional support in cross-sex friendships.
    *c. Sexuality may play a different role in heterosexual and gay relationships.
    d. There is a clearer distinction between "lover" and "friend" in heterosexual than in gay relationships.

17. Which intercultural relationship dialectic is concerned with sensitivity toward power differentials?
    a. differences–similarities dialectic
    *b. privilege–disadvantage dialectic
    c. static–dynamic dialectic
    d. personal–contextual dialectic

18. Which of the following contribute to the initial anxiety in intercultural relationships?
    *a. being worried about negative consequences
    b. overly positive stereotypes
    c. distrust because of power differentials
    d. nonverbal space differences

19. The greatest cultural difference Lewin found in his cross-cultural studies of self-disclosure was
    a. the degree to which people were motivated to share personal information.
    b. the degree to which men and women differ in the type of information they self-disclose.
    c. the degree to which cultures vary in how disclosure about sexual topics contributes to intimacy.
    *d. the degree to which the outer boundary was more or less permeable.

20. The dialectic that is concerned with the way intercultural relationships grow and change is the
    a. differences–similarities dialectic.
    *b. privilege–disadvantage dialectic.
    c. static–dynamic dialectic.
    d. personal–contextual dialectic.

21. One of the ways in which intercultural relationships are different from intracultural relationships is that
    a. they typically become more intimate and committed than intercultural relationships.
    b. partners generally have more tolerance of each other's differences in intracultural relationships.
    *c. there is a greater challenge to explain in intercultural relationships.
    d. there is less initial motivation in intracultural relationships to learn about dissimiliarities.

MATCHING QUESTIONS

For each of the following intercultural relational strategies for dealing with cultural differences in relationships, select the letter that best describes it.

22. submission (c)

23. obliteration (d)

24. consensus (a)

25. compromise (b)

   a. Partners temporarily suspend cultural ways to adapt to contexts.

   b. Partners give up parts of their cultures to accommodate each other.

   c. One partner gives up his or her culture and adopts the ways of the other.

   d. Both partners give up their cultural practices and form a third culture with new practices.

TRUE/FALSE QUESTIONS

26. The matching hypothesis suggests that men are generally attracted to partners they believe have a higher level of attractiveness; whereas women are attracted to partners with a lower level of attractiveness. (F)

27. Social contexts are often structured in ways that limit people from interacting with those who are very different from them. (T)

28. In some cultures, strangers are perceived as potential relationships. (T)

29. There are fewer rewards and more work in intercultural relationships. (F)

30. People generally tend to feel less anxious when they meet people from other cultures because they know they will not have to measure up to as many expectations. (F)

31. The reason given most often for why people form intercultural dating relationships is because they are attracted to each other. (T)

32. The biggest obstacles to boundary-crossing friendships have come from minority communities. (F)

33. In majority of cultures other than the United States, homosexuality is not considered a problematic behavior. (T)

34. Same-sex friendships play the same roles for gay and straight males in the United States. (F)

35. Once a person has developed a close intercultural relationship, he or she is more likely to form others. (T)

36. Cognitive consistency suggests that we are attracted to people who physically look like us. (F)

37. People with extremely collectivistic value orientations emphasize more love, passion, and physical attraction with romantic relationship partners than people in individually oriented societies. (F)

38. Intimacy is less important in intercultural than intracultural relationships. (F)

ESSAY QUESTIONS

39. Identify some cultural differences in how people are attracted to each other.

40. Describe some benefits of intercultural friendships.

41. If your friend told you she was getting married to someone from another culture, what advice would you give her?

42. How do social and cultural contexts influence the formation of intercultural relationships?

43. If you were going to become friends with someone from another culture, what differences could you expect in the formation of the relationship?

44. Discuss implications of primary principles of relational attraction for intercultural communication.

45. What contextual elements influence intercultural relationships and how?

CHAPTER 11

CULTURE, COMMUNICATION, AND CONFLICT

MULTIPLE-CHOICE QUESTIONS

1. Which is true of conflict in general?
   a. Conflict is found primarily in individualistic cultures.
   b. Conflict is always viewed as destructive to relationships.
   *c. Men and women deal with conflict differently.
   d. There are few cultural differences in how people from other cultures approach conflict.

2. Which of the following is true of the peace-making approach to conflict?
   a. It is based on the notion that the other is not as important as the harmony of one's soul.
   b. This approach attempts to resolve conflict by pretending that it does not exist, until it gradually fades in the memories of the combatants.
   *c. It attempts to find creative negotiation to resolve conflicts when they occur.
   d. It is based on Gandhi's principles of nonviolence.

3. Which of the following is an example of a formal intervention?
   a. a boy's father negotiating a conflict with a teacher for his son
   *b. a lawyer helping negotiate custody of children between divorcing parents
   c. a girl asking her cousin to apologize to her friend on her behalf for a misunderstanding they had
   d. a man asking his brother to help him negotiate a salary dispute with a client

4. What strategy type is being used when there is a high concern for self and other reflected and open and direct communication?
   a. dominating
   b. obliging
   *c. integrating
   d. compromising

5. Which strategy plays down differences and incompatibilities while emphasizing commonalities that satisfy the concerns of the other?
   a. compromising
   b. integrating
   c. reflecting
   *d. obliging

6. Which statement is true about how men and women differ in the way they handle conflict?
    *a. Women feel good about discussing relationships whereas men want to talk about them only when they need fixing, and once they are fixed, talk about other things.
    b. Men give more details in their stories, whereas women get right to the point.
    c. Men like to commiserate by telling about similar situations they have experienced; when a woman does this, she is accused of stealing the stage.
    d. Women are likely to show support by saying nothing, whereas men show their support by making sympathetic noises.

7. In what way does Collier suggest that Mexican American males and females differ in how they handle conflict?
    a. Males are more silent about conflicts than females.
    b. Females use intermediaries more often than males.
    *c. Males feel that talking to work out the conflict is more important than females do.
    d. Females feel that face saving for self is a more important issue than males.

8. Which is true for individualistic societies?
    a. They emphasize less direct forms of communication.
    *b. They tend to use more solution-oriented conflict styles.
    c. They tend to use more avoiding and obliging conflict styles.
    d. They tend to base behavioral decisions on whether or not the other is an ingroup member.

9. Which of the following is true of intercultural interpersonal conflicts?
    a. People usually take more time and care to select the most efficient conflict strategy.
    *b. People who are not fluent in the language may have a difficult time resolving conflicts.
    c. The context has little effect on the conflict compared with elements of the relationship.
    d. Interpersonal conflicts happen more frequently on an international level than on an interpersonal level.

10. Which of the following assumptions is identified by Augsberg for the conflict as opportunity approach?
    a. The social system should not be adjusted to the needs of the members.
    b. Disputants should be disciplined.
    c. Conflict is a destructive disturbance of the peace.
    *d. Direct confrontation and conciliation are valued.

11. In which way is productive conflict different from destructive conflict?
    *a. In productive conflict individuals limit conflict to the original issue.
    b. In productive conflict individuals broaden the conflict in definition.
    c. In productive conflict individuals promote a competitive atmosphere.
    d. In productive conflict individuals use either-or thinking.

12. The key to creating a cooperative atmosphere is
    a. to encourage people to think of innovative and creative solutions.
    b. to step back and explore other options or delegate the problem to a third party.
    *c. to create a cooperative atmosphere at the beginning of the interaction or relationship.
    d. to identify your own preferred conflict style.

13. The main idea of the conflict as opportunity approach to conflict is that
    a. conflict is a way of adding creativity and renewal to stagnating relationships.
    b. conflict is destructive and that it is best to use some type of intervention to resolve.
    c. conflict is a necessary motivator for helping people learn about each other.
    *d. conflict may contribute to more satisfying relationships if handled constructively.

14. Why are economic problems often blamed on cultural differences?
    a. Immigrants from other cultures typically take away the jobs of U.S. citizens and cause the economic difficulties.
    *b. Decision makers blame cultural difference to divert attention away from their own responsibility for the problems.
    c. Economic problems cause cultural groups to become more inclusive of their own members and exclusive of outsiders.
    d. Generally increases in heterogeneity contribute to social turmoil, which has a negative effect on the economy.

15. Exploration is important for
    *a. encouraging people to think about creative solutions to conflict.
    b. creating a competitive relational atmosphere that will motivate people to resolve conflicts.
    c. helping people resolve conflicts using the obliging conflict style.
    d. encouraging men to use more supportive comments in conflicts with women.

16. What is one of the challenges of Western mediation models for helping with intercultural conflict?
    a. They ignore the role of history in resolving conflicts.
    b. Mediation is an uncomfortable approach for people from cultures that do not typically use intermediaries.
    *c. They often ignore cultural variations in the conflict process.
    d. They are more face threatening than other approaches for conflict resolution.

MATCHING QUESTIONS

For each conflict style, select a letter that provides a description.

17. avoiding (c)

18. obliging (a)

19. dominating (e)

20. integrating (b)

21. compromising (d)

   a. one person plays down the differences and incompatibilities and emphasizes commonalities that satisfy the concern of the other

   b. reflects high concern for both self and other and involves open and direct exchange of information in an attempt to reach a solution acceptable to both parties

   c. sometimes reflects a low concern for self and other, at other times may result in harmonious relationships

(continued)

d. reflects a moderate degree of concern for self and others and involves sharing and exchanging information whereby both individuals give up something to find a mutually acceptable decision

e. reflects a high concern for self and low concern for others and has been identified with a win-lose orientation or with forcing behavior to win one's position

For each conflict type below, select the letter that describes it.

22. affective conflict (c)

23. goal conflict (a)

24. cognitive conflict (b)

25. conflict of interest (d)

a. when people disagree about something they have been working for and really want to see happen

b. when conflict emerges because the ideologies of the people differ

c. When conflicts occur because individuals realize they are not experiencing the same feelings about something

d. when people have different ideas about what they would like to do or where they would like to go

TRUE/FALSE QUESTIONS

26. In some cultural groups, conflict is seen as ultimately unproductive for relationships. (T)

27. Ting-Toomey et al. suggest that the conflict as opportunity orientation stems from a value for saving the face of others. (F)

28. The avoiding style is viewed as an appropriate conflict management style in some cultures. (T)

29. People from individualistic cultures tend to prefer more avoiding and obliging conflict styles. (F)

30. The social movement perspective of conflict is "conflict as destructive." (F)

31. In situations of intercultural conflict, we tend to use our universal default style for handling conflict, which is to avoid it. (F)

32. The most common view of interpersonal conflict in the United States is "conflict as destructive." (F)

33. Relationships without conflict are seen as not very healthy and potentially problematic by U.S. interpersonal scholars. (T)

34. "Avoiding" is not an effective strategy of dealing with conflict. (F)

35. Confrontation has often been an effective strategy for bringing about social change. (T)

36. Mediation is more sensitive to cultural variations in conflict than most other conflict strategies. (F)

37. Conflict as approached from the interpretive and critical approaches is less complex than conflict as approached from the interpersonal perspective. (F)

38. Either-or thinking is one of the most important skills for successful mediation of intercultural conflicts. (F)

ESSAY QUESTIONS

39. Describe differences between the "conflict as opportunity" and "conflict as destructive" orientations to interpersonal conflict.

40. Identify three benefits for groups that work through conflicts.

41. A friend is working on a class project with an international partner. What suggestions could you give your friend for dealing with any possible intercultural conflicts that arise?

42. Explain the differences in how collectivists and individualists approach conflict.

43. What are some of the benefits of forgiveness in conflict situations?

44. Describe how people develop their conflict style preferences.

45. Explain the role and types of conflict in social movements.

46. Explain how historical and political contexts affect interpersonal conflicts.

47. Describe the three aspects of intercultural conflict.

CHAPTER 12

THE OUTLOOK FOR
INTERCULTURAL COMMUNICATION

MULTIPLE-CHOICE QUESTIONS

1. Linguistic knowledge is important to intercultural communication competence so that interactants know what the other is saying. Why else is it important?
   a. The process of learning the language causes people to develop less tolerance for ambiguity.
   b. People who speak multiple languages are more competent communicators than those who know only one.
   *c. Learning additional languages increases one's empathy for culturally different individuals.
   d. Learning a second language increases one's sensitivity to ethical dilemmas.

2. Which of the following is an example of macro-level behavior?
   a. Taking your shoes off before you enter a home.
   *b. Interaction management in communication interactions.
   c. Raising your hand before speaking in group meetings.
   d. Bringing a gift to the host family when you arrive for dinner.

3. When a person realizes that he/she is not experiencing success in intercultural interactions, it is a case of
   *a. conscious incompetence.
   b. unconscious competence.
   c. conscious competence.
   d. unconscious incompetence.

4. If John is communicating with his friend Koji from Japan and accidentally offends Koji, who never tells him, what approach may John have been using to communicate?
   a. unconscious competence
   b. conscious competence
   *c. unconscious incompetence
   d. conscious incompetence

5. The term *category width* refers to
   a. the range of attitudes toward people who are different from us.
   b. the number of linguistic categories we have.
   c. our categorical knowledge useful in intercultural communication.
   *d. the range of things we can include in one category.

6. In the intercultural context, empathy refers to
   a. being able to judge according to our own frame of reference.
   *b. the capacity to imagine oneself in another role within the cultural context.
   c. the ability to make correct interpretations of the other's behavior.
   d. consciousness of one's own intercultural behavior.

7. Which of the following is the most important dimension of intercultural competence?
   a. knowledge
   b. attitudes
   c. skills
   *d. motivation

8. Linguistic knowledge leads to higher intercultural competence because
   a. knowing the language of the other culture gives us access to cultural patterns.
   b. we can be competent only if we can conduct interactions in the language of the culture we are visiting.
   *c. knowing the difficulty of learning a second language helps us appreciate challenges others face in new cultural contexts.
   d. fluency in a foreign language lowers our anxiety and increases tolerance for ambiguity.

9. The D.I.E. exercise is helpful in understanding intercultural dynamics because
   *a. confusing the different levels of processing information can lead to misunderstanding and ineffective communication.
   b. evaluation is the most important method of understanding intercultural processes.
   c. people should always stay at the descriptive level while interacting with someone who is culturally different.
   d. people should never make negative evaluations of intercultural processes.

10. Which of the following is true about the role of motivation in intercultural communication?
   a. Most of the time the communicators' skill levels are more significant than motivation in intercultural communication.
   *b. Historical and political contexts may influence a person's motivation to communicate.
   c. The amount of information a person has about another culture will determine his or her level of motivation to communicate.
   d. Motivation to communicate in intercultural contexts is more often found in women than men.

11. Transpection refers to
   a. the ability to "walk in another person's shoes."
   b. the ability to adjust our interaction posture.
   c. the ability to evaluate our own perceptions and their influence on our communication.
   *d. the ability to see the world exactly as the other person sees it.

12. What is Bennett's Platinum Rule for competent intercultural communicators?
   a. Try to understand, try to resolve conflicts creatively, and if all this fails, forgive.
   b. To understand others, you must try to see the world as they see it from their context.
   *c. Do unto others as they themselves would have done unto them.
   d. The multicultural person is the person who is not afraid to change his or her preconceptions.

13. Which is an example of an interpretive statement?
   a. You said you wanted to go to the library.
   b. I am happy you have decided to come to our party.
   c. I saw you in Professor Brown's class at 3:30 this afternoon.
   *d. I think you are getting behind in your classes.

14. If Heidi is really trying hard to communicate as competently as possible with her roommate Lin Sue from Taiwan, which competence approach is she using?
    a. unconscious competence
    *b. conscious competence
    c. unconscious incompetence
    d. conscious incompetence

15. The critical approach to intercultural communication competence reminds us that
    a. good communicators need to be sensitive to the many contexts in which intercultural communication occurs.
    b. good communicators need to think about how cultural variations influence the process of communication.
    *c. good communicators realize that political, economic, and historical contexts constrain an individual's competence.
    d. good communicators need to aggressively question existing social structures and inequalities.

16. Which of the following characterize intercultural alliances?
    *a. orientations of affirmation
    b. coalitions or equilateral power
    c. criticisms of dominant power structures
    d. gender and racial equality

17. What does Dace say Whites must do before any real interracial communication can occur with African Americans?
    a. They have to forgive one another.
    b. They need to balance out economic disparities.
    c. They need to make a greater commitment to affirmative action policies.
    *d. They need to make a commitment to really listening.

18. Which of the following is NOT found in Kivel's list of suggestions from people of color for White people who want to be allies?
    *a. Experience some of the pain yourselves.
    b. Don't make assumptions.
    c. Interrupt jokes and comments.
    d. Don't ask me to speak for my people.

19. Which of the following is true about building coalitions?
    a. It will not happen until more resources are made available to groups of color.
    b. It is generally quite easy once people sit down and talk to each other.
    *c. In the process, people may find their own identities become injured.
    d. It is impossible to accomplish while people continue to transcend some of their identities.

20. Which characteristic of intercultural alliances have intercultural friends achieved who recognize that powerful people see the importance of history differently from those who are less powerful?
    a. power and unearned privilege
    b. orientations of affirmation
    c. tolerance for ambiguity
    *d. impact of history

21. The authors suggest that the most important knowledge a competent intercultural communicator needs is
    *a. self-knowledge.
    b. linguistic knowledge.
    c. other-knowledge.
    d. micro-cultural knowledge.

22. Tolerance for ambiguity refers to
    a. the ability to withhold judgment until facts are obtained.
    b. the ability to perceive the world from the perspective of another.
    c. the ability to transcend one's own identity.
    *d. the ability to feel comfortable in situations with many unknown elements.

MATCHING QUESTIONS

For each type of statement below, select the letter that identifies an example of that type of statement.

23. evaluative (b)

24. descriptive (c)

25. interpretive (a)

a. "I do not think that you really want to go to town with me."

b. "It makes me angry when all of the stores shut down for two-hour lunch breaks."

c. "Mario is yawning."

TRUE/FALSE QUESTIONS

26. The best way to learn how to become a good intercultural communicator is to read as many books as possible about different cultural groups. (F)

27. Some behaviors are likely to work in all cultures at a macro level. (T)

28. Conscious competence occurs when the person is attitudinally and cognitively prepared but lets go and uses holistic cognitive processing. (F)

29. One of the best preparations we can make for becoming competent intercultural communicators is to develop our abilities to think using narrow categories. (F)

30. The highest level of communication competence requires a combination of holistic and analytic thinking. (T)

31. Expressions of respect are universally valid as macro-level behaviors. (F)

32. Intercultural alliances are generally formed by oppressed cultural groups to take power away from dominant cultural groups. (F)

33. Evaluative statements are nonjudgmental statements. (F)

34. For real interracial communication to occur, African Americans need to make a commitment to really listen to Whites. (F)

35. Most African Americans want the opportunity to speak for their people. (F)

36. Intercultural alliances are bonds between individuals or groups across cultures that are characterized by a shared recognition of power and the impact of history and by an orientation toward affirmation. (T)

37. Forming coalitions can be emotionally injuring. (T)

38. Linguistic knowledge is the most important component of intercultural communication competence. (F)

ESSAY QUESTIONS

39. Describe some important reasons competent intercultural communicators should be self-reflexive.

40. Discuss why it is problematic to identify universal behaviors that work well in all cultural contexts.

41. Identify and explain the four levels of intercultural competence.

42. Discuss the components of intercultural competence.

43. What needs to occur so that people can form intercultural alliances?

44. List some of the suggestions people of color have for White people who want to be their allies.

45. Why is it important to learn the D.I.E. skills to increase one's level of intercultural communication competence?